The Talavera Campaign 1809

The Talavera Campaign 1809

Tim Saunders

Pen & Sword
MILITARY

First published in Great Britain in 2023 by
PEN & SWORD MILITARY
an imprint of Pen & Sword Books Ltd
Yorkshire – Philadelphia

Copyright © Tim Saunders, 2023

ISBN 978-1-39904-003-7

The right of Tim Saunders to be identified as the author of this work has been asserted by him in accordance with the Copyright, Designs and Patents Act 1988.

A CIP catalogue record for this book is available from the British Library.

All rights reserved. No part of this book may be reproduced or transmitted in any form or by any means, electronic or mechanical including photocopying, recording or by any information storage and retrieval system, without permission from the Publisher in writing.

Typeset by Concept, Huddersfield, West Yorkshire, HD4 5JL
Printed on paper from a sustainable source by
CPI Group (UK) Ltd, Croydon CR0 4YY

Pen & Sword Books Ltd incorporates the imprints of After the Battle, Aviation, Atlas, Family History, Fiction, Maritime, Military, Discovery, Politics, History, Archaeology, Select, Wharncliffe Local History, Wharncliffe True Crime, Military Classics, Wharncliffe Transport, Leo Cooper, The Praetorian Press, Remember When, White Owl, Seaforth Publishing and Frontline Books.

For a complete list of Pen & Sword titles please contact
PEN & SWORD BOOKS LTD
47 Church Street, Barnsley, South Yorkshire, S70 2AS, England
E-mail: enquiries@pen-and-sword.co.uk
Website: www.pen-and-sword.co.uk
or
PEN & SWORD BOOKS
1950 Lawrence Rd, Havertown, PA 19083, USA
E-mail: uspen-and-sword@casematepublishers.com
Website: www.penandswordbooks.com

Contents

Acknowledgements vi
Introduction vii
  1. The Peninsular, 1809 1
  2. The Douro Campaign 15
  3. Preparation and Planning 33
  4. The Campaign Opens 59
  5. The Advance to Battle 79
  6. Talavera – The First Day of Battle 105
  7. The Day of Battle, 28 July 1809 133
  8. The Main French Attack 153
  9. The Final Phase and Aftermath 179
10. The Withdrawal to Portugal 203
11. The End of the 1809 Campaign 233
Appendices
    I: An Example of Wellesley's General Orders 243
    II: Orders of Battle 245
Notes 249
Index 255

Acknowledgements

As the Battlefield Companion series progresses and Covid lockdowns become a memory, writing is easier and with access to archives and that repository of knowledge in regimental museums it is very much business as normal. However, I have continued to use the proliferating number of digital resources and I continue to be surprised at quite how much documentation can be found online with a bit of determined digging. To the forums and online libraries that I have used, many thanks.

As has been the case in the past, I have been helped and encouraged by friends and colleagues with historical advice and the battlefield guide's knowledge of the ground in the Peninsular. I particularly thank fellow guide and historian Rob Yuill, who has again helped with the loan of books from his extensive library.

Napoleonic living historians, as always, have played a significant role in helping me understand the drill and tactics of the Peninsular armies. The insight they provided has enabled me to go into greater detail, with a clear understanding and ability to interpret those passages in accounts that I for one have tended to pass over quickly. I would particularly like to thank Jonathan S. Cabrera Asensio and Luis Sorando Muzás, chairman of the Asociación Napoleónica Española, who have helped me understand the situation and open my eyes beyond outright condemnation of the Spanish armies without context.

In my first book I thanked the late David Spinney, inspirational history teacher at Claysmore School, for encouraging my fascination with military history. Twenty years on, I think it is time to thank him again for setting me on a thoroughly rewarding path.

      Tim Saunders
      Warminster, 2023

Introduction

The conduct of Lieutenant General Sir Arthur Wellesley's 1808 campaign in Portugal had displayed both his ability to command in the field and the quality of his troops, but this was against Junot's small, isolated and dispersed corps. In contrast, the Talavera Campaign of 1809 was an altogether sterner test in which some near fatal mistakes were made in confronting veteran French formations. Wellesley himself confessed that his biggest error was to enter Spain and risk his army with only the most rudimentary lines of communication back to Portugal in case of difficulties. Now working as brigades and divisions in a much larger army, Wellesley's subordinate commanders and staff officers down to battalion level revealed that they had much to learn about the practicalities of campaign and operating as a part of larger formations. The failure of the piquets to prevent the rearguard being taken by surprise on the Rio Alberche during the afternoon of 27 July and that evening the mal-deployment of the army that almost led to disaster are just two examples.

Though mistakes were made, they were in most cases made up for by the fighting qualities of the British soldiers, but often at cost and lessons were learned. On the other hand, even though some of the French battalions and commanders in King Joseph's army had fought the British the previous year, they persisted in attacking in their tried and tested column with clearly little or no intent of deploying. Although there were some close calls, the firepower and unnerving stillness of the British two lines prevailed over the French columns attempting to bludgeon their way through.

During the Talavera Campaign, General Wellesley's eye for ground was revealed in his rejection of a seemingly acceptable position to fight on the Rio Alberche in favour of one that few if any others had spotted on the Portina north of Talavera. The decisions he made as commander of the British army in the field during the 1809 campaign were a foretaste of the constraints he would operate under for the next five years. Not only did Wellesley have to keep an eye on political maneuvering at home but also deal with the sundry needs and sensitivities of his Portuguese and Spanish allies. For Wellesley as much as anyone in his army, Talavera was a learning experience that would form the bedrock of the Peninsular Army.

In writing I have had, of course, to record the overwhelming disappointment from top to bottom of the British army, not to say bitterness, over the

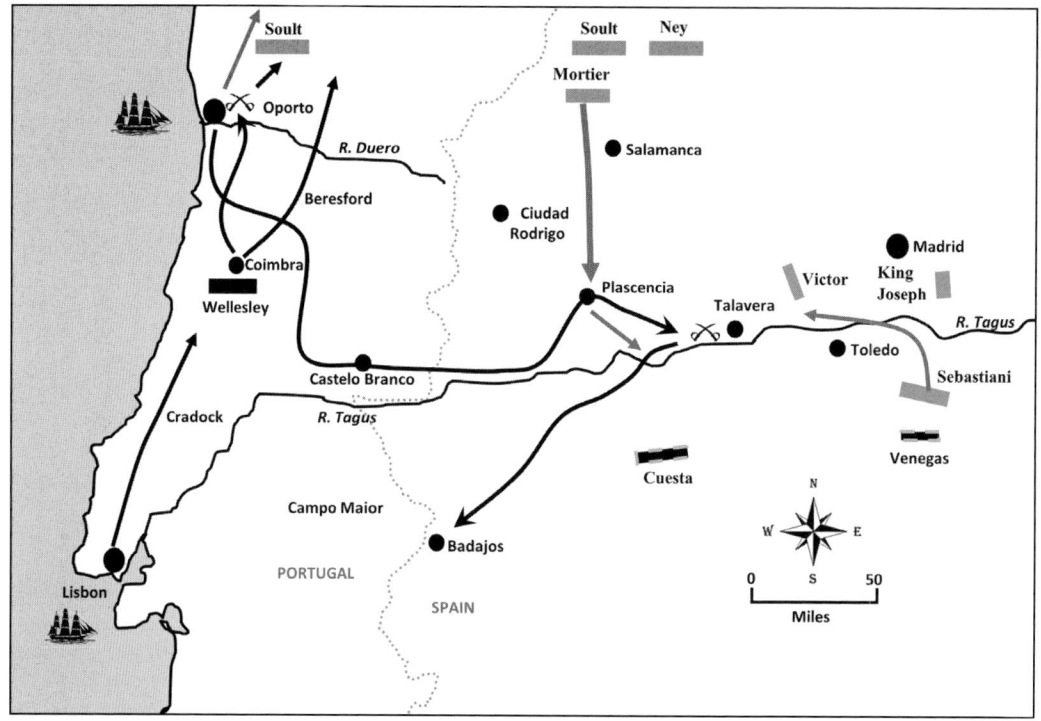

Outline of the 1809 Duero and Talavera campaigns.

way they were let down by their Spanish ally's inability, and at times unwillingness, to deliver the promised supplies of food. Near starvation is a consistent theme in virtually every memoir of the campaign and placed firmly at the feet of the Spanish without recognising the deficiencies of their own commissariat. Another point to be mentioned here is the equally oft-cited state of the Spanish army. It is, however, worth remembering that soldiers then and now tend to look at other armies through the prism of their own 'excellence', with precious little regard to the circumstances of that army, while of course forgetting their own areas of inadequacy. In both these areas I have attempted to be even handed.

Chapter One

The Peninsular, 1809

With the defeat of the Austrians and Russians at Austerlitz in 1805, and the Prussians at the twin battles of Jeana and Auerstadt in October 1806, Napoleon was reaching the zenith of his power. A month later, installed in the Prussian capital, he issued the Berlin Decrees, as a response to the Royal Navy's blockade of ports along the north coast of Europe from Brest to the River Elbe and the great trading city of Hamburg. Following the Battle of Trafalgar and the breaking up of the invasion camp at Boulogne, the only way of defeating Britain and cutting the supply of the silver funding coalitions against France was to close ports of Europe to British trade. The Continental System did hit Britain, that 'nation of shopkeepers', financially but the embargo on British goods leaked badly, thanks to wholesale smuggling and the issue of trading licences by the emperor's government in Paris. Not only that, Sweden and Portugal, at the extremities of Europe, flagrantly ignored the Continental System, which was, of course, an insult to Napoleon's power and imperial dignity following the 1807 Treaty of Tilsit.

Despite threats from Napoleon, impounding shipping and a humiliating acquiescence by their government, Portuguese merchants at home and in the colonies were heavily reliant on business with Britain and continued to trade openly. Consequently, as part of a wider plan to bring the whole of Iberia under his sway, General Junot's 25,000-strong Gironde Corps of Observation was dispatched to launch a Franco-Spanish invasion of Portugal. Riven by indecision and its fear of France, the house of Braganza and the government were paralysed into inaction. Thus, even when just a handful of ragged French soldiers dribbled into Lisbon after a march of over 500 miles in appalling weather across Spain and Portugal, there was no resistance. General Foy wrote of:

> ... those formidable warriors before whom Europe was dumb and whose looks the [Portuguese] Prince Regent had not dared to encounter. A people possessed of a lively imagination had expected to see heroes of a superior species, colossuses, demigods ... A forced march of eighteen days, famine, torrents, inundated valleys, and beating rain, had debilitated their bodies, and destroyed their clothing. They had hardly strength enough left to keep the step to the sound of the drum. A long file of lean, limping, and mostly beardless soldiers, followed with lagging

The departure of the Prince Regent of Portugal for the Brazils on 30 November 1807.

pace the scantily filled masses of the battalions ... For the purposes of attack and defence, the troops had nothing but rusted firelocks, and cartridges imbued with water.[1]

They arrived in time to see the ships bearing the Portuguese Royal family along with much of the country's nobility and wealth passing the Rock of Lisbon under escort of Admiral Sir Sidney Smith's Royal Navy flotilla. Foy concluded that: 'The Portuguese had been prepared to feel terror; the only feeling which they now experienced was that of vexation, at having been astounded and brought under the yoke by a handful of foreigners.'

Ruling by decree, General Junot occupied the whole of Portugal and disbanded most of the army, with the little that remained being sent to Germany initially for garrison duties. Meanwhile, across the country money was extorted for the exchequer in Paris, once of course French pockets had been filled with loot.

The other part of Napoleon's carefully laid plan for Iberia was to bring Spain into his empire, initially using the alliance with Spain to send troops into Iberia, with Spain hoping to secure southern Portugal was part of the deal. Napoleon, however, betrayed his allies and in 1808 usurped the Spanish throne from the unpopular and venal Bourbon monarchy. King Ferdinand VII and his father were lured to France, where Napoleon would mediate in the dynastic dispute, but they and members of their court were detained and forced to renounce the throne in favour of Joseph Bonaparte. Despite the unpopularity of the Bourbons, this proved to be one of Napoleon's greatest errors, giving rise to his Spanish Ulcer that for the next six years bled away money, manpower and credibility.

Initially there was little resistance to the French by the establishment or senior military commanders. Resistance, when it came, was from the outraged peasantry and the middle classes across the country. The population of Madrid revolted against the occupation on 2 May 1808 and was brutally suppressed by French troops under Marshal Murat, which set the nascent independence struggle on fire. The problem with this rebellion and war against the French occupation of Iberia was that there was no central authority in Spain. In the absence of a legitimate monarchy, the regional and local juntas took a self-interested control of their affairs, which both Sir John Moore and General Wellesley found to their cost immediately they entered Spain.

Enter the British

At the beginning of 1808 the British were long-standing enemies of Spain, having most recently sunk a large proportion of the Spanish fleet at Trafalgar and only the year before intervened in South America, where General Whitlock was rebuffed by the garrison of Buenos Aires. However, on the basis that Spain was now effectively at war with France, she now represented a potential ally.

By 1808, the threat of French invasion of southern England had receded and the British Government turned to further small-scale operations around the globe, readying a series of expeditions. One under Sir John Moore was to sail to the Baltic to support Sweden, another to the Mediterranean was to be found from General Spencer's garrison of Gibraltar, and a third was to be a new attempt to seize Spanish colonies in South America. This latter expedition was characterised by the Leader of the Opposition, Richard Sheridan, in Parliament as a 'policy of flitching sugar islands'. In the case of this latter expedition, Lieutenant General Sir Arthur Wellesley was mustering a 9,000-strong expedition in Ireland to seize Venezuela. Preparations were well under way when a delegation from the Asturias in northern Spain brought word of the changed situation in the country, which offered the Portland Government an opportunity to promote the rebellion against the French, as this was a useful case of 'my enemy's enemy being my friend'.

In redirecting the expedition, Lord Chatham, the Minister for War, gave General Wellesley considerable latitude of action: he was to sail for the Tagus to support the revolt against the French occupiers of Lisbon and Portugal. He was, however, also given leave to conduct operations in Spain should the opportunity present itself. Wellesley would be joined by Sir Brent Spencer's 5,000-man expedition from Gibraltar and other brigades being assembled in

4 The Talavera Campaign, 1809

Major General Sir Arthur Wellesley, painted in India by Robert Holm after the Battle of Assay.

England and Ireland. With these reinforcements, which would increase the force to some 40,000 men, would come two more senior commanders; Generals Sir Hew Dalrymple and Sir Harry Burrard, who would take command above the relatively junior Wellesley.

General Wellesley sailed ahead of his main force aboard HMS *Crocodile* to assess the situation in Iberia, but arriving in Coruna he found that enthusiasm engendered by the Spanish victory at Baylen had been reduced following the disaster of Medina de Rioseco. The Galician Junta nonetheless gave the British general an unreasonably healthy view of the situation. They 'vain-gloriously' overestimated the number of their troops, who were in fact falling back on to the River Esla and Benavente pursued by Marshal Bessières, whose numbers in turn they underestimated. The Junta was reluctant to accept British help beyond money and muskets, but informed Wellesley of a Portuguese revolt in Oporto.

Arriving in Oporto, Sir Arthur found the mood there very different. The Junta had abandoned hope of Spanish aid to rebellions across northern Portugal, which until the recent French victories had seemed possible. What is more, they were willing to accept British military help, lacking their own forces capable of confronting the French.

As a landing place closer to Lisbon that offered some shelter from the Atlantic swell, the Junta recommended the mouth of the River Mondego, some 65 miles south. An added advantage of Mondego Bay was that Fort Figueira[2] was already garrisoned by 300 Royal Marines and it dominated the mouth of the river.[3]

After two days during which local boats were hired to supplement those of the Royal Navy to take the army and its stores ashore, the landings began on 1 August 1808. First to be loaded into boats and rowed ashore were Major Robert Traver's companies of 2nd 95th and the 5th 60th Rifles, both of Fane's Brigade. Transferring from the rolling hulls of the transports into the tossing boats was problematical but crossing the sandbar at the mouth of the estuary was treacherous thanks to a dangerous surf, which cost several riflemen their lives at the very outset of the campaign. The Rifles had advanced 2 miles inland to deploy piquets and patrols to cover the beachhead[4] throughout the five days it took to disembark Wellesley's force and the further three required to land Spencer's troops from Gibraltar. Once ashore, the army numbered 13,000 men.

Wellesley advanced south on 9 August, making contact with the French at the town of Óbidos and on the following day, 17 August, had its first proper engagement with General Henri de Laborde's force of 5,000 men at Roliça. The French fought a skilful action but were outnumbered[5] and without reinforcement by Loison arriving in time, de Laborde was saved from destruction by Wellesley's lack of cavalry, which prevented an effective British pursuit.

General Wellesley continued his march south and drew up his forces on a ridge overlooking the village of Vimeiro to cover the landing of British reinforcements at Maceira Bay. Along with the fresh troops, General Sir Harry Burrard had arrived aboard the sloop of war HMS *Brazen*. Wellesley was

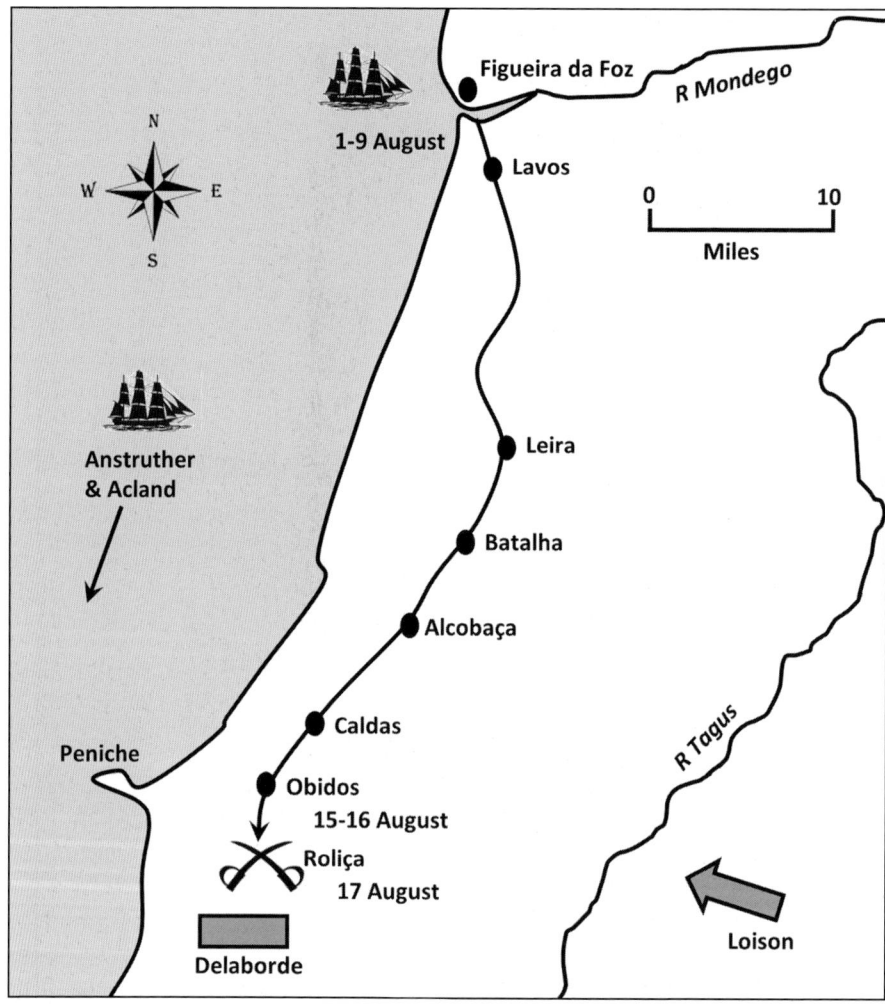

General Wellesley's 1808 campaign in Portugal – The advance to Roliça.

taken out to the ship to report to Burrard, who allowed his junior to command the forthcoming battle. The resulting fighting against General Junot was hard and the British two-deep line volley fire and charge prevailed against French attacks in column. The enemy began to withdraw but with the expectation of the arrival of Sir John Moore's reinforcement, Sir Harry forbade any resumption of the march on Lisbon.

Following a period of negotiation, the Convention of Cintra was signed, agreeing to ship Junot's army back to France in Royal Navy ships complete with weapons and loot. The resulting outcry at home saw generals Dalrymple, Burrard and Wellesley recalled home. Fortunately, Wellesley

General de Laborde, Wellesley's first opponent in the Peninsular.

was absolved but Sir John Moore was left in command, with Portugal liberated from the French, to take the fight into Spain.

Meanwhile, news of events in Portugal and the disaster at Baylen, where the French had been defeated by the Spaniards in July, reached Paris. These affronts to French power had Napoleon preparing to personally lead a campaign in Spain to restore his brother's kingdom and to 'drive the leopard into the sea'.

General Wellesley's 1808 campaign in Portugal – the manoeuvres before Vimiero and reinforcement.

Sir John Moore's Campaign

Fresh orders for Sir John arrived in Lisbon from the Government at the end of the first week in October.[6] This time the overall intent was clear:

> His Majesty having determined to employ a corps of his troops of not less than 30,000 infantry and 5,000 cavalry in the north of Spain, to

co-operate with the Spanish armies in the expulsion of the French from that kingdom, has been pleased to entrust to you the command in chief of His forces.

The specifics, however, were vague and dismissed by Moore as 'a sort of gibberish': '... take the necessary measures for opening a communication with the Spanish authorities for the purpose of framing the plan of campaign, on which it may be advisable that the respective armies should act in concert.'

Instructions to advance into northern Spain were easily given but Sir John commented that: 'They talked of going into Spain as if going into Hyde Park.' With military operations for many years previously confined to small-scale expeditions, the army had little practical experience of conducting a campaign on the scale the Government ordered.

Most problematic of the army's departments was the Treasury-controlled commissariat, about which Moore said that 'a knowledge of their duties in the field was almost entirely lacking' and without a decent military chest, Moore could not purchase the army's necessities, even if they had been available. In reply to his orders, he complained to the Government that:

> The army is without equipment of any kind, either for the carriage of light baggage of regiments, artillery stores, commissariat stores, or other appendages of an army and not a magazine is formed in any of the routes by which we are to march.

Sir John Moore worked sixteen hours a day to prepare the army for taking to the field. Leaving a garrison at Lisbon along with the army's sick on 26 October 1808, the British marched from their cantonments around Lisbon for the Spanish frontier on roads that were rapidly deteriorating in the autumn rains. As so little was known about the geography of Portugal and the road condition that the army would encounter on its march, Moore was forced to split his army, with General Hope taking the cavalry, artillery and some infantry into Spain via a supposedly better but long loop south.[7] The main force (the infantry) would take three separate but more direct routes to the Spanish border and Ciudad Rodrigo. All, it was envisaged, would ultimately head via Salamanca for León.

While the army marched into Spain, another reinforcement was arriving at Corunna, but General Baird's 15,000 men could not at first be landed. This was partly due to the Spanish reluctance to embrace their erstwhile enemy but also the inability to feed their new ally. When ashore, Baird also lacked cash; without money he could not procure the necessary mules and bullock carts to move his army's food and stores. These problems were not resolved until November, when he finally set out to join the rest of the army at Salamanca.

10 *The Talavera Campaign, 1809*

Sir John Moore, having marched into Spain to support Britain's new ally, also found that it was almost impossible to deal with the fractured Spanish government or the self-interested local juntas, which were all still deluded as to the true situation by their victory at Bailén. Moore wrote to Castlereagh a despairingly from Salamanca:

> If ever I had a conception of the weakness of the Spanish armies, the depleted state of the country, and the apparent apathy of the people and the selfish imbecility of the government I should certainly have been in no hurry to enter Spain or to have approached the scene of the action, until the army was united.

He prophetically concluded that advancing into Spain 'may prove to be the worst thing I could have done'.

During the late autumn Napoleon, at the head of the *Armée d'Espagne*, had crossed the Pyrenees with 40,000 men, bringing the total of French forces in the Peninsular to 250,000. By 6 November Napoleon had seized a central position at Vitoria, between the Spanish armies of Blake and Castaños. The French were successful at virtually every turn in two sweeping enveloping movements, and Napoleon was able to march on Madrid.

Sir John Moore's advance into Spain.

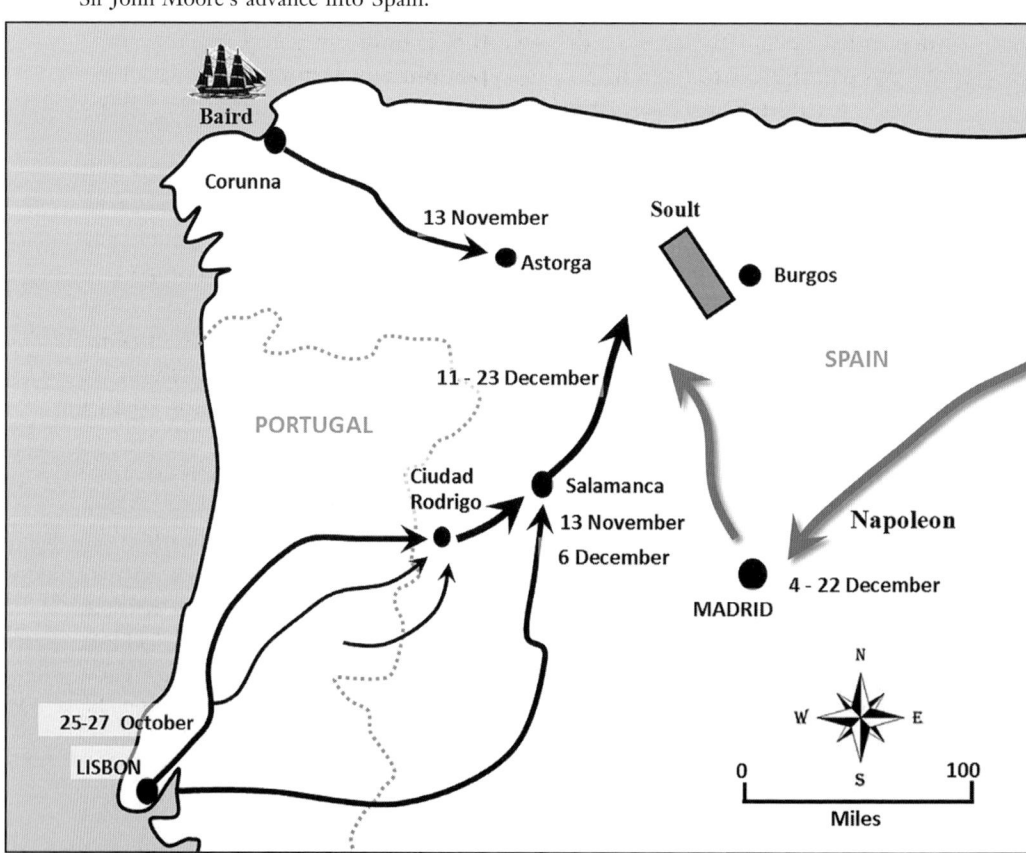

Meanwhile, the Supreme Junta 'in their blind self-confidence' calculated that the French had just 80,000 men and dismissed any serious danger of an attack on Madrid. Consequently, an inadequate force fell back before Napoleon, leaving a rearguard to hold the Pass of Somosierra on the road to Madrid, which was forced on 30 November. Demands for the surrender of Madrid followed and on 4 December Napoleon entered the Spanish capital unopposed.

The emperor only belatedly realised how exposed the small British army was and set out to cross the Sierra de Guadarrama in full winter conditions. Meanwhile, unaware of the threat posed by Napoleon, Moore was advancing into León to confront an isolated French corps and was only informed at what proved to be the last moment that Napoleon was marching to cut him off from safety.

Ordering a precipitate retreat to the River Elsa at Benavente, Moore's army, now numbering 35,000, narrowly avoided being cut off by a small margin by Napoleon's force of nearly 125,000. Reaching Astorga only hours after the allies had left, the emperor realised that the opportunity to destroy the British had passed, and he handed over the pursuit through the Galician mountains to Marshal Soult.

The epic winter retreat across the mountains to Corunna was marked by steadfast rearguard action that was sadly matched by the drunken looting by much of the rest of the army, a disgrace that is only mitigated in part by the soldiers' willingness to fight when the opportunity presented itself. Reaching Corunna with the Royal Navy arriving to evacuate Sir John's army, the enemy were hard on the heels of the British and a battle was inevitable.

There were plenty of potential defensive positions on the ridges around Corunna for Sir John Moore to position the army, but the length of line he could occupy was constrained by having just 15,000 men still ashore. He chose the Monte Moro Ridge, across which the El Burgo road snakes to the port. Here he deployed Hope and Baird's divisions supported by eight 6-pounders, but the problem was that this ridge was easily outflanked around its eastern end. Consequently, Sir Edward Paget's division was tucked out of site behind the hill to counter any turning move and had reserves just outside the city.

Marshal Soult's plan was to attack the Monte Moro and fix the British divisions on the ridge in battle with two divisions and then, as Moore expected, turn and envelop Baird's flank with Mermet's division. To assist with this, Soult's cavalry was concentrated on this flank.

With a French assault looking unlikely, the 1st Division was ordered to follow the cavalry and most of the artillery back to Corunna but, at 1400 hours, Soult attacked. His plan was to assault the main British position in order to fix them in place, while as expected Mermet's division attacked the

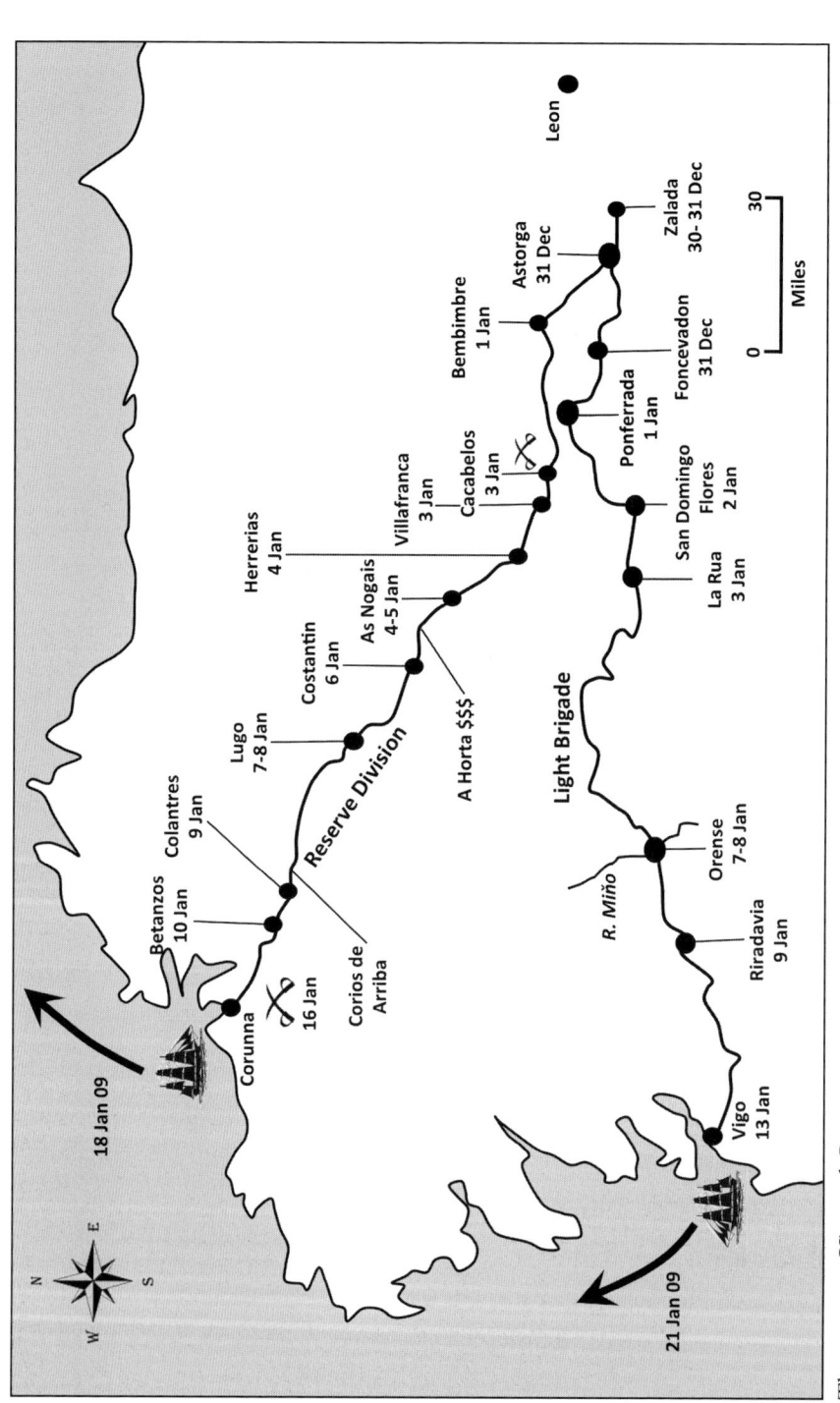

The retreat to Vigo and Corunna.

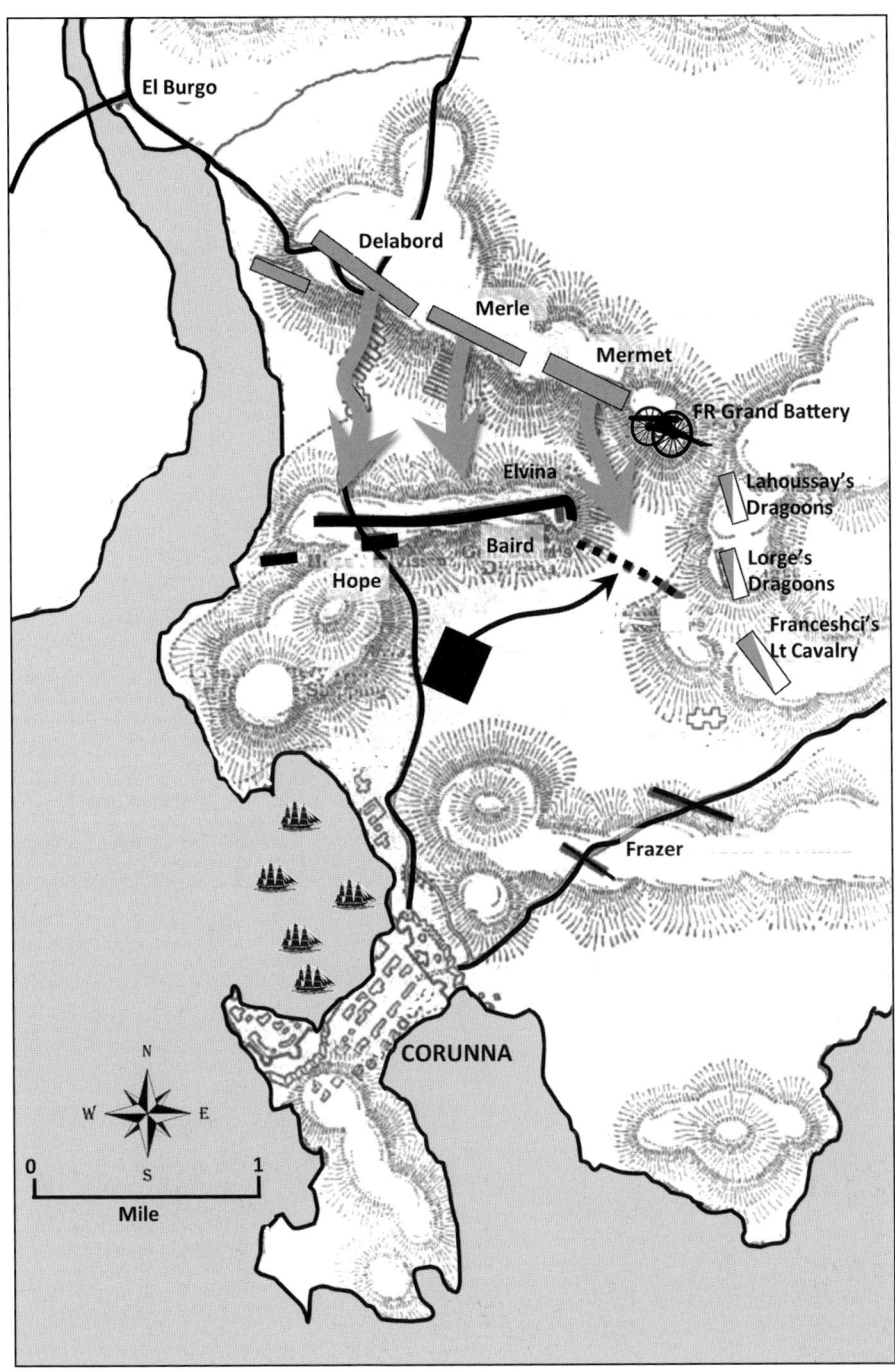

The Battle of Corunna.

British right flank near Elviña, with one of his brigades aiming to envelop that flank and finally destroy Moore's army.

The focus of the fighting on the Monte Moro Ridge was for Elviña and the British were outgunned by the French artillery firing across the valley. The battle ebbed and flowed across the ridge. Sir John Moore had ordered up the Guards of his reserve when he was mortally wounded by a cannon shot and was taken off the field, leaving Hope to take command.

To the west of the ridge the French cavalry advanced on the flank of Mermet's division, but were impeded by walls and ditches. Consequently, dismounted dragoons were deployed in skirmish order but, led by the 95th Rifles of Paget's division, they were forced withdraw. In the more open area off to the British, right Franceschi's light cavalry attempted to cut the British off but were delayed by broken ground and were stopped by Fraser's division on the Santa Margarita Ridge.

As daylight faded over the Monte Moro Ridge, Mermet committed his last reserves, which in accordance with the pattern of the day were counterattacked by Manningham's brigade, culminating with a sustained exchange of volley fire. As darkness fell the French retired back across the valley.

The evacuation of the army from Corunna left a force of 12,000 British soldiers under Sir John Cradock in Lisbon. These were mainly the sick left there in the autumn, now formed into two provisional battalions, and the troops that had remained as a garrison.

Sir John Moore was mortally wounded during the battle.

Chapter Two

The Douro Campaign

Despite the evacuation of the Peninsular, in early March 1809, Lord Castlereagh considered a return to Portugal and contemplated a British role in the defence of the country. In his deliberations he had divided opinion to consider. During the autumn of 1808 Sir John Moore, based on the most basic topographical knowledge of Portugal, wrote to the Government:

> I can say generally that the frontier of Portugal is not defensible against a superior force. It is an open frontier, all equally rugged, but all equally to be penetrated. If the French succeed in Spain, it will be vain to attempt to resist them in Portugal.

In contrast, however, Sir Arthur Wellesley gave his own opinion in a Memorandum on the Defence of Portugal written in early March 1809, gauging perfectly the situation and difficulties of the French:

> I have always been of opinion that Portugal might be defended, whatever might be the result of the contest in Spain, and that in the meantime measures adopted for the defence of Portugal would be highly useful to the Spaniards in their contest with the French. My notion was that the Portuguese military establishment ought to be revived, and that in addition to those troops His Majesty ought to employ about 20,000 British troops, including about 4,000 cavalry. My opinion was that, even if Spain should have been conquered, the French would not be able to overrun Portugal with a smaller force than 100,000 men. As long as the contest may continue in Spain, this force, if it could be placed in a state of activity, would be highly useful to the Spaniards, and might eventually decide the contest.

These encouraging and far-sighted thoughts were very far from universally supported among the military, who agreed with Moore's view that the frontier was indefensible, as did Whig politicians, but there were several other factors that convinced Castlereagh's government to reinforce the British presence in Portugal. Firstly, diplomatic moves were under way with Austria to form the Fifth Coalition against Napoleon and, secondly, Wellesley and Moore had proved that at the extremity of Napoleon's suzerainty, a British army could take on the French and be successfully evacuated if necessary. By fighting in the Peninsular the Government could demonstrate a commitment to arms as well as money, safe in the knowledge that for the time being Napoleon's armies would be fully committed. Thirdly, there was the small matter of the Government's prestige following scandals and Whig criticism of Cintra and Corunna that a resumption of military action and further victories in Portugal and Spain promised. In short, military action would distract attention from the Duke of York's corruption accusations that beset Castlereagh. Consequently, on 2 April the prime minister courageously announced that a second expedition to Portugal would be mounted under the command of Sir Arthur Wellesley.

With Sir John Moore killed at Corunna and General Wellesley absolved of blame for the disgraceful Convention of Cintra, Sir Arthur was the only available commander who had enjoyed significant success against the French in Continental Europe. In addition, thanks to his success in 1808, those who believed that Wellesley's experience in India during the period 1797–1805 was not relevant to fighting the French had been placated. He was, therefore, the natural choice to lead the British return to Portugal, despite Whig political opposition to Sir Arthur himself and the Wellesley family in general.

The newly appointed Commander in Chief promptly embarked for the Peninsular in April 1809, landing in Lisbon on the 22nd with a plan to defend the capital and ultimately Portugal. However, first he had to deal with Marshal Soult and the 20,000 men of the French II Corps that had seized Oporto a month earlier The marshal had been ordered south from Galicia by

Wellesley returns to the Peninsular, landing in Lisbon.

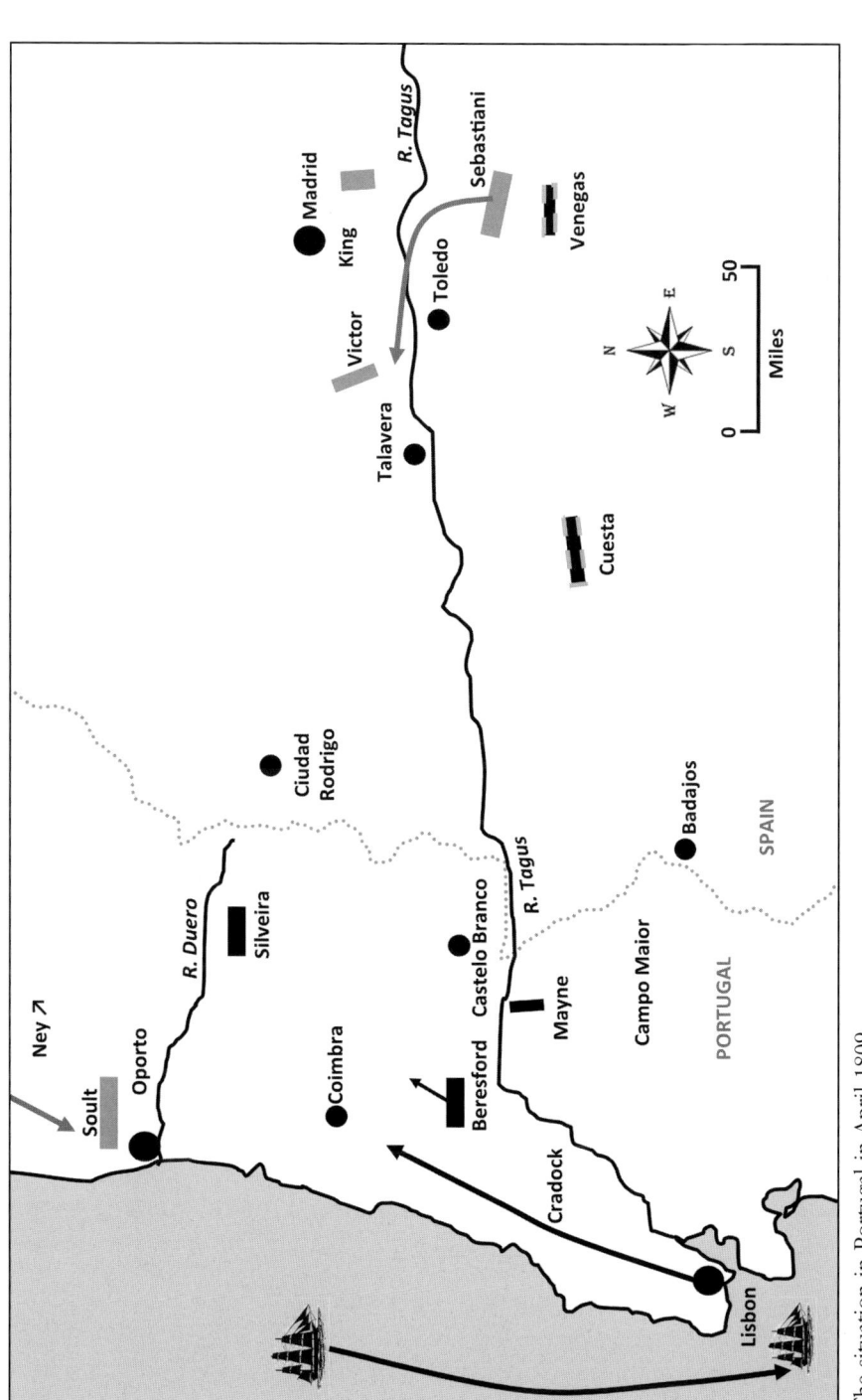

The situation in Portugal in April 1809.

Napoleon to invade Portugal for a second time following the British evacuation of Corunna but, with few resources, he had to cope with bad weather and appalling roads. Napoleon's unrealistic expectations for II Corps were dealt a further blow by the constant attacks of the increasingly numerous Portuguese guerrillas. As a result, Soult's campaign stalled at Oporto.

The other arm of Napoleon's plan for the invasion of Portugal was also in difficulty and similarly stalled. Marshal Victor's I Corps was to have advanced along the Tagus valley with a view to advancing on Lisbon from the east but with General Cuesta's Spanish army threatening him from the south, he was unable to cross into Portugal. Even when Victor defeated Cuesta at Medellín on 28 March, his corps was under-resourced and overstretched, and with a large area of Estremadura to hold, he was incapable of playing his part in the emperor's plan.

With Victor and Soult separated by a circuitous route and some 130 miles of hostile country, neither marshal knew the situation of the other until much later. For the British, even with internal lines of communication it still took nearly a week for information from the southern front to reach Wellesley to the north.

The Douro Campaign

For the 1809 Talavera Campaign to be fully appreciated, a brief account of the Douro Campaign of April and May that year is necessary. It helps explain the degree of confidence with which Wellesley and his army advanced into the Tagus valley to join with General Cuesta's Army of Extremadura and to confront King Joseph and two French corps.[1]

By the time Wellesley arrived in Portugal, Marshal Beresford's reorganisation of the Portuguese army was under way and reinforcements from England under generals Sherbrooke and Hill had boosted the strength of the allied armies to 25,000 British and 16,000 Portuguese. The latter included Silveira's division. Under pressure from Hill and Beresford, General Cradock left the environs of Lisbon and by the time Wellesley arrived was marching north via Leiria and Coimbra to confront Soult. The possibility of Victor advancing on Lisbon was covered by the deployment of General Mackenzie's force of 11,500 men, consisting mainly of Portuguese but strengthened by his brigade of British infantry. Wellesley assumed command of the main army, now consisting of 17,000 British and 7,000 Portuguese effectives, on 2 May at Coimbra.

Within a day and a half, he had produced a campaign plan. The army would continue the advance north towards the Douro with the main body, while Beresford was detached with 7,000 men to march north via Viseu and Lamego to join Silveira's Portuguese division beyond the Douro. This part of the plan, however, had already unbeknown to Wellesley, miscarried with

The Douro Campaign   19

Wellesley's predecessor, General Cradock, sailed to Gibraltar, where he became the Governor.

Silveira's loss of the Rio Tâmega bridge at Amarante. Nonetheless, Beresford joined the Portuguese division at Lamego on 10 May. The army at that stage was not divided but while at Coimbra, Wellesley organised his new command into divisions with brigades that balanced the experience of his battalions and commanders across the army.[2]

Marshal Soult in Oporto was soon aware of both the arrival of Wellesley and the advance of the allied force towards him and promptly ordered

20   *The Talavera Campaign, 1809*

Franceschi's cavalry screen to withdraw north to less advanced positions. He also realised that he would probably have to retire back to Galicia, however, he made two fundamental errors of judgement. Firstly, he believed that the broad Douro would in the short and medium terms protect his position in the city and that it would take the Royal Navy or a fleet of fishing boats to conduct an amphibious landing north of Oporto to outflank him. Secondly, he miscalculated the rate at which Wellesley's army would cover the distance to the Douro. Consequently, when the allies approached the southern bank of the river having completed the final stage of the advance in just four days,

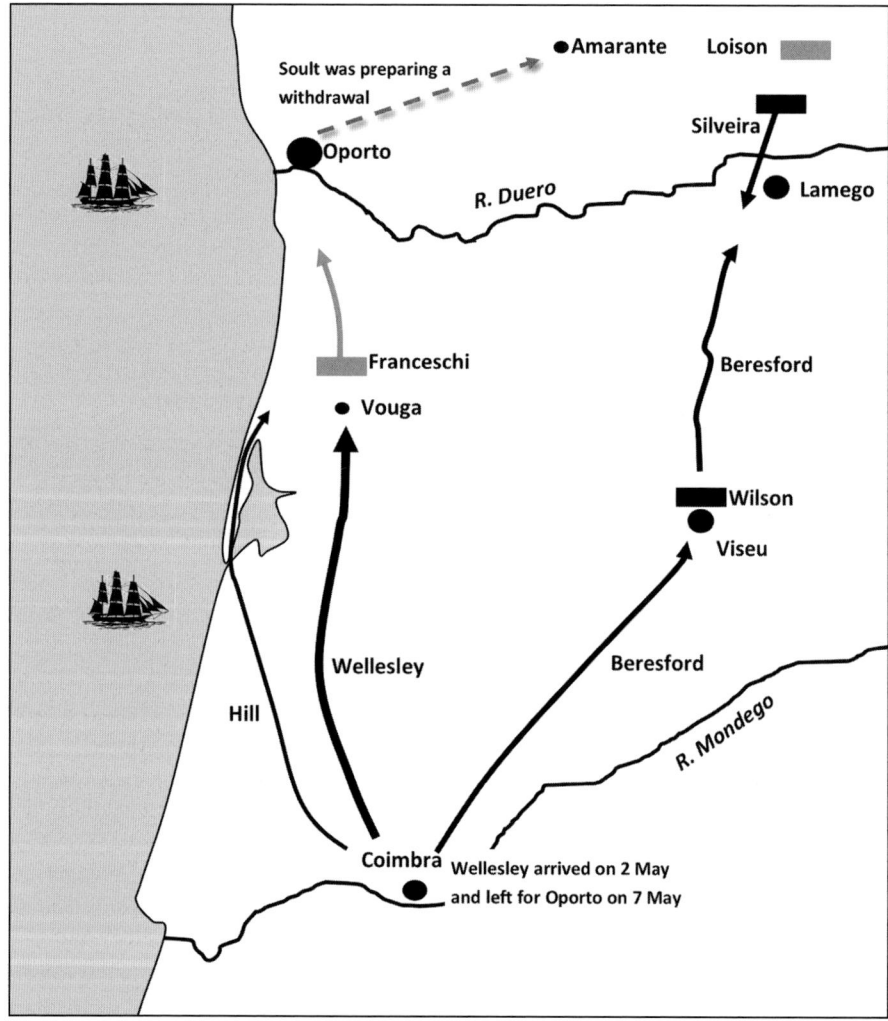

The advance to the Rio Douro.

Soult was not fully prepared for his withdrawal on the roads leading northeast to Braga or east to Villa Real, intending to remain in Oporto to cover the withdrawal for another two days.

Having failed to intercept the French cavalry the previous day, on 11 May the British came up against Soult's rearguard provided by Mermet's division and Franceschi's cavalry in the Grijó valley, where they were positioned to hold their ground. Following a speculative attack by Stewart's brigade, Wellesley manoeuvred the French out of their position by flanking marches without loss. The French rearguard then withdrew across the Douro, destroying the bridge of boats behind them.

Second Battle of Oporto

When the leading British troops reached the river at Villa Nova, opposite Oporto, on 12 May, Wellesley was careful to conceal their numbers behind the Convent of Serra do Pilar on the high ground on the southern bank. As a result, the French remained unconcerned, believing that an attempt to conduct an assault crossing of the Douro was all but impossible. Soult and his staff's confidence in the protection of the broad river inland from Oporto was based on the fact that their troops had either sunk or taken all the boats they had found to the northern bank.

Wellesley viewed the river, city and the broken bridge from the garden of the convent, where he received intelligence from local people on the French deployment and patrol reports. According to Lieutenant FitzClarence, ADC to the Adjutant General, 'doubts came fast and thick upon us, respecting the passage of the Douro in the face of an enemy'. Reports from British patrols soon confirmed that there were no boats to be found on the southern bank, and that the French troops were concentrated between Oporto and the mouth of the river. However, few French troops were to be seen upstream of the city, from which Mermet's infantry and wagons loaded with II Corps' wounded and Soult's loot were heading north.

A potential solution to the lack of boats was provided when word arrived that a partly scuttled ferry boat had been found at Barca d'Avintas just 4 miles upstream and that the villagers were already repairing and refloating the sizeable craft. General Murray was immediately ordered to march to the ferry site and cross the river with the brigade of King's German Legion (KGL) Infantry and a squadron of the 14th Light Dragoons. This crossing, however, was initially at least only intended as a diversion as other news had arrived.

Around dawn, Lieutenant Colonel Waters,[3] on a reconnaissance, encountered a Portuguese hairdresser who had that night crossed the river in a skiff and spotted four apparently unguarded wine barges on the northern bank. These barges, beyond the eastern bounds of the city, were below a substantial high-walled seminary. Lieutenant FitzClarence recalled that General

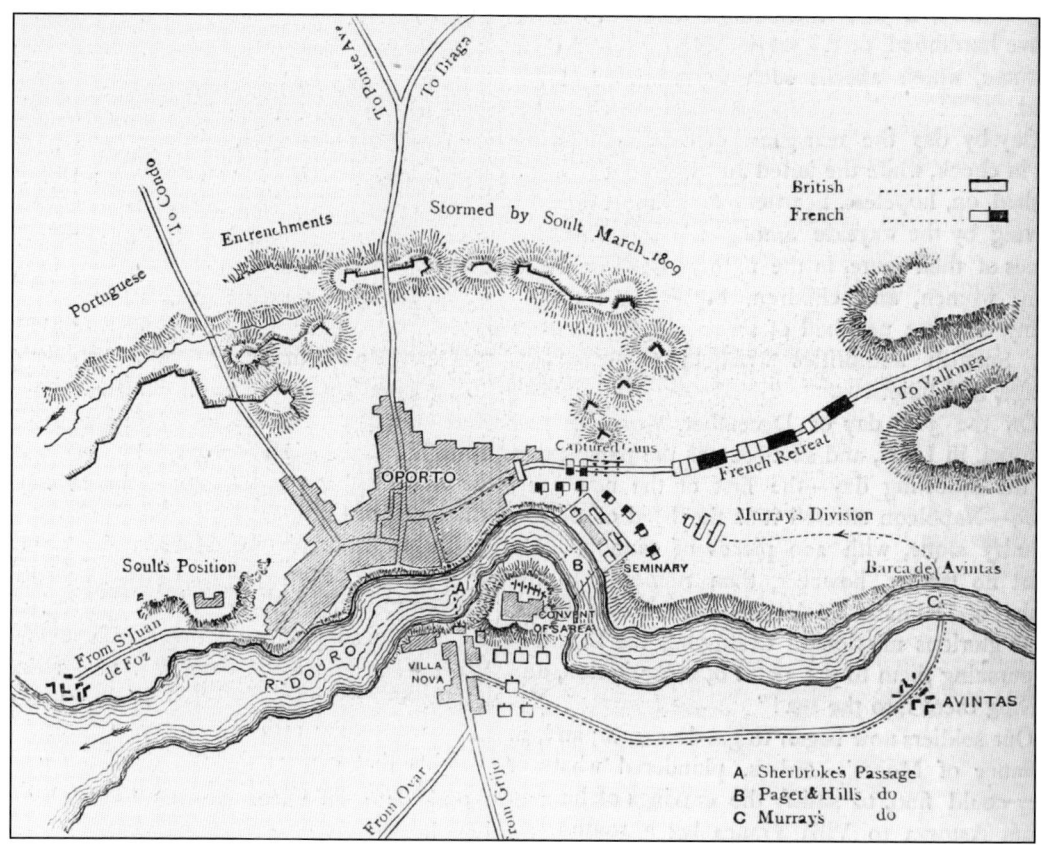

Second Battle of Oporto.

Wellesley promptly ordered Colonel Waters to cross the river in the skiff and bring back one of the barges. Waters, with the aid of the Prior of Amarante, persuaded four local Portuguese to cross in the skiff and undetected they managed to bring back all four of the barges. FitzClarence continued:

> When our doubt and fears were at their highest this agreeable information arrived, and was received by all with the greatest satisfaction, while three companies of the Buffs, accompanied by General Paget, were immediately conveyed to the other side.

Wellesley had immediately appreciated the strength of the isolated seminary and how, once occupied by the Buffs, it could be effectively defended by his artillery fire from south of the river. While the barges were making their first crossing, batteries were ordered up with little fuss into the convent gardens. FitzClarence again watched the progress of the buffs:

> The spot at which they passed over and landed was about half a mile above the city, at the foot of a steep cliff, up which a zigzag road, or winding path, led to a vast unfinished brick-building, standing on the brink ... being surrounded by a wall with a large iron-gate, opening on

The seminary has today been absorbed into the city.

the road to Vallongo. It was a strong post, and the three companies, on gaining the summit, threw themselves into it, as it at once covered the place of disembarkation, and was for themselves a good means of defence. Our artillery was posted on the high bank, on the other side, completely commanding the Prado and the Vallongo road.

It had taken just fifteen minutes for the first barge to cross with an officer and twenty-five men – in all two crossings were made by each of the four barges during the course of almost an hour before the French discovered what was happening to their rear and the first musket shots were heard. With the French drums beating the assembly, Hill's Brigade continued to cross the Douro.

Soult had his quarters on the side of the city nearest the sea overlooking the presumed British threat. Word of the crossing was received while the marshal was breakfasting and he reputedly ridiculed the first reports, having secured all the boats on the north bank. He even persisted in this belief until gunfire from south of the river incontrovertibly proved otherwise. Fortescue pointedly commented:

> As to Soult and his officers at large, it can only be said that their carelessness in the matter of watching the river and the boats was extraordinary, though it can be matched by some of the proceedings of the French army in Italy in 1806. For the marshal [Soult] there is some excuse in so far as

Opposite the Seminary, the Convent of Serra do Pilar stands on the southern bank of the river.

he was in bad health: but the truth was that he despised his enemy, as indeed did every one of his brethren and the great emperor himself, until convinced by bitter experience of the error. There is no greater danger for an army than to be the spoiled children of victory.

General Foy was the first French commander to realise that a serious crossing by the British was under way. At 1130 hours, following a forty-five-minute delay, the 17th Légère was assembled and marching out of the city to attack the allied lodgement in the seminary, while guns were sent down to the river to stop the crossing of the barges. At this point the three British batteries opened fire from the area of the convent, sweeping aside the French attack and the guns with shot, shell and grape. Meanwhile, the crossing by barges continued apace with Hill's command aboard. The scale of the fighting grew, as not only were the number of defenders in the seminary steadily increasing but also the French were reinforced by three battalions of the 70th Line. Their attack was, however, halted.

Watching through his telescope from the convent, FitzClarence had a good view of the fire effect of the British batteries and described the fighting:

> More boats, in the meantime, were brought across, and more troops; the 48th, 66th, and a Portuguese battalion, landed, and not only defended themselves successfully, but even drove the enemy from the walls between the town and the bishop's palace. This petty success was seen by Sir Arthur and his staff, who cheered our soldiery as they chased the enemy from the various posts. The enemy's troops now came through

the town in great numbers and obliged our troops to confine themselves to the enclosure. They continued running along the road towards and beyond the iron gate, while our shells and shot were whizzing through the trees and between the houses into the road as they passed. They brought up a gun through the gate to batter the house; but this proved an unfortunate experiment, as our troops, increasing in number by fresh embarkations, though General Paget was wounded, charged and captured it. They also brought some *guns* to bear from the open spaces in the town, but they were tamely, if not badly served.

While the fight grew in intensity around the seminary, General Murray had also crossed to the north bank of the Douro and was soon seen 'making as much show as possible, marching with his ranks open towards the Vallongo road'. This very visible move threatened to cut off the French from the division that had already marched on the road north-east. Consequently, as FitzClarence recalled, the French soldiers 'now began to think of nothing else and directed their march toward Amarante'. As Soult's men hurried out of the city, the Portuguese civilians took their boats across the river to transport the Guards Brigade to the city's quays 'amidst the cheers of the people, and the waving of pocket-handkerchiefs by the women from the windows'. Oporto was cleared 'with the greatest speed' by Sherbrooke's guardsmen.

The French suffered some 300 casualties and lost about the same number of prisoners, including a battery of gunners and six pieces of artillery. In addition, Soult had abandoned 1,500 men left behind sick in hospital. Allied losses totalled 150 men, including General Paget who numbered among the wounded.

British infantry advance on the enemy with bayonets fixed and arms charged.

A combination of the speed of advance from Coimbra, Wellesley's daring plan and Soult's complacency had delivered a significant victory. Captain Fitzroy Stanhope, one of the commander-of the-forces' aides-de-camp, was sent to London with Wellesley's dispatches aboard one of the naval ships that had been cruising off Oporto, whose crews had seen the smoke of the fighting during the actions of the 11th and 12th.

The Pursuit

What remained for Wellesley's army was the pursuit of Soult's corps to northern Spain, with the aim of inflicting as heavy losses as possible, in order to neutralise the French threat from Galicia for some time. As most of the allied army was still south of the Douro and required ferrying across the river, Wellesley was unable to follow the enemy with his full force for the best part of a day.

By nightfall on 12 May, however, Soult's men had marched 10 miles from Oporto, with the intention of following Loison's division, which was several days march ahead of him on the road back to Spain, via Amarante. That night, however, the marshal received word that Loison's 9,000-strong division had retreated from the Rio Tâmega bridge near Amarante and that he was marching to the north-west. What had happened was that the advance of Silveira's

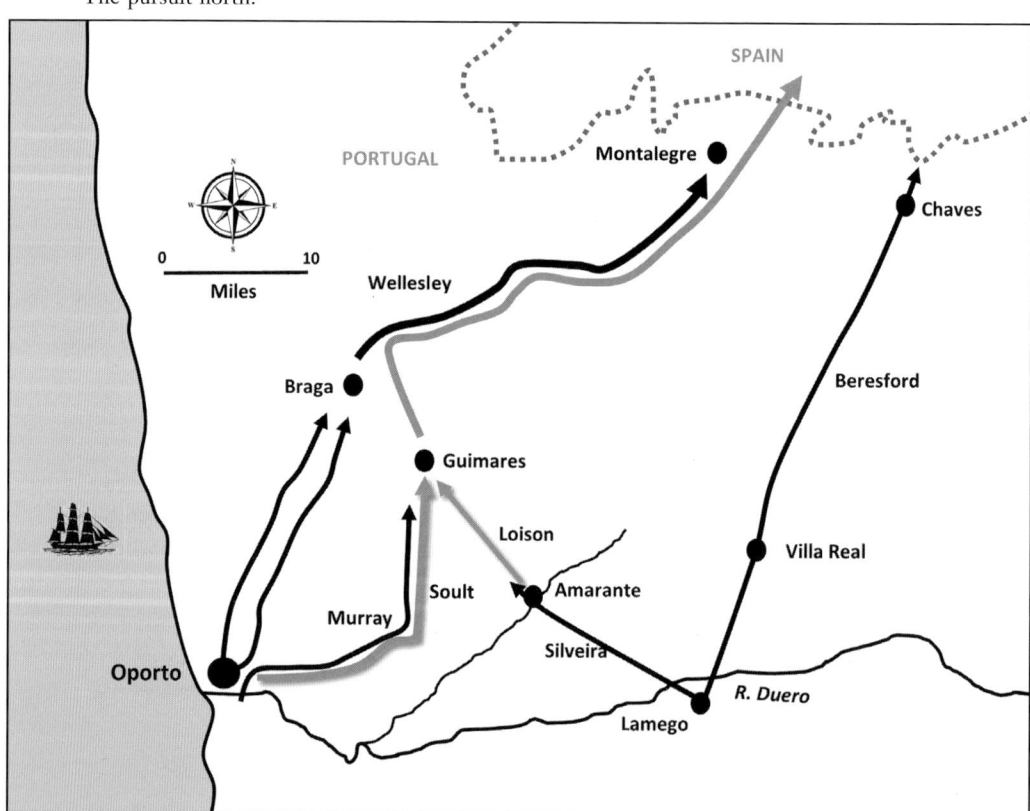

The pursuit north.

> **Spain – a Nation Resists**
>
> Across the Iberian Peninsular, particularly in Spain, the usurpation of the throne by the French, and indeed most of the country, famously led to resistance at almost every turn and to guerrilla warfare. Quiet how debilitating this was to the French cause in the Peninsular and how much it contributed to the liberation of Spain is exemplified by the words of Albert Rocca, an officer of Hussars, writing of the 1809 campaigns in Galicia and Extremadura.
>   The French found that, led by the all-powerful church and their priest:
>
>> The character of the Spanish of these provinces has no parallel of resemblance with other nations of Europe. Patriotism is with them another name for religion … it is patriotism alone, either religious or political, that can render a nation invincible.
>>   No Spaniard would give credit to the misfortunes of Spain or believe she could be subdued. This sentiment animated every heart, in defiance of individual losses, and the frequent discomfort of her armies.
>
> The French regiments accustomed to living off the land found that food had been hidden from them and the population had taken to the hills:
>
>> When the army departed, the peasants descended from the neighbouring heights, and came from their hiding places in every direction, as if they had risen from the bowels of the earth. … Our soldiers could not stray an inch from the road, or halt a single step behind the columns, without running the risk of being instantly despatched by the revengeful mountain folk. We dared not here, as we did everywhere in Germany, form detached patrols, or send our sick without escort to the hospitals.
>
> It was not only individual French soldiers that were attacked:
>
>> Not a day passed without bringing us disastrous intelligence of some of the small parties left behind to preserve our communications. All our communication posts, stationed in our rear as in Germany, consisting of only nine or fifteen men, were annihilated.
>>   Whole squadrons, whole battalions, were butchered by the peasants [guerrilla attack] in a single night. Seven hundred French prisoners were drowned in the Minho all at once, by command of Don Pedro de Barrios, Governor of Galicia, for the Junta.
>
> This, of course, necessitated larger garrisons on the lines of communications and substantial escorts of squadron size for messengers, which significantly weakened the French forces. The brutality of the guerrilla war, where excess begat excess, is another matter:
>
>> Nothing can exceed the horrible sight I next beheld. At every step I stumbled over the disfigured bodies of Frenchmen, recently murdered,

Two sketches by Goya depicting French atrocities (above) and Spanish revenge (below).

The Douro Campaign

Albert Rocca's regiment was the 2nd Hussars, who wore a brown dolman and pellise with blue breaches, although these were normally replaced on campaign by overalls.

and bloody shreds of their garments. The still vivid marks in the sand, declared how some of these hapless beings must have wrestled, and the prolonged torments they must have endured, before they expired. The copper-plates of their caps, scattered around, could alone show that they had been soldiers, or to what regiments they belonged. Those who had thus attacked the French on the Toledo road, were the keepers of the Royal stud, and some peasants who had abandoned their villages on the arrival of our troops. They had acquired a high degree of barbarity by their vagabond and solitary way of living.

Try as they might to subdue their areas of responsibility with increasingly brutal methods, the marshals invariably failed. Lieutenant Rocca of the 2nd Hussars wrote:

Every effort of Marshal Ney's [VI Corps] to terrify Galicia to submission, was vain. Instead of being restrained by severity, their hatred against the

> French was more indignantly roused. Violent measures were answered with even more violent reprisals, which always happens where there is a spark of patriotism . . . Instead of diminishing with our weakness, the rage of the people became daily more inflamed.*
>
> When Napoleon talked to Colonel Campbell on St Helena, he confessed that underestimating the Spanish and the resulting drain on his military resources was his greatest mistake.
>
> Later in the Peninsular War, Lieutenant Rocca commanded Marsal Marmont's cavalry escort during the 1812 Campaign. Such bodies were necessary not only for sake of a marshal's status as army or corps commander but also because of the very real threat in the guerrilla infested country of the Peninsular to even sizeable bodies of staff officers and headquarters. Also, commanders could get themselves into dangerous situations. In 1810, for instance, during the retreat from Santarem back to Spain, Marshal Masséna found himself left behind having an evening meal with just his staff and escort, thanks to one of Marshal Ney's precipitate withdrawals. He only narrowly avoided capture.
>
> An escort could be from company strength of approximately ninety troopers up to a full squadron of nearly 200 men. Soldiers detailed as escort were normally detachments of about fifteen men from the red plumed elite companies of the various cavalry regiments under a marshal's command. Their duties included acting as orderlies around the headquarters and escorting ADCs when delivering orders to formations. Invariably they took some of the best troop horses with them, which was of course unpopular with their parent regiment.
>
> *Rocca, Albert, *Hussar Rocca* (Leonaur, 2006).
> †Campbell, Neil, *Napoleon at Fontainebleau and Elba* (John Murry, London, 1869).

division, reinforced by Beresford, had provided Loison with an excuse to withdraw, which disrupted Soult's plans for a march to north-east Spain on relatively good roads via Villa Real and Chaves. Consequently, 'in imminent danger' and cut off from Loison, with just under half of his corps, Soult had to pursue the only option available to him and take to the very poor mountain roads north through the Sierra de Santa Catalina. Wasting no time on councils of war or elaborate orders, he instructed his men to abandon everything, except the food in their knapsacks, and for his military chest to be blown up. He then had to embark on 'a desperate attempt to cross the Serra de Santa Catalina' but not before he also destroyed his artillery by firing cannon barrel to barrel and burning their gun carriages and limbers.

On 13 May, in pouring rain, Soult marched his corps north-west over the hills via the Ave valley to Gaimarâes, where he was joined by Loison, and on the evening of 14 May reached Póvoa de Lanhoso. Here, having escaped from one perilous situation, II Corps now had to outpace Wellesley, who with intelligence on the French withdrawal was forced marching via Braga to intercept the marshal. Further east, Beresford was conducting a similar march to intercept the French via the Villa Real–Chaves road. Soul marched hard north-east on the Braga–Chaves road, but Silveira had been dispatched by Beresford across the Sierra de la Cabrera and blocked his path at the Ponte Nova across the Rio Cávado east of Salamonde. With the British hot on their heels, II Corps only escaped from this second perilous position thanks to a surprise night attack by 100 picked men from 31st Légère that forced the bridge. Nonetheless, Soult lost heavily crossing the Cávado but the French continued to march hard and reached the border into Spain minus their guns and equipment near Montalegre on 17 May. In doing so they had passed ahead of Beresford and brushed aside an attempt to block the corps by some Portuguese *Ordenanza* led by a British officer.

With the threat to Portugal growing as Marshal Victor's I Corps advanced west along the Tagus valley, and having seen Soult across the border into Spain, Wellesley called off the pursuit. Leaving Silveira in the north covering the Rio Douro and deploying Beresford to the Beira frontier, he marched the British component of his army south to concentrate on the Tagus at Abrantes.

The second French invasion of Portugal had cost Marshal Soult's II Corps, originally numbering some 23,000, between 4,000 and 5,000 men and they had been ejected in just nine days of action, minus their artillery and baggage. Having reached safety, Soult withdrew into Galicia and joined Marshal Ney at Lugo on 30 May. Wellesley now calculated that it would be some weeks before II Corps could again take to the field and that, having left a force to cover the northern borders of Portugal, he could turn his attention south-east to Marshal Victor in the Tagus valley.

Water Canteens

Personal accounts by the participants in the Talavera Campaign all mention water at some point, particularly a lack of it when on the march.

British soldiers had been issued the Board of Ordnance (BO) canteen since 1793 and by 1803, the main contractor, Trotter and Sons, had produced 200,000 of them. It had a barrel like construction and was held together with metal loops, contained around 1.5 pints and was painted in ordinance blue. As a company stores item issued only when in the field, it had the unit, company and item number painted on it in white.

The canteen was carried in a leather strap 1 inch wide and 68 inches long, with a buckle so that the canteen could be adjusted to sit on the soldier's haversack.

A reproduction of the British Board of Ordinance canteen and strap.

The French, meanwhile, used a variety of canteens, including glass bottles slung on a rope loop in rush covers to give them some protection, through to the increasingly popular gourd canteen. This readily available squash was hollowed out and the thick skin dried before melted bee's wax was applied to the inside to make it waterproof.

Spanish soldiers mostly carried the traditional *recuerdo* leather water/wine carrier, which was often brought to the army by the man himself. With General Cuesta's regiments being rapidly raised, a variety of containers were invariably pressed into use as canteens.

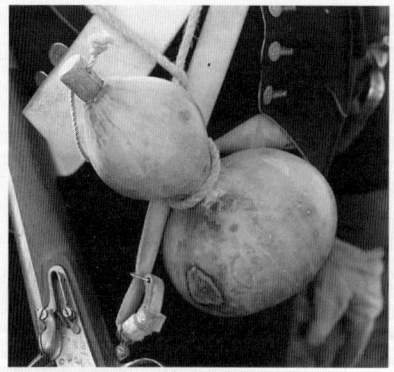 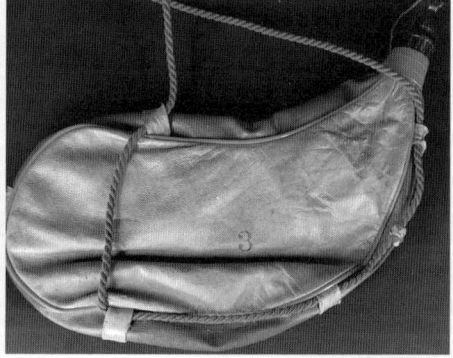

(*Left*) A gourd canteen being carried by a French soldier. (*Right*) A modern copy of the traditional leather *recuerdo* water carrier.

Chapter Three

Campaign Planning and Preparation

When Napoleon had hurried away from Astorga, handing over the pursuit of Sir John Moore, he took with him his Imperial Guard and numerous veteran units, eventually including Marshal Mortier's V Corps. This, however, still left 280,000 French troops to hold down an increasingly guerrilla-infested Spain, which was not enough to subjugate such a large and rugged country. Of those French corps still in Spain, following Wellesley's Douro Campaign Marshal Soult's, minus his artillery and loot, was reorganising, General Sébastiani was fixed south of Madrid by the Army of La Mancha that threatened King Joseph's capital and others were too far afield with their own local difficulties to help. Only Marshal Ney's VI Corps up in Galicia presented any semblance of a threat. In short, with the Fifth Coalition drawing French forces away and Wellesley's return, between January and June 1809, the strategic situation in Iberia had changed significantly and the initiative lay with the allies.

With too few troops widely spread across Spain, the normal French system of corps remaining within supporting distance of each other was not possible; they were essentially on their own. If defeated, as in the case of Soult at Oporto, they could, however, fall back on the nearest corps for succour. With the French corps rarely able or indeed their commanders willing to concentrate, the comparatively small Anglo-Portuguese army was able to join the Spanish in mounting operations against them.

With the short preliminary campaign to bundle Marshal Soult out of Oporto and back into Galicia complete, Wellesley could turn to address the next threat to Portugal: Marshal Victor in the Tagus valley. Planning for a swift transfer of the army to the new front was already under way when, during 17 May, word reached Wellesley's headquarters at Montalegre on the northern frontier that Victor was apparently on the offensive. The French had captured the great Roman bridge across the River Tagus at Alcántara on the Portuguese border. It was one of the few crossings of the great river that could be used throughout the year, with the next bridge at Almaraz being 70 miles by road upstream.

Victor, lacking intelligence or information about Soult's operations, fully realised that his inactivity in the Tagus valley, fixed by General Cuesta's Army of Extremadura to his south, was contrary to Napoleon's orders. When General Mackenzie, commanding the 3rd Division, deployed as the Lisbon

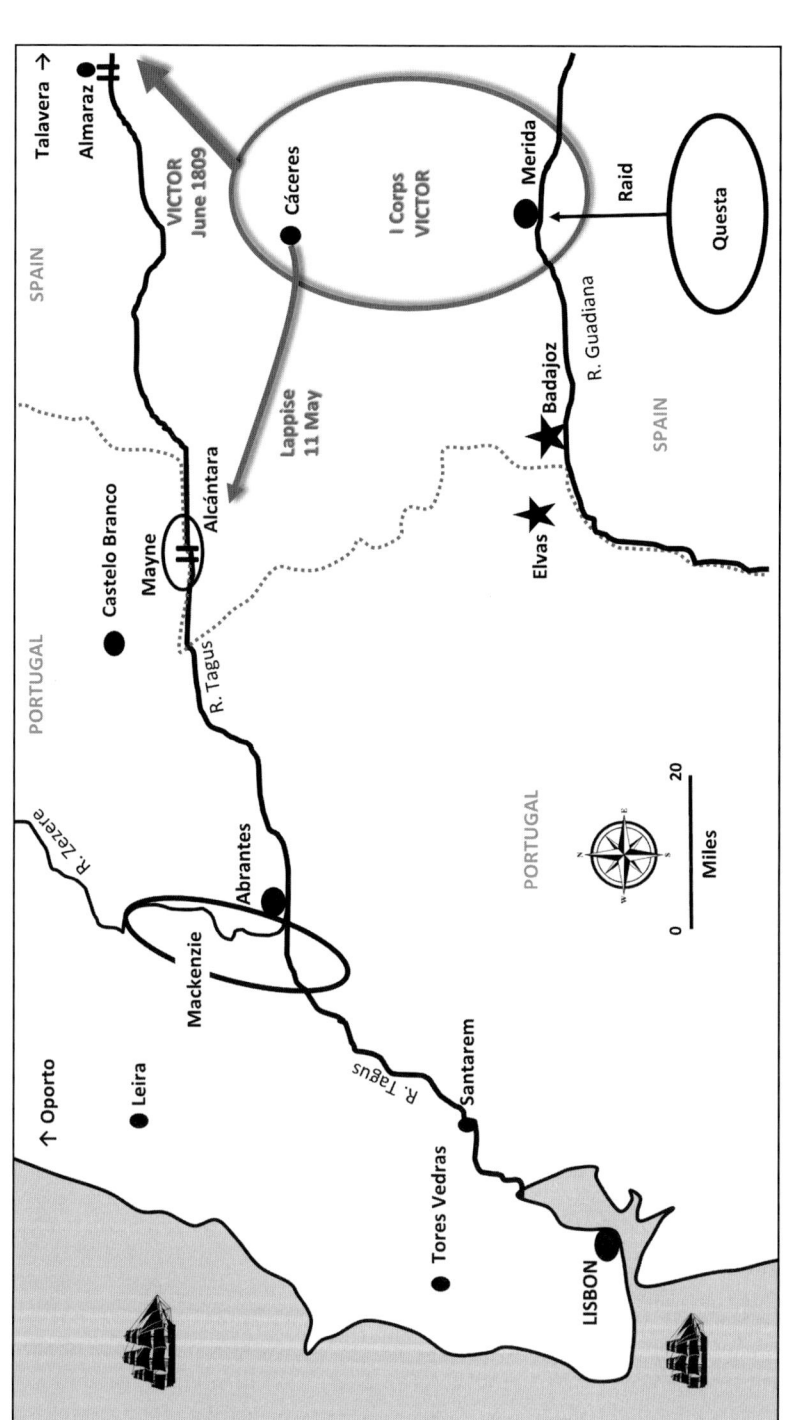

Operations in the Tagus valley, May–June 1809.

covering force,[1] sent Colonel Mayne forward in early May to hold the Alcántara bridge, this represented an opportunity for the alarmed Victor to demonstrate offensive activity. Mayne's force consisted of his own, the 1st Battalion Loyal Lusitanian Legion and the Idanha Militia Battalion, plus a squadron of dragoons and a supporting battery of six guns, totalling some 2,000 men. Victor promptly concentrated his corps and dispatched General Lapisse's 2nd Division and a brigade of dragoons from La Tour-Maubourg's division to secure the bridge against this being the opening of an allied offensive into the Tagus valley.

Colonel Mayne's battalions were deployed in entrenched positions on the northern bank of the Tagus opposite the town of Alcántara. To his front were the normal piquets and well beyond them Lieutenant Colonel Grant was patrolling the approaches with the Legion's cavalry and he:

> retired before the enemy's corps, after some skirmishing on the 12th of May, on which day the enemy entered Alcántara, which on account of its being on the left bank of the Tagus it was necessary to evacuate, for the purpose of defending the passage of the river, which was the only object, consequently this unfortunate city was again exposed to the ravages of its wanton enemies.

On 14 May General Lapisse reached Alcántara and formed his division to attack. Colonel Mayne later wrote:

> The enemy's columns having come within range of our batteries, our guns commenced a fire on them with a good deal of effect, and many shells were pitched directly into the centre of their columns, which did considerable execution. The parapets and walls of the town were soon lined by the infantry of the enemy, while they constructed batteries, which afterwards bore with a good deal of effect on our position, and particularly two which were brought to bear on our flanks. In the meantime, a heavy and destructive fire of musketry had commenced on both sides.

Unable to attack across the bridge, the battle became a firefight in which the weight of French numbers counted. Lapisse's artillery was heavier and started to dismount the Portuguese guns, while the French infantry fired from the cover of Alcántara's houses on the opposite side of the river. Mayne continued:

> we were obliged to give way; but much to the credit of the brave soldiers engaged, be it recorded, that they sustained that tremendous fire for the space of nine hours, during which the enemy could not succeed in any attempt made at carrying the bridge by storm, having suffered most

considerably from the well-directed fire of our sharpshooters, covered by the rocks, &c. within forty or fifty yards of the bridge ...

It was, however, obvious that with superiority of French numbers they would eventually overcome the Portuguese. With night approaching, the militia soldiers started to drift away and with the guns dismounted and 'the loss of seven officers, and 250 men killed and wounded, Colonel Mayne was induced, to prevent the complete sacrifice of these brave fellows under his command, to retire'. Mayne ordered the bridge to be blown but the demolition only damaged one arch of the strongly built structure. Napier suggests that, knowing that the bridge had been prepared for demolition, Lapisse's whole aim was to induce Mayne to blow the structure, thus denying the avenue of advance into Spain via Alcántara.[2]

The badly damaged span of the Trajan bridge at Alcántara soon collapsed. Temporary repairs were made both during the war and afterwards, but it was only properly repaired in 1857.

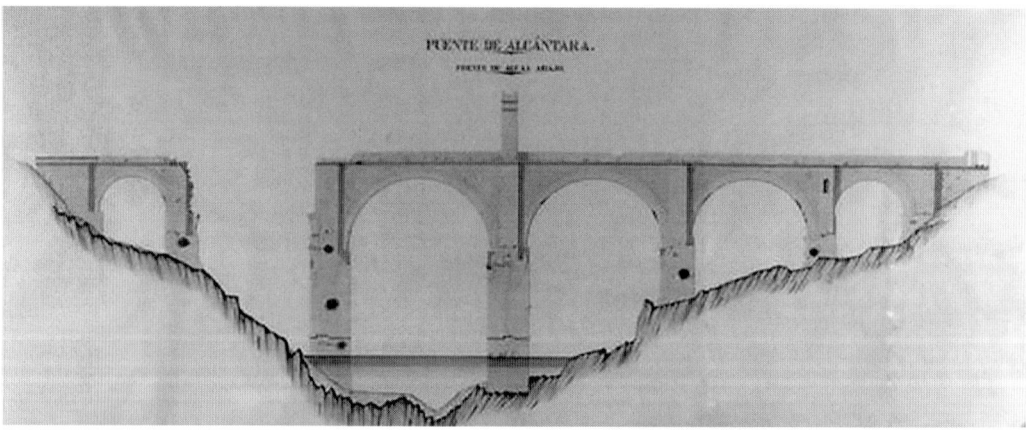

A rearguard of cavalry, under Lieutenant Colonel Grant, covered the withdrawal of some 6 miles to another river line:

> which was effected with the greatest steadiness and regularity, and proved these young troops to be worthy of the ancient military character of the Portuguese nation, having evinced that fortitude and gallantry at so early a period of the campaigns.

Over the following three days Lapisse deployed cavalry patrols to the northwest and when they reported that there was no sign of enemy forces assembling for an offensive, he withdrew back to join the rest of I Corps. News from General Mackenzie of the action at Alcántara could well have been interpreted by Wellesley as a possible opening of an offensive by Marshal Victor. If so, it would threaten his line of communication to Lisbon but he calculated that with just 10,000 men available to Victor, this was not a serious probability. Nonetheless, word of Lapisse's withdrawal and Mayne's reoccupation of Alcántara was greeted with some relief by a nervous General Mackenzie.

Meanwhile, with Victor having concentrated his corps further north to guard the Tagus valley, General Cuesta raided the Mérida garrison and the two German battalions in French service that had been left to hold the city. These troops in the stout and extensive monastery withstood the attack and when Victor sent forces back south to confront the Spanish advance, Cuesta quickly withdrew across the Rio Guadiana and into the mountains.[3]

The perennial problem suffered by French troops in Spain now came to haunt Victor – a lack of food. Expected to largely live off the land, I Corps' foraging parties soon stripped the part of impoverished Extremadura they occupied of scant resources. Spreading formations and units out helped in the short term but this was limited by the need to be able to quickly concentrate if necessary. Albert Rocca, a French officer in the 2nd Hussars in Victor's corps, wrote:

> On account of the scarcity of forage and other necessities, we were obliged to change our cantonments frequently. Almost the whole country occupied by our troops had been abandoned by its inhabitants. Before going, they used to brick up, in a secret place of their dwellings, everything of value which they could not remove. The first thing, therefore, our soldiers did in coming to their empty and unfurnished houses, was to measure like architects the outside walls, and then the inside rooms, to examine if any space had been taken off. Sometimes we also found vessels of wine concealed in the earth. We were thus taught to live on chance offerings, passing whole weeks without a supply of bread, and without being able to procure barley for our horses.

38 The Talavera Campaign, 1809

Thus, to avoid starvation vulnerable foragers had to eventually travel further and further afield to find food, increasingly dispersing the corps. Victor wrote of the exhausted country to King Joseph's headquarters:

> 24 May. The troops are on half rations of bread: they can get little meat – often none at all. The results of starvation are making themselves felt in the most deplorable way. The men are going into hospital at the rate of several hundreds a day ...
> 29 May. We have no flour to issue for a bread ration, so cannot bake biscuit. The whole population of this region has retired within Cuesta's lines, after destroying the ovens and the mills, and removing every scrap

Marshal Victor, commander of I Corps. After ten years as an artillery private, with the Revolution Victor rose rapidly to the command of a battalion and under Napoleon his career advanced steadily, becoming a marshal in 1807.

of food. It seems that the enemy is resolved to starve us out, and to leave a desert in front of us if we advance ... Carefully estimating all my stores I find that I have barely enough to last for five days in hand. We are menaced with absolute famine, which we can only avoid by moving off, and there is no suitable cantonment to be found in the whole space between the Tagus and the Guadiana; the entire country is ruined.

Victor, in a continuing exchange of letters, wrote: 'If I could even get together enough biscuit to feed the army for merely seven or eight days, I should not feel so uncomfortable.' He also reported the growing strength of General Cuesta's army and pressed the King to be allowed to withdraw towards Madrid and redeploy north of the Tagus. Joseph's response, recognising I Corps' perilous logistic situation, was to promise to send 300,000 rations of biscuit and demand Victor move west to threaten Portugal and relieve pressure on Soult, who he believed to be still around Oporto. Not only was Joseph conscious of countermanding Napoleon's orders but a withdrawal would entail the loss of substantial parts of Extremadura, including Mérida. A move to the frontier would, of course, have taken Victor's command into greater danger, as had been exemplified by Cuesta's action when he concentrated and sent Lapisse to Alcántara.

Eventually, after no fewer than three weeks, when the much-delayed news of Soult's retreat reached Madrid, Joseph and his chief of staff Marshal Jourdan issued orders for Victor's withdrawal, which took place during the second week of June. I Corps took up less exposed positions in richer country north of the Tagus, securing the crossings between Talavera and Almaraz.

> **General Cuesta – Commander of the Army of Extremadura**
> General Don Gregorio García de la Cuesta y Fernandez de Celis was 68 years old in 1809 and was no longer the vigorous officer noted for his bravery of previous years. His unenviable situation as commander of the Army of Extremadura reflected the divisions amongst the ruling juntas, plots against him and the deeply felt patriotism of the Spanish people following the French usurpation of the Bourbon throne.
>
> Cuesta had risen from the Royal Guards to the rank of lieutenant general and following success in the 1790s against the French he became the President of the Council of Castile. Defeat on the battlefield and court politics led to him being exiled from the court in 1801. War with Britain in 1805 and the consequent alliance with France saw Cuesta returning as Commander in Chief of Old Castile, with his headquarters at Valladolid.
>
> The Dos de Mayo rebellion against the French usurpers in 1808 changed everything. Despite his reservations regarding success, Cuesta agreed to lead the rebellion in Castile and set about raising an army. However, with very few

General Cuesta.

regular battalions and even fewer men of military experience, this was, to say the least, difficult. He managed to form a force of some 7,000 poorly equipped men but was quickly defeated at Cabeza and withdrew west to regroup in the mountains of Galicia. Throughout the Liberation War the French may have repeatedly defeated Spanish armies, but they were rarely destroyed and constantly re-joined the fight against them, despite being hampered by the lack of a functioning central junta for much of the conflict.

Amidst intriguing and self-centred political manoeuvring by regional juntas, Cuesta was placed under house arrest but following a brief period of Spanish battlefield success, the arrival of Napoleon at the head of a substantial army put the Spanish armies in a desperate situation. Consequently, on 29 December 1808, Cuesta was released and appointed to command the Army of Extremadura. This appointment was not, however, universally popular and throughout Cuesta's time in command, plotting against him continued.

Though distinctly ad hoc and ill-equipped, Cuesta did as much as possible to reorganise his army along modern lines. However, with a renewed French offensive in the Tagus valley, he was defeated at Medellín, where he was wounded, and his lack of tactical ability starkly revealed. Again, Cuesta withdrew to recruit and to reconstitute his army.

Incapacitated by his wound to a significant extent and surrounded by disloyalty, plotting and jealousy, it is hardly surprising that Cuesta made a difficult ally to work with, as highlighted by the universal criticism levelled at him by British officers. General Cuesta, however, did his duty to Spain in very difficult circumstances, with few good officers and supplies or a substantial cadre of trained soldiers.

The Anglo-Spanish Campaign Plan

Wellesley's contact with the Spanish juntas and armies during early May had received enthusiastic support along with promises of co-operation and, most importantly, pledges to supply the British army with food and fodder. At this stage, however, following Sir John Moore's experience deep in Spain, Wellesley was only authorised to conduct operations for the immediate defence of Portugal. Wellesley's letter to General Mackenzie at Abrantes makes the situation very clear:

> To Major Gen. Mackenzie.   Oporto, 24th May 1809.
> It has occurred to me, that you may be in the neighborhood of Gen. Cuesta, and that he may propose to you to make some movement in aid of his operations. You will recollect that your corps is destined to the defence of Portugal; and it must not be risked in any offensive operations. Gen. Cuesta's corps is by no means equal in point of strength to that of the French opposed to him; and it is not impossible that he may wish to strengthen himself by a co-operation or a junction with that under your command. All that is very well, as long as the defence of Portugal is the object; but I cannot be responsible for the safety, or for the risk, for an inadequate object, of the King's troops, in an operation with the Spanish troops under the command of Gen. Cuesta. If, therefore, Gen. Cuesta should press you to undertake any service beyond the line of your instructions, you will tell him that your corps is destined to defend a particular line of country, beyond which you cannot go without orders, so long as the French remain on the Tagus; and that in case they should move northward, you have orders, which I now give you, to join the British army.
> P.S. The troops will be on the Mondego on the 26th and 27th [May].

When Wellesley was able to turn his attention to the borders of central Portugal at the end of May, Victor's corps, still located between Mérida and Càceres, numbered 23,000 men. The British army was still growing but less than 20,000 strong, therefore, operations in conjunction with the 35,000 Spanish soldiers of the Army of Extremadura would, of course, provide the allies a decent superiority over both Victor and King Joseph's reserve of 5,500 men. A number of plans and variations were formulated with General Cuesta, who wanted Wellesley to join far wider-ranging operations than permitted by the British Government's orders. Wellesley wrote to Castlereagh:

> Upon my arrival at Coimbra, in the end of last month, I dispatched Lieut. Col. Bourke and Lieut. Col. Cadogan to Gen. Cuesta's headquarters, with a view to arrange with him a plan of co-operation for the British and Spanish armies; with a view also to attack Victor, and to

oblige him to retire from the menacing position which he had assumed in relation to the seats of government of Portugal and Spain. I propose now to extend the objects of this co-operation, Gen. Cuesta having expressed himself, but little satisfied with the limits which I had assigned to it …

Without a timely response from London, Wellesley wrote:

> I shall soon be in Spain, and if Victor does not move across the Tagus, he will be in as bad a scrape as Soult. I hope to receive from you, before long, some orders respecting my conduct, supposing I should drive Victor away from the frontiers of Portugal and should be required by Cuesta or the Junta to pursue him.

In anticipation of authority to operate in the Spanish border provinces, Sir Arthur began examining his options, with Victor's corps being 30–40 miles from the frontier. Having enquired from the aging General Cuesta how he thought they should co-operate to drive Victor back during the third week in May, within days of writing that: 'I hope to soon hear from your Excellency in what manner I can be of assistance to your operations', Wellesley was complaining to Castlereagh about Cuesta. The Spanish general was obstinate, proud and conscious of his position above his younger allied general, which

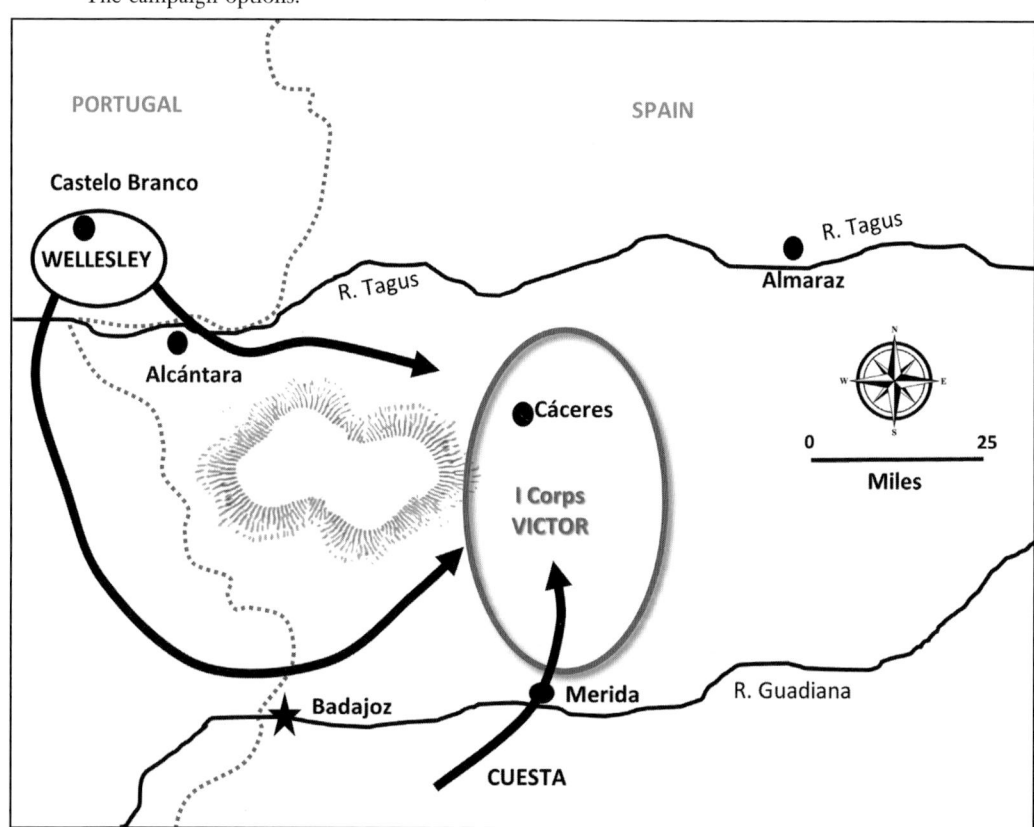

The campaign options.

made him a significant obstacle not only to efficient planning but to the conduct of operations as well.

The withdrawal of I Corps to the north-east and across the Tagus required Wellesley and Cuesta to reformulate their plans. Their courses of action boiled down to independent advances down the Tagus valleys astride the river or linking up with Cuesta in the Guadiana valley on the right. A lack of viable routes through the Sierra Guadeloupe ruled out a central approach.

Over the course of a month, proposals and counter-proposals were made along with at least one significant volte-face. Options were discussed in an exchange of letters that would by turn have seen the British army first marching south to the Rio Guadiana and Badajoz and then continuing along the Tagus valley from Abrantes towards Plasencia. One iteration forwarded from Cuesta through his liaison officers was a thoroughly dangerous deployment of isolated flanking forces that again had Wellesley near to exasperation. On 12 June 1809, however, Wellesley wrote to Castlereagh:

> I have the honour to acknowledge the dispatch of the 25th ult, in which your Lordship conveys to me, by His Majesty's commands, an authority to extend my operations in Spain beyond the provinces immediately adjacent to the Portuguese frontier.

Working with General Cuesta to make a plan to deliver that advance deeper into Spain presented even more difficulties that operations in the border area. The problems saw Wellesley writing: 'I can only say that the obstinacy of this old gentleman is throwing out of our hands the finest game any armies ever had.' At least a part of the problem was that with the intriguing among the Junta and the army, Cuesta feared being replaced, possibly, despite national pride, by Wellesley. The British general had been made aware of a proposal to make him the commander of all allied forces. Sir Arthur replied:

> I am much flattered, by the notion entertained by some of the persons in authority at Seville, of appointing me to the command of the Spanish armies. I have received no instruction from Government upon that subject: but I believe that it was considered an object of great importance in England that the Commander-in-chief of the British troops should have that situation. But it is one more likely to be attained by refraining from pressing it and leaving it to the Spanish themselves to discover the expediency of the arrangement, than by any suggestion on our parts.

He concluded that with the current state of jealousy and resentment such a proposal was doomed to failure, and it would be several more years of success before Wellesley was able to exert any real authority over allied operations in the Peninsular.

General Don Gregorio García de la Cuesta, commander of the Army of Extremadura.

Hiatus

Speed, of course, was of the essence if the allies were to have cut off and destroyed Victor in his isolated forward position. The state of Wellesley's army after its exertions at Oporto and in the mountains proved, however, not to permit a speedy redeployment to central Portugal and an immediate offensive into the Spanish border lands. Exhaustion, the poor performance of the commissariat and the wet weather had reduced battalions to a sickly state and clothing and equipment needed repair or replacement, particularly the soldier's shoes.[4] (See Appendix I for an example of the measures published in a General Order to establish a workable logistic system.)

Not only that, but Wellesley also wrote: 'I fear that I must delay making any movements whatever till the army shall receive a supply of money.'[5] With need to fund the Fifth Coalition, British silver for Wellesley's military chest was short and the army had to increasingly resort to treasury promissory notes, which at this stage of the campaign were generally accepted in Portugal. Nonetheless, Commissary Schaumann recorded in his diary the trials of collecting forage for the horses of the 14th and 16th Light Dragoons during this period at Thomar in Portugal:

> Every day I have to forage for my regiment in the surrounding fields, which are allotted to me in turn by the magistrate, and I have to cut the poor people's corn down. The latter stand by lamenting, howling and crying, and tearing their hair, begging me, often on their knees, to spare their property; but alas! in vain. When one of the townsmen from whom

Deputy Commissary Schaumann, one of 410 commissaries who served in the Peninsular. He was a lot happier when transferred to the 1st Hussars, KGL, who did not look down on him as 'trade'.

I was taking forage this morning saw that his prayers were of no avail, he went mad with rage, and fetching a gun from his cottage, was on the point of firing at me when he was seized by the arm by his wretched wife and one of my dragoons, and was just prevented from hitting me, the ball flying into the air above my head. What a horrible thing war is![6]

At least payment for the Portuguese would eventually be forthcoming but both the French and the British faced different perennial problems in the Peninsular. For the former it was, of course, the need to forage and take food from wherever they could, while for the British, it was the lack of cash to pay for food and transport in friendly Portugal and Spain, as well as paying the army. One of the results of this were penniless soldiers, not just 'the incorrigible rogues' that every regiment had, 'marauding', which forced Wellesley to write in General Orders:

> 10. The Commander of the Forces is concerned to have to announce to the army that private —, of the 53d regt., has been wounded, and has probably died of the wounds he received from some peasants in the neighborhood of Coimbra; and that corporal — and private — have probably met with the same fate: this is one of the consequences of the irregularities of which the soldiers have been guilty, which have had the effect of turning into enemies a people who were grateful for the benefits which they had received from the British nation, and manifested their gratitude by affording to the soldiers every comfort and assistance which was in their power.

At this early stage in the war march discipline and fitness were lacking across much of the army. Many of those 'marauding' across central Portugal were from Colonel Donkin's Brigade of 3rd Division. A note to Donkin from Wellesley is revealing:

> The number of men absent from these regiments [2/87th and 1/88th] as a result of the late marches is scandalous; and I desire that an officer from each regiment go back immediately the whole road by which the Brigade has moved since 5th May, in search of the missing men.

This kind of straggling and looting was not confined to any one brigade or group of regiments. Early in his command, Wellesley told Castlereagh that he knew what he had to do:

> The army behave terribly ill. They are a rabble who cannot bear success any more than Sir J. Moore's army could bear failure. I am endeavouring to tame them; but if I should not succeed, I must make an official complaint of them, and send one or two corps home in disgrace. They plunder in all directions.

Lieutenant Sherer described a typical overnight during the army's march to the Tagus:

> We bivouacked daily. It is a pleasing sight to see a column arrive at its halting ground. The camp is generally marked out, if circumstances allow of it, on the edge of some wood, and near a river or stream. The troops are halted in open columns, arms piled, piquets and guards paraded and posted, and, in two minutes, all appear at home. Some fetch large stones to form fire-places; others hurry off with canteens and kettles for water, while the wood resounds with the blows of the bill-hook. Dispersed, under the more distant trees, you see the officers; some dressing, some arranging a few boughs to shelter them by night; others kindling their own fires; while the most active are seen returning from the village, laden with bread, or, from some flock of goats, feeding near us, with a supply of new milk. How often, under some spreading cork-tree, which offered shade, shelter, and fuel, have I taken up my lodging for the night; and here, or by some gurgling stream, fanned by whatever air was stirring, and sat down with men I both liked and esteemed, to a coarse, but wholesome meal, seasoned by hunger and by cheerfulness. The rude simplicity of this life I found most pleasing.[7]

While the army was assembling and refitting in the Tagus valley centred on Abrantes, which they started to reach by the middle of June, orders were issued for the deployment of assistant provost marshals and their detachments to each brigade. They were to address the problem of absence and straggling and deal harshly with those who fell out from the ranks without permission, along with soldiers found thieving. Private Cooper of the 7th Royal Fusiliers described the flogging of those caught breaching regulations:

> At this time punishment in the army was generally flogging and the number of lashes dreadful. Frequently from 200 to 500 were given; nay sometimes more. In some cases half the sentence was inflicted at once and the remainder when the culprit's back was healed ... A practice, also most fearful, had been introduced of flogging to the beat of the drum. The manner was, ten taps of the drum were beaten between each stroke. Many were lashed into insensibility ... It has been frequently stated that the Duke of Wellington was severe. In answer to this, I would say he could not be otherwise. His army was composed of the lowest orders ... it is true they plundered when an opportunity occurred ... By the discipline he enforced, the British Army became more than a match even at the greatest odds, to the best of Napoleon's bloated legions.[8]

The poor performance of the commissariat and consequent looting was at least partly due to a lack of transport. On 22 May Wellesley complained to

On the better routes in Portugal the local bullock cart was used, but the mainstay of Wellesley's emerging logistic system was to become the brigade of mules.

the British Government minister in Lisbon that: 'I cannot be certain of the subsistence of this army, unless the Portuguese Government will let us have 300–400 good mules, with saddles and drivers. It is ridiculous that in Portugal that number cannot be found.' To make matters worse, mules supplied to formations and units for the carriage of camp kettles, company books and medical stores were being misappropriated for other regimental and officers' baggage. This was addressed in one of a whole series of General Orders issued before crossing into Spain, on a variety of administrative topics. As this was the first campaign of any scale for most regiments and battalions, they were largely relearning by experience the simple practicalities of waging war in the Peninsular, such as camp hygiene that prevented numerous cases of sickness.

The short rest after the Douro Campaign was welcome and Sergeant Cooper records that they were bivouacked out of the summer sun. 'The camp near Abrantes was formed of pine trees and branches, each hut being capable of containing 18–20 men. When the rain fell, it found easy entrance, to our great discomfort.'

The Corps of Mounted Guides

During the hiatus for rest and reequipping, following the navigational embarrassments of the Douro Campaign and Soult's escape through the mountains, the Corps of Guides was re-formed. Wellesley reported to the military secretary at Horse Guards that he had issued a General Order on 23 May 1809:[9]

> This corps is essentially necessary in all operations in Portugal. It is most difficult to obtain any information respecting roads, or any of the local

Campaign Planning and Preparation 49

circumstances which must be considered in the decisions to be formed respecting the march of troops; and this difficulty obliged me last year, and all those who have since conducted operations in this country, to form a corps of this description.

The object is not only to have a corps whose particular duty it will be to make inquiries, and have a knowledge of roads, but to have a class of persons in the army who shall march with the heads of columns, and interpret between the officers commanding them, and the people of the country guiding them, or others from whom they may wish to make inquiries.

The Mounted Guides were not on the establishment of either the British or Portuguese armies but fell under Colonel George Murray, the Quarter Master General.[10] Their function was initially to produce itineraries for the movement of the army and to guide divisions and brigades on the march. Later on, when the roads in Portugal and the border areas became well known to the army and maps of central Portugal were produced to a scale of 4 miles to the inch, the guide's role widened to include the gathering of intelligence.

The task of assembling the corps was given to one of the junior Deputy Assistant Quarter Master Generals, Captain Scovell, who was quickly promoted to major without purchase and elevated to Assistant Quarter Master General.[11] The initial strength, divided between two troops, was to be four lieutenants and four cornets, and twenty-five NCOs and soldiers, but the corps soon grew to 100 strong, which would rise by 1813 to nearly 200 officers and men.

At the beginning of the Talavera Campaign, Captain Scovell was still training and equipping the guides. Their uniform was based on that of the light cavalry, except that the blue dolman was replaced by red cloth. Tarleton helmets were worn by all ranks, and officers at least wore a pelisse.

Reinforcements

The arrival of further fresh troops equivalent to two brigades of infantry and one of cavalry, which had been hastily prepared in southern England for campaigning in the Peninsular, was another reason for delay. They arrived throughout May and into June, having been badly delayed by contrary winds, with the Light Brigade for instance being embarked on shipping for almost a month. As a result, with negligible acclimatisation to the Iberian summer those handful of battalions that had been rushed forward by the time the campaign started suffered considerable losses through sickness.

These reinforcements were, however, counterbalanced by having to send several battalions and cavalry squadrons back to the UK or on to Gibraltar for an expedition to Sicily. The net result was that with the addition of the

A working likeness of Major George Scovell made for a larger picture.

23rd Light Dragoons, the 1st/48th and the 61st Foot, plus sundry replacements, the strength of the army only rose from 18,000 to 22,000, which was only marginally larger than during the Douro Campaign.

It was not just the soldiers that arrived from Britain that took time to adjust to the climate and conditions of service in the Peninsular but particularly cavalry. The 23rd Light Dragoons disembarked at Lisbon in early June and Wellesley wrote to Lieutenant Colonel Seymour with instructions as to how best preserve the condition of his regiment's horses, which would already have been lowered by time spent aboard transports:

> I am particularly anxious that your horses should join the army in a condition for service, and in that view, I recommend your attention to the following objects:
>
> 1st, to their shoeing: the greater the number of sets of spare shoes and nails the better. 2dly, you should at an early period accustom the horses to eat barley, or Indian corn and straw. We find that by giving them half barley and half oats, and by degrees diminishing the proportion of oats, they soon eat the former as well as the latter. The same with hay and straw. I shall take care that, when you get your route for marching, you shall not be made to go marches of too great length. Some of the stables at Lisbon are infected by glanders; and, indeed, at all events, it is desirable that after the first day or two you should have your horses picketed rather than stabled.

Later, still keeping abreast of the circumstances of units newly arrived in Lisbon, 170 miles to the west, Wellesley wrote:

> I am concerned that I do not agree in opinion with you respecting the propriety of sending one regiment of dragoons to Castello de Vide; particularly not one which will have been but just landed. Neither officers, men, nor horses are, in the first days after their disembarkation, fit for any duty, and particularly not for that description of duty to be performed by one regiment of dragoons opposed to a whole army.

Those reinforcements that had yet to join the army included Brigadier General Robert Craufurd's veteran Light Brigade, which had fought under Sir John Moore. As the army started its march to the Spanish frontier, Wellington's headquarters reached Castello Branco on 30 June, from where the following day he wrote to Craufurd:

> I am glad to find by a letter which you have addressed to the Adjutant General on the 28th, that you arrived on the 28th June. You do not mention the troop of horse artillery, and I therefore conclude it is not come with you.[12] You will find orders at Lisbon upon all points on which you can require them.
>
> I beg that if the troop of horse artillery should not be ready to march when your brigade will be ready, you will not wait for them.
>
> We have here two battalions composed of detachments from all the regiments which composed the army under the command of the late Sir John Moore, and among others, of the 43rd, 52nd, and 95th; of which three I enclose a return. I believe that these men belong, generally, to the

Brigadier General Robert Craufurd's Light Brigade had been reconstituted on its return from Corunna, with the 2nd 52nd Light Infantry and 2nd 95th Rifles being exchanged for their 1st Battalions.

2nd battalions of those regiments[13] I propose to send these battalions of detachments down to Lisbon immediately, in order that they may embark for England, if I should find that the enemy do not make a stand on this side of Madrid, in a position which I understand they can occupy near Talavera de la Reyna. I beg that you will inquire from the Commanding Officers of the 43rd, 52nd, and 95th, whether they wish that the officers and men belonging to these regiments respectively should be detained in Portugal, and of course, with the army to join the regiments; or whether I shall send them down to Lisbon to go home with the other detachments.

With the arrival and departure of battalions and regiments, and also having left most of the Portuguese battalions and guns that had fought alongside the British as a corps of observation on the northern frontier, Wellesley

The Battalions of Detachments

Following the evacuation of Sir John Moore's army from Corunna and a renewed French threat to Portugal, General Cradock reorganised the small British force left in the country, numbering between 13,000 and 14,000 men. Among them were 1,500 soldiers that had been left behind sick in Lisbon or had re-joined the army having fallen out from its ranks as Sir John marched to Salamanca during the short-lived offensive phase or most numerously having been left behind during the retreats to Corunna and Vigo. Most of the latter, including prisoners who escaped, were collected at Oporto by General Cameron, who noted that some of them were '... committing every possible excess that could render the name of a British soldier odious to the nation'.

During January and early February 1809 two battalions of detachments were formed and on 6 February, the muster rolls for the two battalions detailed their composition:*

Lieutenant Colonel Bunbury 1st Battalion of Detachments			Lieutenant Colonel Copeson 2nd Battalion of Detachments		
	Officers	NCOs & Soldiers		Officers	NCOs & Soldiers
3rd Foot	1		2nd Foot	4	96
20th Foot	2	47	4th Foot	5	78
28th Foot	8	120	5th Foot	4	93
32nd Foot	1		6th Foot	1	38
38th Foot	6	59	32nd Foot	10	74
42nd Hldrs	3	23	36th Foot	6	75
43rd LI	4	119	42nd Hldr	1	
50th Foot	1		50th Foot	3	75
52nd LI	6	123	71st Hldrs	3	107
79th Hldrs	5	64	82nd Foot	9	96
91st Hldrs	4	164			
92nd Hldrs	5	74			
95th Rifles		35			
Total	46	828	Total	46	734

The strength of both battalions fluctuated but generally grew as men returned to the army or from extended periods of sickness. By the eve of Talavera, however, the 1st Battalion had shrunk to just over 600 effectives, while the 2nd Battalion numbered 625 men.

During the Talavera Campaign, the 1st Battalion served in Stewart's Brigade of the 2nd Division and the 2nd Battalion with Kemmis's Brigade of the 4th Division.

*Napoleon Series Archive. The Waterloo Association.

A soldier wearing his undress uniform replaces the hobnails on his shoes.

> Wellesley acknowledged that the battalions of detachments fought well but he was very critical of their behaviour at other times. The Adjutant General wrote that:
>
> > they are the cause of great disorder – no esprit de corps for their interior economy among them, though they will fight. They are careless of all else, and their officers do not look to their temporary field officers and superiors under whom they are placed, as in an established regiment.
>
> At Talavera the 1st Battalion was heavily engaged in the Battle of the Medellín and suffered 203 casualties, while the 2nd Battalion lost just 25 men. General Wellesley kept the battalions of detachments intact until after the Talavera Campaign, when both were broken up in September and the soldiers returned to their parent regiment if serving with the Peninsular Army or sent back to England or Ireland. For instance, men originally of the 2nd 95th Rifles joined the 1st Battalion of their regiment in the Light Brigade along with those of the 43rd and 52nd Light Infantry, which made a welcome reinforcement of some 150 men.
>
> Those soldiers of the battalions of detachments who were present during 26–27 July 1809 and were still living in 1848 earned the MGSM with the bar 'Talavera' but as they were detachments no battle honour was awarded to their parent regimental.

reorganised his thirteen brigades into divisions. There were four infantry divisions of unequal size and a cavalry division under General Cotton of three brigades, one of which was heavy and the other two light (see Appendix II for the Order of Battle). This greatly eased the passage of orders from headquarters, but they were through the hands of at this stage mostly inexperienced staff officers.[14]

The Final Plan

All the while urging caution, Wellesley had finally agreed an outline plan for the campaign with General Cuesta, which now that Victor had withdrawn beyond the river, was plainly to take place in the Tagus valley, which greatly simplified the debate. While maintaining a safe distance, the Army of Extremadura was already moving north into the area vacated by I Corps, with the eventual aim of securing and repairing the bridge of boats at Almaraz in order to facilitate the junction of the armies. Wellesley would, meanwhile, advance north of the Tagus, crossing the border at Zarza la Mayor and march towards Plasencia with the aim of turning Victor's right flank.

The planned junction of the armies west of Talavera would create a mass of 55,000 allied troops to face Victor and potentially Joseph's reserves, which could total between 40,000 and 50,000 French troops. With the campaign

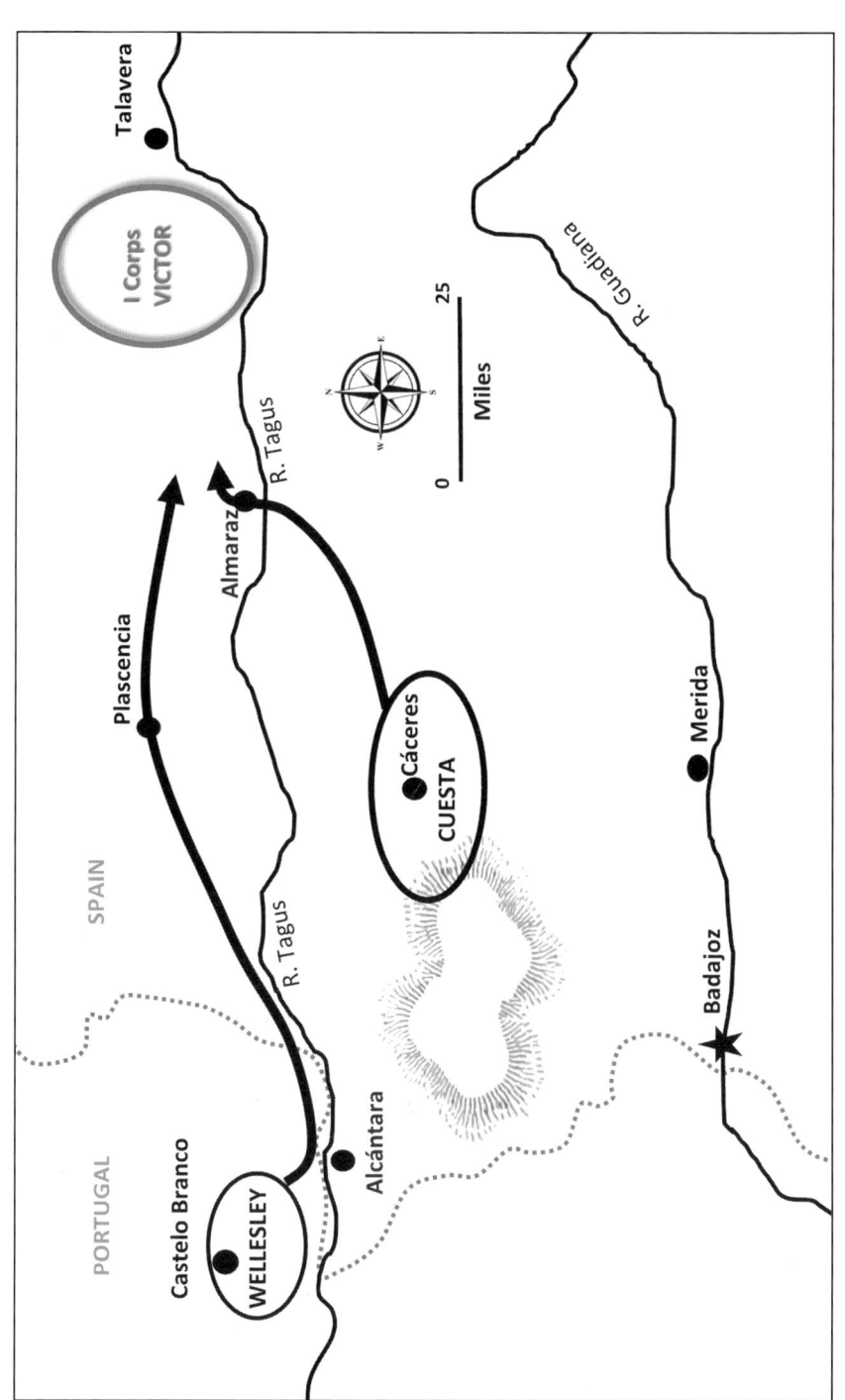

The revised campaign plan.

now taking place in the Tagus valley and the French corps now within two days' march of mutual support, General Venegas's Army of La Mancha was well placed to contribute to maintaining a favourable numerical balance around Talavera. His part in the plan was to cross the Guadiana, keep General Sébastiani's corps fixed south of Madrid and draw elements of Joseph's central reserve away from his capital.

Colonel Sir Robert Wilson, with a force of 1,500 Portuguese troops of the Loyal Lusitania Legion, was to cover the northern flank of the British advance. Wellesley was, however, concerned about the passes over the Sierra de Gata near Perales and that at Baños, which would be guarded by a small force of Portuguese troops, who would later be replaced by Spanish ones. These important passes were taken by the north–south route between Old Castiel and Extremadura and would have considerable importance later in the campaign.

After a month concentrating and refitting or completing unit stores, with food and some money also having arrived to pay the army and help fund the coming advance, the march from Abrantes began on 26 June. On 3 July Wellesley's leading brigades crossed the frontier into Spain; the Talavera Campaign had at last begun in earnest.

Colonel Sir Robert Wilson.

French Shakos, Plumes and Pompoms

By 1809 the revolutionary and early Napoleonic bicorn had been replaced by the 1805 substantial leather and felt shako, which, though heavier, offered far better protection to the wearer's head in battle and cut a better dash on parade or when walking out. Shako covers of various materials were locally manufactured, but in the Peninsular a white cloth cover was preferred as it at least reflected some of the Iberian heat.

In accordance with the regiment's authorised brass or white metal work, shako plates bearing the regiment's number was in either one of these materials, along with the other metal fittings, such as hanging for the cords.

The tall plumes were favoured by the French early in the Napoleonic Wars as they made soldiers more impressive and, allegedly, led to the enemy firing at too long a range and too high, but of course they were impressive on parade. In battle, however, tall plumes were a distinct disadvantage when using cover in an attempt to gain surprise in thick country, attracting the attention of the enemy's skirmishers and artillery. Consequently, the two elite companies increasingly wore pompoms on their shakos while on campaign.

There was a standard colour scheme of plumes and pompoms to distinguish the various companies in a battalion, but this was distinctly theoretical, with regiments frequently adopting their own variations, particularly in respect of differences between battalions. Numbers 1, 2 and 3 on white discs were the most common divergence from standard.

- Grenadier Company – red
- 1st Fusilier Company – dark green
- 2nd Fusilier Company – sky blue
- 3rd Fusilier Company – orange
- 4th Fusilier Company – violet
- Voltigeur Company – yellow and/or green

The French infantry wore braided cords on their shakos for parades: red for the grenadiers, yellow/green for voltigeurs (to match their fringed epaulets) and white for the fusilier companies.

Chin scales in brass or white metal to match the colour of the plate were only introduced in 1810.

A French shako of a fusilier company without the cords, which were added for parade.

Chapter Four

The Campaign Opens

After a halt that for most of the army was about three weeks, with routes of march issued that initially took them astride the Tagus, the divisions proceeded by relatively easy stages to the frontier of Spain and Portugal. Sergeant Cooper recorded that:

> We marched in the direction of Madrid and crossed the Tagus at Villa Valha, by a bridge of boats. Here the Tagus is deep and rapid, being confined between two rocky hills. Next day to Sarnades and encamped in a field of newly reaped flax. Having made hut of sheaves we rested tolerably, but next morning some rascals set fire to the flax and made a terrific blaze. Of course, nobody did it.

With the infantry already on the march, General Cotton's 2nd Cavalry Brigade broke up from Thomar on 2 July. Commissary Schaumann recorded in his diary that:

> The road which stretched away across the hills, was bad in parts, but good on the whole. Large herds of goats were grazing on the heights all round, while in the valley you could see a plough drawn by bullocks, laboriously tearing up the parched ground. It was a picture of beautiful contrasts, a wild, and at the same time, cultivated landscape. In Cortizados we found a horrible place with buildings hardly worthy of the name of houses. The inhabitants were obliging and friendly but complained bitterly of having been robbed of all they possessed by the French, when the latter had marched to Lisbon [in 1807]. We were therefore obliged to content ourselves with their goodwill and satisfy our needs with what we had brought with us. Here, as elsewhere, we were shown with great triumph pieces of clothing and arms belonging to French soldiers who, having fallen into the hands of the peasants one by one, had been miserably murdered.

The routine adopted by the army while on the march was that on arriving at their billets or bivouac, normally by late morning, routes for the following day cascaded down the chain of command via divisional deputy assistant quarter master generals to majors of brigade and were issued to battalion adjutants during the afternoon. Orders of march were confirmed, and officers were told off for various duties, including the battalions' baggage. The

A post-war image of General Sir Stapleton-Cotton, who commanded a light cavalry brigade during the Talavera Campaign.

following morning the bugles sounded, and the drums beat reveille in the early hours and the day's march was under way well before dawn to enable 12 to 15 miles to be completed before it got too hot.

Normally, a brigade advance party of a staff officer and the battalion's camp colour men (two per company) would have marched ahead of the column and marked out the ground where company lines were to be established. This

Camp colours mounted on 7ft poles on campaign were deliberately plain and functional. They were made of cotton in the regimental colour with minimal adornment, so that if captured, the enemy could not claim to have taken 'enemy colours'. For the same reason, French infantry battalion *fanions* were supposed to be similarly plain.

enabled captains to lead their men straight to their ground and begin the business of posting piquets and sentries without delay. In the broken country of the Peninsular, where cover from rain and sun was of importance, company bivouac areas that offered shelter were occupied rather than the prescribed battalion lines.

French Intelligence

Of the march, Ensign Aitchison of the 3rd Guards wrote in a letter home:

> The weather is dry but uncommonly hot. In the whole of our march we have encamped every night – the men make huts and the few officers who have tents make use of them – we march every morning at half-past two. Our division [Sherbrooke's] amounts to about 7,000. On the march we have had to pass many rivers, some of which were of a considerable depth but we forded them all.[1]

Despite Wellesley's own intelligence system being still very much a work in progress, as the Talavera Campaign opened his awareness of the French situation was so much more comprehensive than that of King Joseph. It is apparent that the King's headquarters in Madrid was unaware of the serious threat developing to their west. Not only were French dispatches being intercepted by the guerrillas, but they were forcing ADCs carrying them to be escorted by cavalry detachments, which reduced the speed of delivery to that of ordinary troop horses. In a hostile territory, gathering intelligence was difficult; the French could not send exploring officers out and information freely given by the local population was scant. Consequently, Joseph and Marshal Jourdan were unaware of the assembly of the British in central Portugal and with Victor's withdrawal, the convergence of the allied armies. On 9 June they were still ignorant of the presence of the British army just a week's march to the west at Plascencia.

It was not only the French commanders in Madrid who were ignorant of what was happening away from their immediate area, as Wellesley's letter of 9 July to Mr Frere, the British diplomat to the Central or Supreme Junta at Seville, indicates:

> According to the promise ... of advising you instantly of any intelligence which might be received respecting the movements of the Army of Galicia, I dispatch a courier with the enclosed intercepted letters from Marshal Soult: they are infinitely curious in many respects; but as he seems to have been shut out from all intelligence and correspondence for some months past, it is very difficult to form any conjecture as to the plans which he may form in a state of things which must be entirely new to him; though I should conclude at any rate that his talk about an

attempt on Portugal on the side of Braganza is a mere vapour to palliate his retreat.²

The intercepted letters referred to above were among the items found in the possession of General Franceschi, who was captured along with his ADCs on the road near Toro and had been quickly passed to Marshal Beresford in northern Portugal.

The Army of La Mancha

General Venegas with his 21,000 men, as had been planned, started to advance north from the Sierra Morena, driving Sébastiani's cavalry back towards the Guadiana. Thoroughly alarmed, the French general exaggerated the strength of the Army of La Mancha in his reports, doubling it in size. For the allies this exaggeration had the satisfactory effect of firmly focusing the attention of the King to the south of his capital.

Venegas had, however, pushed forward somewhat rashly but on receiving information that Joseph had reinforced Sébastiani's IV Corps on 25 June, he promptly turned and retreated with haste back to the safety of the mountains. The French, now numbering 27,000, followed but could not bring the Spanish to battle before word reached Joseph that Cuesta was carrying out repairs to the Almaraz bridges and that other allied troops were manoeuvring in the Tagus valley. Consequently, the King, equally promptly, withdrew to the Guadiana, and leaving IV Corps covering the south, he took his reserve back to Toledo on the Tagus, from where he could support either Victor or Sébastiani, a position that he would certainly not have vacated had he known of the allied activity to the west.

Victor's Second Withdrawal

While Cuesta and Wellesley were beginning their advance up the Tagus valley and the King was away driving Venegas south, Victor's situation, just a week after the last of his troops had crossed to the north of the Tagus, was again critical. He wrote to Joseph on 25 June that:

> The position is desperate. The 1st Corps is on the eve of dissolution: the men are dropping down from mere starvation. I have nothing, absolutely nothing, to give them. They are in a state of despair ... I am forced to fall back on Talavera, where there are no more resources than here. We must have prompt succour, but where can it be found? If your Majesty abandons me in my present wretched situation, I lose my honour, my military record – everything. I shall not be to blame for the disaster which menaces my troops, but I shall have to bear the blame. Tomorrow I shall be at Talavera, waiting your Majesty's orders. The enemy has a pontoon-train: if he wishes to cross the Tagus he can do so, for the

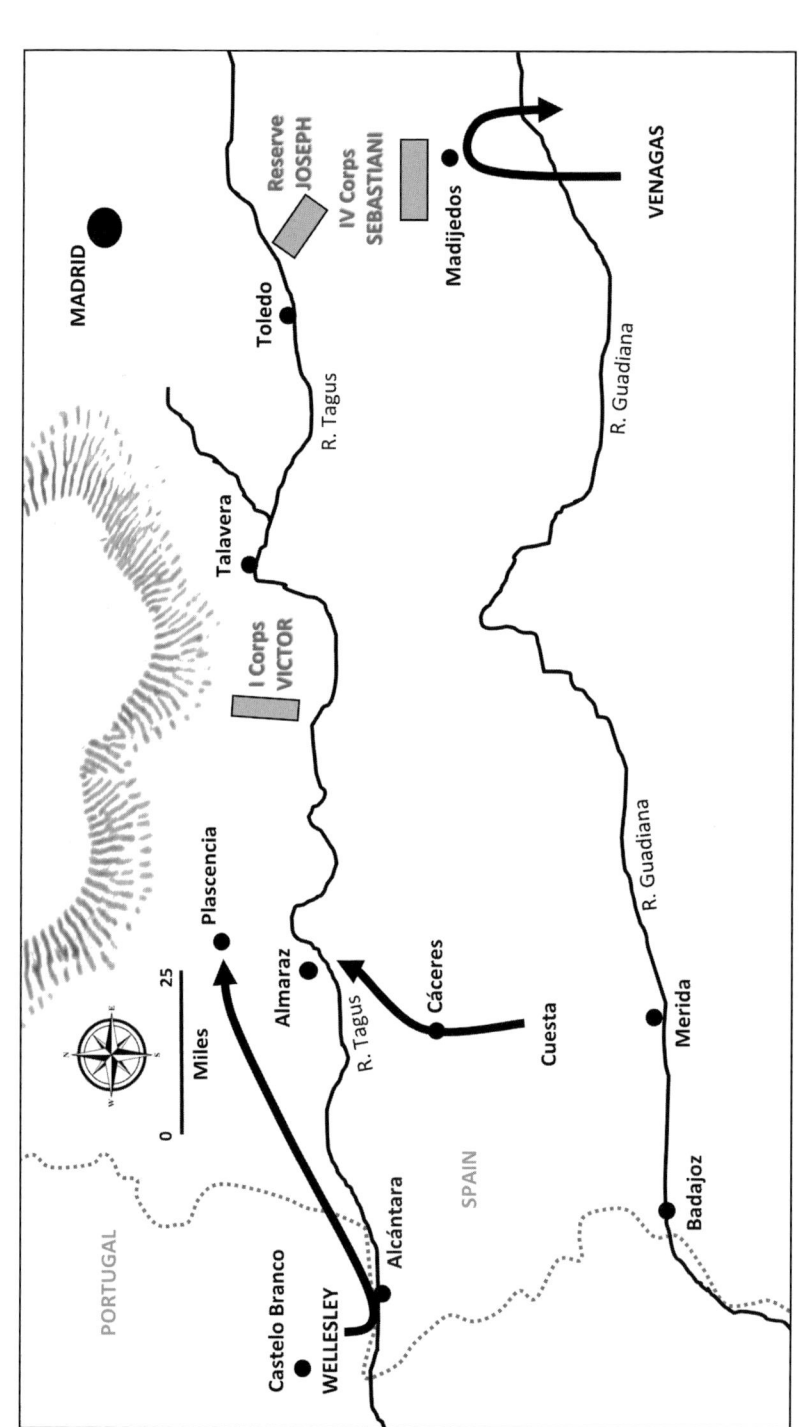

The situation at the opening of the Talavera Campaign.

1st Corps can no longer remain opposite him. Never was there a more distressing situation than ours.

Victor fell back behind the River Alberche just to the east of Talavera and Wellesley, anticipating the scene of the coming fighting by a full three weeks, wrote to Lieutenant Colonel Roche, one of his officers attached to Cuesta's army, from Zarza la Mayor on 4 July:

> I shall be very much obliged to you if you will endeavour to obtain for me an accurate account of the course of the Alberche, the nature of its banks, the depth of water, &c., particularly low down towards Talavera; whether there are many bridges over that river besides that which has been broken up, or fords, or ferries, the nature of the roads leading to such passages on both sides the river, through what towns they pass ... I think it would be very desirable, if possible, to get some intelligent person to examine the lower part of the Alberche, and the enemy's position upon that river ... it will be impossible to employ an officer in this reconnaissance, unless in disguise.

Administration

'If the people of Spain are unable or unwilling to supply what the army requires, I am afraid that they must do without its services.'

[Wellesley to Frere and Beresford]

The army arrived at Plascencia between 8 and 12 July and it was here that logistic problems became obvious. The Junta of Seville's lightly given promise of food for the army in the forthcoming campaign was immediately shown to be 'without foundation'. The problems were threefold: a lack of food and transport in a generally impoverished part of Spain and a paucity of hard cash.

With French troops having passed that way in 1807 and most recently with I Corps living off the country, food in the Tagus valley was short, which given intercepts of Victor's communications on the subject perhaps should not have been a surprise. Fodder and food were, however, available further to the north but therein lay the second problem. Despite assurances that transport to hire would be available, there was a lack of mules and vehicles to both form a magazine at Plascencia and supply the army on the march through a friendly country. At this stage in the war, the British logistic system simply lacked sufficient transport under its own control to collect and distribute supplies. Oman explained the essence of the issue:

> Wellesley sent officers to scour the countryside as far as Bejar and Ciudad Rodrigo, but they could procure him neither mules nor carts. He also pressed the Spanish commissary-general, Lozano de Torres, to hunt up every animal that could be procured, but to small effect. The fact was

Mule trains such as this followed armies into difficult terrain well into the modern period.

that Estremadura was not at any time rich in beasts or vehicles, and that the peasantry had sent away most of those they owned while the French lay at Almaraz, lest they should be carried off by the enemy.[3]

Judging by the comments of Lieutenant Charles Leslie, the French were not the only army that the Spanish were hiding their animals from. He records that on 17 July, while he was on the road down from the mountains to the north to re-join the army:

> I started on my return to Placentia. I was much surprised to meet on the road at intervals herds of cattle, mules, &c., coming up to the mountains. On inquiring, I was informed that the proprietors of these animals, afraid of their being impressed for the use of the armies, were driving them to a place of security. I likewise passed immense drove of sheep.[4]

It had also been agreed that the British were to pay for their supplies when they entered Spain, having moved beyond their own regular supply lines. Details of the agreement to regularise the procedure were explained in an administrative general order at Plascencia on 9 July:

> The Commander of the Forces having arranged with the magistrates of the different districts and towns in Spain that the officers, soldiers, and others belonging to the army, are to be furnished with what they require at the market prices of each place where they may be quartered, makes known to the troops, that the magistrates will cause to be put up, in the square or market place of each town or village, a list of the various articles of provisions, &c. &c., with their prices annexed to them; and in case any of the inhabitants should demand a higher price than that fixed,

the soldiers are to complain to their officers, stating what inhabitants attempted to impose upon them, and the commanding officer of the regiment is to make known the soldier's complaint to the magistrates of the town, who will take proper measures on the occasion.

The soldiers are not, however, to attempt to take things by force, or on their own terms, under pretense that large prices have been demanded from them. Heads of departments and persons attached to headquarters, in addition to putting up their names on the doors of their quarters, will always, on their arrival in a new quarter, immediately send their addresses to the Adjutant-General, and to the Commandant at headquarters.

The Paymaster General, Mr Boys, failed to bring forward sufficient money to pay for food and fodder as agreed, stating that there was insufficient transport to bring the full military chest forward into Spain. Wellesley complained to his commissary general:

> Thus, then, the object for which I stayed so long at Abrantes has been defeated, and the promise which I have made to the Spanish authorities upon the frontier, viz., 'that ready money should be paid for the supplies furnished to the British troops,' will be violated; and the Commissaries will experience all the difficulties in procuring supplies, and the troops will suffer the distress for the want of them, which we suffered in Portugal. All these evils would have been avoided if Mr. Boys had been supplied with 30 carts, which is the largest number that would have

A British soldier's haversack and canteen and the staples of a soldier's life in the field biscuit, bread and a block of tea, which was shaved and added to hot water.

been required to draw £60,000 in silver, which I believe is the utmost of the sum he had in the military chest at Abrantes.[5]

Such cash as was up with the army was being spent in the Coira area to maintain the army assembling at Plascencia and gather sufficient stocks of food before advancing on Victor at Talavera. The result was a further delay in closing with the enemy.

While acknowledging the abiding impression that the Junta were unwilling or simply unable to persuade local juntas to fulfil their commitments without cash, the failure to bring a sufficiently large military chest into Spain contributed to a great extent to the army's subsequent suffering. By 22 July, however, a week before the Talavera, the British logistic system was clearly not working, and Sir Arthur was reporting that 'the army had received no regular supplies'. Finally, it should be added that General Cuesta's own army was little better off 'living hand to mouth' on an already overstretched supply chain.

In a letter to the Junta, Wellesley diplomatically acknowledged that they had tried to supply him:

Upon my entrance into Spain, I certainly expected to derive that assistance in provisions and other means, which an army invariably receives from the country in which it is stationed; more particularly when it has been sent to the aid of the people of that country. I have not been disappointed in the expectations I had formed of receiving supplies of provisions, and I am much obliged to the Junta for the pains they have taken upon that subject, and I am convinced that they did everything in their power to procure for us the other means we required, although I am sorry to say we did not receive them.[6]

Wellesley's Visit to Cuesta

Having reached Plascencia on 10 July, Wellesley rode with his staff the 40 miles to Cuesta's headquarters in order to co-ordinate the next phase of the campaign. Due to a navigational error by the escort of Spanish dragoons, it was dusk when the British general crossed the bridge of boats at Almaraz and reached the plain where the seventy-year-old Captain General had formed his army up for inspection by the British commander. Wellesley's party were four hours late and the Spanish soldiers and their commander had been waiting all afternoon; this was not a good start to their first face-to-face meeting. The army's adjutant general, Brigadier Charles Stewart[7] described the scene at 'Casa del Puerto, where the headquarters of the Spanish army were established in a wretched hovel':

Our arrival at the camp was announced by a general discharge of artillery, upon which an immense number of torches were made to blaze up,

Brigadier Charles Stewart, later Marquis of Londonderry.

and we passed the entire Spanish line in review by their light. The effect produced by these arrangements was one of no ordinary character. The torches, held aloft at moderate intervals, threw a red and wavering light over the whole scene ... here and there cast into the shade, while the grim and swarthy visages of the soldiers, their bright arms and dark uniforms, appeared peculiarly picturesque as often as the flashes fell upon them. Nor was Cuesta himself an object to be passed by without notice: the old man preceded us, not so much sitting upon his horse as held upon it by two pages, at the imminent risk of being overthrown whenever a cannon was discharged, or a torch flamed out with peculiar brightness. His physical debility was so observable as clearly to mark his unfitness for the situation which he held. As to his mental prowess, he gave us little opportunity of judging, in as much as he scarcely uttered five words during the continuance of our visit: but his corporal infirmities were ever at absolute variance with all a general's duties.[8]

With the parade over and first impressions of the Army of Extremadura and its commander not being particularly favourable, Wellesley's party retired to the Spanish headquarters. Brigadier Stewart continued:

as soon as we entered, Cuesta, who seemed quite overpowered by fatigue, retired to rest, but he returned again at eleven o'clock to supper, and sat with us till past midnight. He sat, however, as he always did under similar circumstances, in profound silence, neither seeking to take a share in the conversation, nor, apparently at least, paying the slightest attention to it. I was much struck by this singularity of manner and inquired of those around me whether it were assumed; but they all represented it as being perfectly natural, and gave rather a curious account of the aged chief. Everything, it appeared, went on throughout the army, rather in his name than by his immediate orders; for he governed his followers wholly by a system of silence and terror, of which all stood wonderfully in awe.

The four-hour meeting to discuss plans the following morning was laden with pride, jealousy and suspicion and did nothing to ease the concerns of either Wellesley or Cuesta. Against a background of intriguing within the Junta and factions in the army, talk of the forty-year-old Wellesley supplanting him and his own fragile reputation, the Spanish general's concerns were understandable. Wellesley was, however, already verging on exasperation thanks to weeks of the elder general's prickly changes of mind.

Of the meeting Wellesley wrote: 'The General received me well and was very attentive to me; but I had no conversation with him, as he declined to speak French, and I cannot talk Spanish,' and Brigadier Stewart recalled that: 'I heard that O'Donoju, who assisted his general [as chief of staff], was the chief speaker, and that Cuesta was, as usual, almost wholly silent.' Wellesley's main issue was straight forward: 'I stated to the General my opinion that the principal attack upon the enemy's posts on the Alberche ought to be made by the united force of the British army and the Spanish army under his command.' It was also agreed that General Venegas would drive Sébastiani's

IV Corps across the Tagus and that he would threaten Madrid. It is worthy of note that there was no intent of fighting the united army of Joseph's reserve and I and IV corps as happened at Talavera.

The meeting's difficulty lay in protecting the armies' left flank and turning the enemy's right, to which end Wellesley proposed a detachment of 10,000 from the much larger Spanish army. This was rejected by Cuesta, who argued that this was a British task. A compromise that would see two Spanish battalions remaining with Colonel Wilson's Loyal Lusitania Legion, which totalled about 3,500, was agreed. The disadvantage of this was that Wilson's advance on the left flank would leave the mountain passes across which the road from Salamanca wound its way through the mountains substantially unguarded.

With the meeting over, that afternoon Wellesley's staff took the opportunity to view the rest of the Spanish army. Stewart was again with the party:

> Our meal did not occupy us long; and on Cuesta retiring, as was his custom, to enjoy his siesta, we mounted our horses, and rode out into the camp. By this means we were enabled to see more of the regiments separately than we had seen during the torch-light review. We saw,

A section of Spanish infantry on the march.

however, nothing which served, in any degree, to raise our opinion of the general efficiency of our allies; and we returned to our host at a late hour, more than ever impressed with the persuasion, that if the deliverance of the Peninsula was to be affected at all, it must be done, not by the Spaniards, but by ourselves.

The impressions of the previous evening were confirmed and on his return to his own headquarters on 12 July, Wellesley gave vent to his feelings to his quarter master general: 'I'm sure I don't know what we can do with these people. Put them behind some stone walls, and I dare say they would defend themselves but to manoeuvre with such a rabble is impossible.' In frustration he concluded:

Oh Lord, Murray, they are so useless I can't attempt Victor now – not at 3 to 2 against me, still less 5 to 2, unless I can get that fellow Vinegar or whatever he is called to keep Sébastiani out of it. Let's go home and leave the dam Spaniards.

The Spanish Army

When they crossed into Spain before Talavera, soldiers of Wellesley's army were almost universally critical of what they saw of the Spanish army of Extremadura and its commander. It should, however, be borne in mind that when viewing other armies, soldiers then and now, invariably do so through the prism of their own military environment, often without giving due credit to different cultural, economic or political factors – among others. It is fair though to say that the state of Spanish arms in 1809 was at a low ebb and that the country's armies were at the beginning of a process of renewal.

Despite being beaten regularly in battle, the Spanish armies were still in being, in the field and willing to take the fight to the French. In that respect they were certainly not defeated but they were rarely a match for French formations, leavened as the enemy corps were with veteran units and experienced commanders. There was certainly no lack of Spanish pride and determination to eject the invader and the raw material, their ordinary soldier, was very good but he was hamstrung in many cases at this stage of the war by poor leadership, equipment and training.

The Spanish army of the 1790s had seen attention spent on lavish uniforms but precious little else. The armies of Spain had deteriorated seriously in the years before the French infiltration and usurpation of the Bourbon throne, having been mismanaged as a fighting force by Charles IV and his First Secretary of State Manuel Godoy. This venal monarchy and corrupt government during the 1790s left the army lacking money to maintain itself let alone improve, and the old adage that 'there are no bad soldiers, just bad officers' applied. The nobility took it a right to take senior positions in the army with

An example of the range of Spanish infantry uniforms.

virtually no training or experience, with their only core military value being personal bravery on the battlefield. This left the actual management of units to poorly regarded, paid and trained subordinates.

With the Central Junta lacking significant sway over the regional juntas, local self-interest and corruption prevailed. Consequently, resources – money, weapons, uniforms and equipment – tended not to be distributed as needed for the cause as a whole. British silver and military hardware, for example, was often hoarded in the regions. Captain Charles Vane passed a critical but not wholly uncomplimentary eye over the parade assembled at Casa del Puerto on 10 July 1809:

> they were all, with a few exceptions, remarkably fine men. Some, indeed, were extremely young – too young for service particularly among the recruits which had lately joined; but take them for all in all, it would not be easy to point out a better made, stouter, or more hardy-looking body of soldiers in the service of any nation in Europe. Of their appointments, it is not possible to speak in the same terms of commendation. There were, indeed, some battalions whose arms, accoutrements, and even clothing, might be pronounced respectable; but in general, they were very deficient, particularly in shoes. It was easy to perceive, likewise, from the attitude in which they stood, as well as from the manner in which they

held their arms, that little or no discipline prevailed among them; and hence that in general they could not be regarded in any other light than as raw levies. Some corps there doubtless were, such as the Irish brigades, a battalion or two of marines from Cadiz, and the remnants of their grenadier battalions, which deserved a higher military character; but speaking of them in the aggregate, they were little better than bold peasantry, armed partially like soldiers, but completely unacquainted with a soldier's duty. This remark applied fully as much to the cavalry as to the infantry. The horses were many of them good, but their riders manifestly knew nothing of movement or discipline; and they were, as well on this account as on the score of a miserable equipment, quite unfit for general service. The artillery, again, was numerous, but totally unlike, both in order and arrangement, to that of other armies; and the generals appeared to have been selected according to one rule alone, namely, that of seniority. They were almost all old men, and, except O'Donaghoe and Largas, evidently incapable of bearing the fatigues or surmounting the difficulties of one hard campaign. It was not so with the colonels and commanders of battalions, who appeared to be young and active, and of whom we had every reason to believe that many were rapidly learning to become skilful officers.

Lieutenant Albert de Rocca, a French officer in the 2nd Hussars, has an interesting explanation how the patriotic Spanish armies, despite their defeats, reappeared not far from their original strength:

The Spanish Junta[s] ... sent orders to the *Alcaids* and clergy, even of the places we occupied, to invite the soldiers of the Spanish militia to join their respective corps. These soldiers of their country, seeking to avoid our troops, travelled by night through unfrequented paths; and thus the dispersed Spanish armies constantly recovered from their disasters, with wonderful celerity and ease. When the army of Castanos arrived at Cuenca after its defeat at Tudela, it was reduced to 9,000 infantry and 2,000 cavalry. One month afterwards, at the engagement of Ucles, the same army numbered more than 25,000 men. After the defeat of General Blake at Espinosa, the Marquis of Romana could scarcely bring together 5,000 soldiers in Galicia. By the beginning of December, he had 22,000 recruits around the city of Leon.*

General Wellesley always held the opinion that it was not his job to defeat the French armies in Spain on his own but to tie down sufficient enemy forces that Spanish arms would be ultimately victorious. In 1809 the allies were still in the early stages of a war that would last six years.

*Rocca, Albert, *Hussar Rocca* (Leonaur, 2006).

Final Preparations

Despite Wellesley's private expostulation, there was no intention of doing anything but carrying on with the attack on Marshal Victor. The 18th had been agreed as the day the British would advance east from Plascencia, during which time further vain efforts were made to gather supplies for the army. In a letter to General O'Donoju at Cuesta's headquarters, several days before he marched east, Wellesley summarised his logistical problems, covered above, and their implications on operations beyond the immediate attack on Victor on the River Alberche:

> I am sorry to say that we shall march but ill provided with many articles which we require, owing to the deficiency in the means of transport in our possession; and this country is either unable or unwilling to supply them. I have sent a Commissary to Gata and Ciudad Rodrigo, but he has not been able to procure one mule; and I fear that he will not be more successful at Bejar, as there appears a general disinclination to give that assistance to the army which every army requires, more particularly in a country unprovided with magazines or strong places.
>
> Nothing shall prevent me from carrying into execution the arrangements which I settled with Gen. Cuesta when I had the pleasure of seeing him, although to do so will be attended with the greatest inconvenience, on account of the deficiency of the means of transport ... but I think it but justice to the army under my command, and to His Majesty, to determine that I shall undertake no new operations till I shall have been supplied with the means of transport which the army requires; and but fair and candid towards Gen. Cuesta to announce to him this determination at the earliest moment. The British army does not require much assistance of this description; none for the baggage of individuals; and what is wanted is to be applied solely to the transport of provisions, ammunition, money, and medical stores.

Just days after the march began Wellesley duly reported to London that: 'The army has had no regular supply.'

Captain Lieth Hay, now with the army, wrote: 'We remained quietly in our camp, giving the Spaniards time to put their several columns in motion,' and on 18 July, in the full heat of the Iberian summer, Wellesley's army resumed its march to the east. Ensign Aitchison of the 3rd Guards, in a letter home, wrote:

> Accordingly, about half-past eight in the morning of that day we forded the river Tagus and entered Spain and soon afterwards camped about four miles to the east of Zarza. The several divisions of the army which had preceded ours marched again the next day and we followed the day

General Juan O'Donoju, chief of staff of the Army of Extremadura.

after. We arrived at this place yesterday, where we are to remain encamped until further orders. Headquarters is at Plasencia, where our two divisions of the army and Major-General Mackenzie with his division is a little in advance. A brigade of Light Troops under General Craufurd which have arrived from England are on the march to join us.[9]

General Venegas's advance from the mountains via Santa Cruz de Mudela was to force Sébastiani's IV Corps north towards Madrid and keep that general

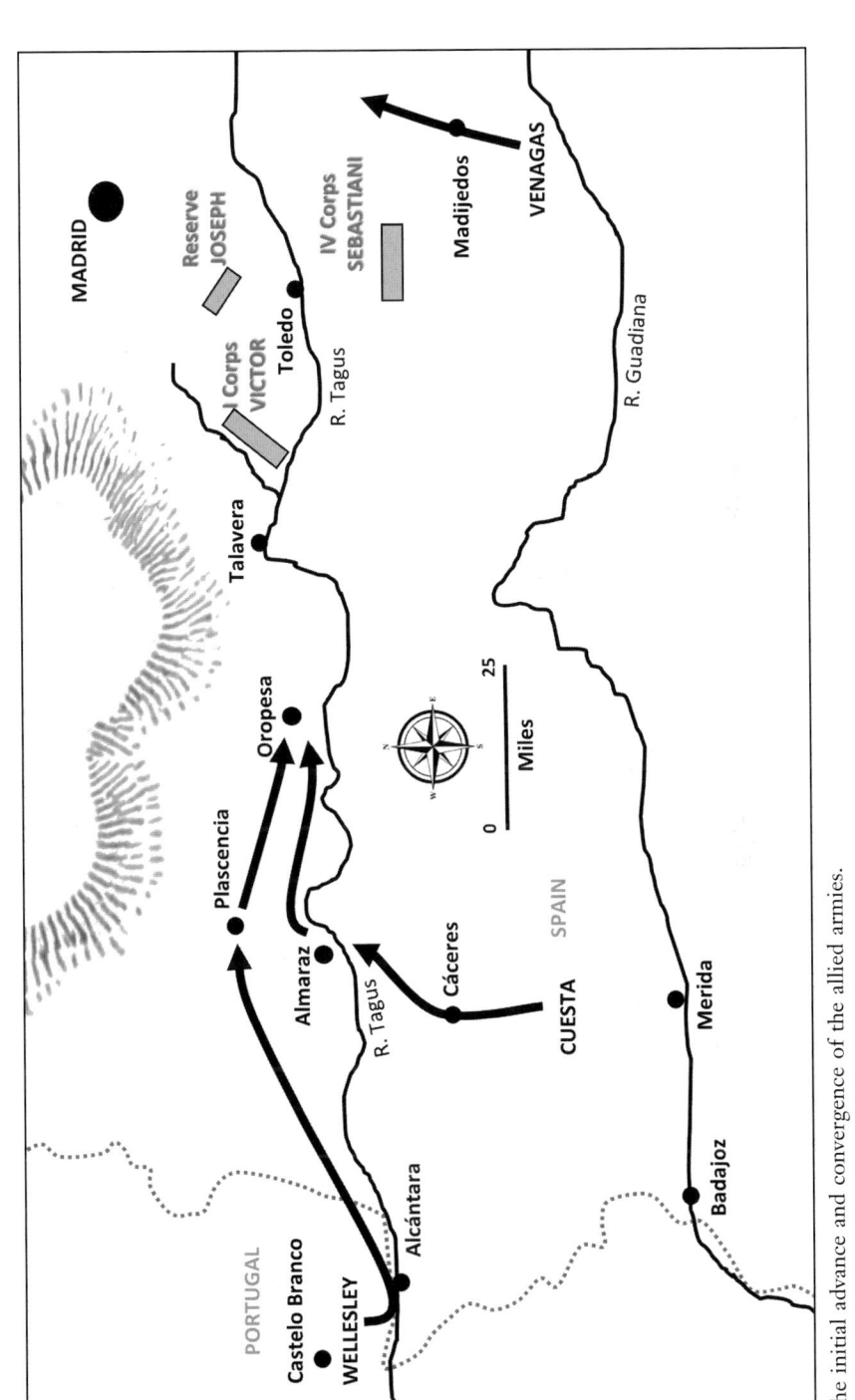

The initial advance and convergence of the allied armies.

fixed and away from the combined forces of Wellesley and Cuesta. To achieve this the Army of La Mancha would have to be in motion on the tail of Sébastiani by the time the main advance began. This Venegas singularly failed to do. Oman observed:

> Even knowing that Venegas was hostile to Cuesta, and that he was a man of no mark or capacity, Wellesley could not have expected that he would disobey orders, waste time, and fail utterly in keeping in touch with Sébastiani or threatening Madrid.

As Wellesley and Cuesta began their march little did they know that Sébastiani was not heading east drawn in by Venegas but falling back out of contact towards Toledo and the seat of the forthcoming operations in the Tagus valley.

With the army finally advancing, Ensign Aitchison reveals in his letters both high expectations and reservation:

> The 21st is said to be fixed on for the joint attack on the enemy and that day we look to as likely to prove as glorious to the British army as any yet reported. The enemy, if he fights at all, has every inducement to resist with desperation, but Spanish patriotism supported by British courage will overcome every obstacle.
>
> In the English papers which have arrived to the 16th ult, they talk of our final success as a matter of course and they even chalk out a plan for us to act upon after the expulsion of the French from the Peninsula. We are not, however, in this quarter yet so sanguine.

A mounted French brigadier general wearing his undress uniform.

Chapter Five

The Advance on Talavera

With Cuesta's Army of Extremadura crossing the Tagus via the bridge of boats at Almaraz, Wellesley, having been joined by the 23rd Light Dragoons and the 1st/61st Foot, put his army in motion towards Victor on the Rio Alberche between 16 and 18 July. They crossed the Rio Tiétar by a hastily laid bridge of boats at Bazagona and marched east. From some distance to the rear, presumably for reasons of fodder supply, Commissary Schaumann was en route with Cotton's light cavalry brigade and described the march:

> On the 16th of July at midday, Sir Arthur Wellesley's cavalry mustered, and the army began to move forward in columns. Our brigade of light dragoons also marched. On the 17th of July the heat was infernal, even in the early morning. From my window I could see one or two infantry regiments laboriously ascending a hill in the sweat of their brow. I shuddered as I thought that in a few minutes I, too, would have to leave my cool room and take the same road.
>
> Our road ran for four leagues through a desolate and, towards the end, wooded district. Again and again we rode through the winding Rio Jerte. A number of dogs which had contracted a warm friendship for our regimental butchers and had followed them out of Plasencia, remained howling and whining on the town side of the river.[1]

Lieutenant Charles Leslie of the 29th Foot recalled the next three days' march towards Oropesa:

> On the following day, the 19th July, we reached Casa de Centinella, after a long march of four leagues, and bivouacked in one of the cork woods. On the 20th we continued on through the same flat country to Oropeza, which is a neat old town situated on a ridge of land rising out of the plain. This was a most distressing march of three leagues. The heat was excessive, and the want of water was severely felt. We learned that a body of French dragoons had left the place only a few hours previous to our arrival. We halted here on the 21st, on which day the Spanish army, under General Cuesta, formed junction with us. They passed on beyond us and took ground in advance of us to our left.

British infantry on the march during high summer in the Peninsular.

In a general order issued at Oropesa on 21 July Wellesley prepared the army to march on Talavera and to receive the Spanish Captain General that evening:

> The army will march to-morrow morning; the regiments to be in the ranks as strong as possible.
>
> The army will parade this evening, in marching order, at five o'clock, on the right of the high road from Oropesa towards Talavera de la Reyna, to be seen by General Cuesta; the infantry and artillery formed in one line from the left ...
>
> The troops will be at open ranks, and will present arms, and officers salute; drums and bands to play a march; each regiment by word of command from its own commanding officer, when the General will approach its left.

Lieutenant FitzClarence, one of the Prince of Wales's illegitimate sons, who was on Wellesley's staff as an ADC to Brigadier General Stewart, the army's adjutant general, recalled that: 'On the 21st, the two Commanders-in-Chief dined together, and in return for the military spectacle Cuesta had given to Sir Arthur at Casa de Puertos, when he visited him from Placentia …' Commissary Schaumann recorded that: 'In the afternoon our army, which is 25,000 strong, was inspected by Sir Arthur at a distance of half and hour's march from the town, on the great high road to Madrid, amidst fields of wheat, ghastly clouds of dust and appalling heat.' Of the inspection Lieutenant Leslie wrote:

> In the afternoon we were ordered to turn out at six o'clock in review order. We paraded accordingly, the whole of our army forming one continued line of great extent. We then understood that this exhibition was for the edification of the Spanish *dons* who were to inspect us. After standing at open ranks for a length of time, we at last perceived a crowd of staff-officers moving up from the left of the line.

Preparing General Cuesta for the review, however, was another demonstration of incapacity that further worried Wellesley's staff. FitzClarence later wrote that:

> The mounting on horseback to proceed to the review, showed how ill-fitted was Cuesta for the activity of war. He was lifted on his horse by two grenadiers, while one of his aide-de-camps was ready on the other side to conduct his right leg over the horse's croup and place it in the stirrup! Remarks were whispered at this moment, that if his mental energy and activity did not compensate for his bodily infirmity, Sir Arthur would find him but an incapable coadjutor. The Spanish General passed along the line from left to right, just as the night fell, and we saw him put comfortably into an antiquated square cornered coach, to proceed to his quarters.[2]

22 July 1808

On the morning of the 22nd, the army was under arms, formed and marching at 0300 hours along the high road to Madrid. In growing heat and a lack of water that even saw Wellesley dismounting to drink from an uninviting pond, after some 9 miles they came up to the Spanish army west of the village of Gamonal, 3 miles short of Talavera. Leslie reported that around midday '… we again met General Cuesta's army, waiting for us in a large plain, and amid loud cheers and cries of *"Viva Inglaterra"* we united on the road. Immediately afterwards there came the sound of guns and musketry fire. 'The inexperienced observer Lieutenant FitzClarence rode forward with the army staff to see what was happening:

> This open country communicated with an extensive plain in front of the town, across which passed the road from Oropesa, being gradually lost

Lieutenant FitzClarence, later 1st Earl of Munster.

as it approached Talavera in the vineyards and woods. In the midst of this plain were posted about 800 or 1000 French cavalry, who, with the utmost indifference, were dismounted, feeling assured that a few skirmishers would check the advance of the Spanish cavalry in their front... Instead of being anxious to show their Allies their activity when at so little cost, being five or six times more numerous than the enemy, they made no attempt to drive them in, but contented themselves with deploying into several long lines, making a very formidable appearance. With feelings of astonishment we rode on to the skirmishers, who consisted of mounted guerrillas, dressed like the farmers of the country. We expected to see them closely and successfully engaged, having heard they were peculiarly adapted for petty warfare; but we found them utterly incapable of coping with the enemy's *tirailleurs*, who were driving them almost into a circle. They were so careless and inexpert in the use of their arms, that one of them nearly shot, by accident, an English officer near him.

The mounted Spaniards were not regular soldiers but, as FitzClarence observed, guerrillas. Effective though they were in petty warfare, the Duke of Alburquerque was wise not to press the French cavalry vedettes, which would have been backed up by formed supports and in this case the rest of La Tour-Maubourg's division of six regiments of dragons numbering 3,270.³ The arrival of Zayas' Spanish infantry division, however, did little to shift the French vedettes but after four hours of skirmishing, Anson's light cavalry brigade (23rd Light Dragoons and 1st Hussar KGL) arrived on the left flank and the French fell back. As they withdrew along the Madrid Road, as they

A dismounted trooper of the 4th Dragoons skirmishing. This regiment was a part of La Tour-Maubourg's 1st Cavalry Division.

passed Talavera the two infantry battalions sent there by Victor marched out of the city and followed the dragoons. FitzClarence recounted:

> On our advancing, the French drew off to the left of the town along the open ground, skirting the enclosures, and exchanging shots with our skirmishers. The Spaniards kept to the right along the great road and could scarcely be brought by the intercession of British officers to enter the town, from whence they learned a body of 4 or 500 infantry had just retired. Brig. General Charles Stewart, who happened to be on the spot, persuaded their officers to follow their retreat along the fine Madrid Road, which was one hundred and fifty yards wide. The enemy were overtaken retiring in two small columns, and to the attack of one, General Stewart led the Spanish cavalry. The result, as indeed all we saw on this day of our allies, was a proof of their total want, not only of discipline, but of courage. On this and two succeeding attempts (to which the English general headed them), on receiving the enemy's fire, when the principal danger was past, they pulled up and fled in every direction; yet in Cuesta's account of this affair, he called it an 'intrepid charge'.

Hurried on their way by Spanish artillery fire, the French withdrew across the Rio Alberche, which ran north at right angles to the Tagus for some 2 miles. Here La Tour-Maubourg's division joined the rest of I Corps. The whole exercise had been to confirm reports that the British were in the Talavera valley. Victor now knew that his corps was almost certainly facing the combined British and Extremaduran armies. ADCs were promptly dispatched to Madrid to pass this vital information on to King Joseph. The King, of course, had up to this point believed that Wellesley was still in central Portugal defending Lisbon.

Meanwhile, Anson's men followed the dragoons but when they reached the wooded banks of the Rio Alberche, the far side of which was swarming with *tirailleurs* and two artillery batteries, the British horsemen were brought to a halt when the enemy opened fire. Wellesley and his staff came forward to examine the French position and divine his intent. FitzClarence was among the officers:

> The enemy had *tirailleurs* in the underwood near the river, and were very jealous of its banks, opening a fire of artillery on all who showed themselves. Sir Arthur and head-quarter staff came unexpectedly in the afternoon under a fire of some light guns on the right in front of the Spaniards, and one of several four-pound shots whizzed close over the General's head.

The stiff resistance indicated a French intent to hold their ground and the British general was able to confirm for himself that Victor was drawn up in

General La Tour-Maubourg, commander of the 1st Division of Dragoons.

an advantageous position on the other side of the Alberche. His army was deployed on some low hills a half mile beyond the river, anchored on the left by the Tagus and on the right by wooded hills and the Alberche, which changed its course to east–west. A detailed reconnaissance of the river revealed an intact wooden bridge on the high road east of the city and that with the summer river level low, the Alberche was fordable at a number of points along its length and was no great obstacle. Wellesley's considered opinion was that Victor's position was too long to be strongly held by the unreinforced I Corps of 22,000, men facing 20,000 British and 32,000 Spanish. Given the numerical advantage of two to one, Wellesley would like to have attacked immediately but as the afternoon was well advanced, there was insufficient daylight to assemble the armies, which were at that point strung out on the road back to Gamonal. All he could do was prepare an attack for the following morning and hope that Victor would not have slipped away east during the short hours of summer darkness.

As the sun set, Anson's cavalry piqueted the river line supported by General Mackenzie's 3rd Division, while the rest of the British army was halted and bivouaced in the area north of Talavera. The Duke of Alburquerque deployed his cavalry facing the bridge on the high road to Madrid on the French left, while the Spanish main body occupied the city to the rear.

General Wellesley and his staff worked to prepare a plan for an attack the following morning, which the British commander took to present to a wavering Cuesta but the general had, however, gone to bed. Once awakened he and his staff seemed oblivious of the opportunity or the necessity for delivering an attack at dawn. He 'received the suggestion with dry civility', and asked for time to think them over. After a conference with his subordinates, he at last sent word at midnight that he would accept the proposed plan of operations.

This prevarication and the Captain General's actions yawing from unwarranted timidity to overconfidence during the subsequent days can, on top of indifferent ability, only be explained as stamping his authority and restoring his reputation after a series of defeats, the most serious of which had been at Medellín. It is only fair to add that Cuesta exasperated his chief of staff General O'Donoju and had argued with a number of his senior officers over his conduct of operations when the advantage so clearly lay with the allies.

23 July 1809

'The state of the campaign to a uniformed spectator appeared extraordinary.' [Lieutenant Leith Hay]

The plan Wellesley had developed was for the Spanish to fix the French in position with an attack on the bridge and the southern length of the Alberche, while he would turn the right flank of the enemy's defensive line. The

A British light dragoon. The dolman and Tarleton helmet were both replaced in the 1812 dress regulations.

3rd Division was already positioned at the bend in the river and at midnight General Sherbrooke's 1st Division was brought up to join them, but at 0300 hours, the agreed time for the attack, there was no sign of the Spanish. Lieutenant Leith Hay, who had arrived with the army the previous evening, provides a flavour of the long wait that morning for a fight that did not materialise. 'It appears difficult to account for the delay in attacking so inferior a force, as regimental officers, we know nothing with certainty, except what we witnessed or read in the orders of the army, all was rumour, exaggeration, surmise or error.'

After waiting until well after dawn, Wellesley rode to find General Cuesta, who according to FitzClarence was in his bivouac 'three quarters of a mile from the Alberche, where, on cushions taken out of his carriage, he sat a picture of physical and mental inability':

> Two soldiers stood near to aid or support him in any little necessary operation, and the scene would have been ridiculous had it not been painful, as we saw the tide, which, 'when taken at its flood,' might, nay, would 'lead us on to fortune' and victory, fast ebbing, without our taking advantage of it.

Cuesta complained to Wellesley that the French defences had not been sufficiently examined, that it would take time to deploy his army at the points it was to attack, that he not convinced of the state of the fords to be used by his left, that the bridge over which his right-hand column would advance

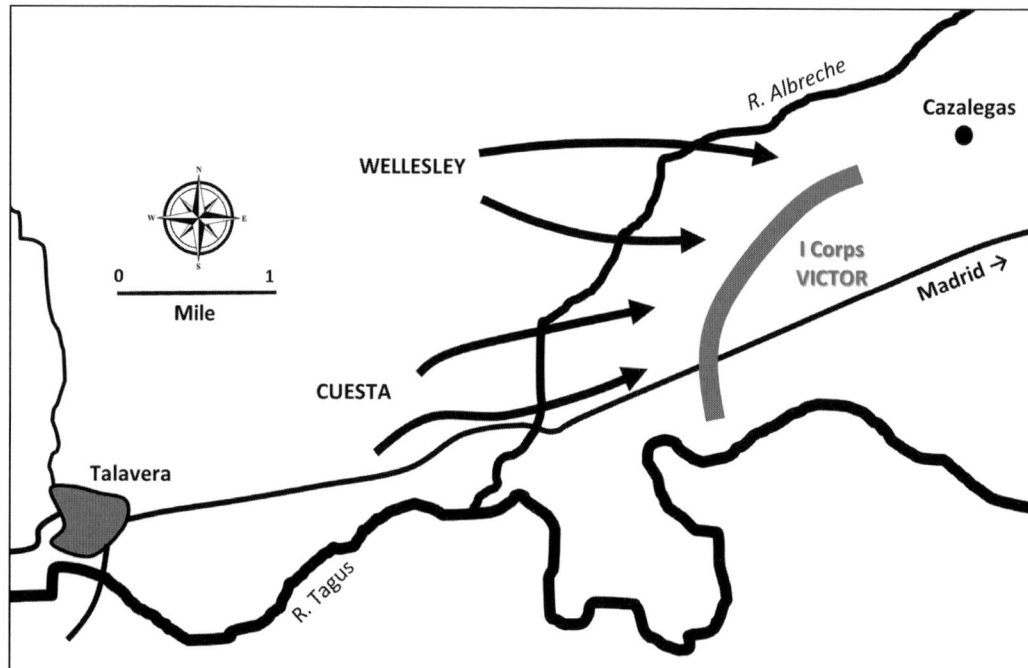

Alberche – the battle that did not take place.

seemed too weak for artillery to cross, 'and many other things to the same effect ...':[4]

> After considerable suspense, it was universally reported throughout the army, that on being pressed and driven to his last excuse, Cuesta pleaded that it was Sunday, at the same time promising to attack at daylight the next morning; and our troops were in consequence ordered back to their bivouacs. It may be fairly considered that pride had considerable weight on this occasion. Cuesta was a true Spaniard and disliked the suggestion of an English general in his own country, and, with recollections of two hundred and fifty years before, could not bring his ideas down to present changes and circumstances. These feelings were national, and ever evinced ...[5]

Almost as inexplicably, Marshal Victor, despite being outnumbered by the combined army twice his size and being at close quarters, remain throughout the morning in a dangerously exposed position. Theories include being ordered to remain in place and to march away at the first sign of allied attack, but this was extremely risky with the armies in such close proximity, and some retrograde movement to facilitate a safe withdrawal would almost certainly have been observed. William Napier,[6] however, theorised that the French had a sympathiser in the Spanish camp who managed to assure Victor that there would be no attack that day.

Eventually, when Victor's outposts were seen to be discreetly thinning out to the rear, General Cuesta was persuaded to see for himself that his concerns were much reduced. Again, the British staff officers were treated with a demonstration of the Captain General's incapacity when mounting his horse. This time Cuesta was persuaded not only to agree to attack but to issue orders to his army. As the day was again well advanced this would have to be the following morning and after a long day of uncertainty the 29th Foot 'were at last informed that the men may cook their dinners'.

24 July 1809

Having spent most of the night with a party filling his company's water canteens, Lieutenant Leslie returned to the bivouac of the 29th Foot at about 0200 hours, where:

> we found the troops getting under arms, with orders to make as little noise as possible. No drums were allowed to beat or bugles to sound; it was therefore clear to everyone that we were now about to attack the enemy. After the disappointment of yesterday, everybody was in high spirits. While the parade was forming, I had the pleasure to find that my school-fellow, friend and country neighbour, Andrew Leith Hay, who

A sketch of British line and highland infantry drawn in 1809.

had got a lieutenancy in the regiment, had just arrived with our senior, Captain Tucker.

We moved off in the greatest silence about three o'clock a.m., diverging to our left hand as we advanced towards the enemy. When the column had marched about five miles we were halted. The 29th Regiment, the leading one, was deployed into line. The next regiment did the same at about ten paces in our rear, and all the following ones did the same, so that the whole division stood in column of regiments in line. We now understood that we were within gunshot range of the enemy's position, and that we were only waiting to hear that our right and centre columns had commenced to attack the enemy's left, for us to dash on and carry the key of his position.

But we waited in vain; no firing was heard; no cheer of success greeted our ears – all was silence. Day was fast breaking. The men became impatient; eager murmurings were heard on every and, 'Why don't we advance?' While we were in this state of suspense, the gallant Lord Hill, commander of our column, came back from the front with evident vexation, and announced that the enemy had retreated and there would be no fighting. This intelligence was received in mortified silence.

Unsurprisingly, Marshal Victor had marched off as soon as darkness fell and by dawn was already 10 miles down the road to Madrid and beyond any hope of catching. With the enemy marching away towards Madrid, General Cuesta performed another volte-face and was full of ardour for a pursuit. Wellesley, however, stuck to his assertion made at Plascencia when his own difficulties and the veracity of Spanish promises of logistic support became obvious, that having seen Victor off from the Alberche he would take his army no further east. Any reservations did not concern Cuesta in the slightest, as he now saw Madrid as a prize for the taking that would frustrate the intent of the Seville Junta to put the city in the hands of his rival, General Venegas.

During the morning of 24 July Wellesley reported to Mr Frere that: 'Gen. Cuesta has since marched to Cevolla; and I do not know whether he intends to halt there, or what are to be his future operations.' He went on to say that without supplies and the means to transport them he could not advance on Madrid, explaining that:

> This intimation has become still more necessary within the last 2 days, in which I am concerned to say that, although my troops have been on forced marches, engaged in operations with the enemy, the success of which I must say depended upon them, they have had nothing to eat, while the Spanish army have had plenty; notwithstanding that I have returns of engagements made by the alcaldes of villages in the Vera de Plasencia to furnish this army before the 24th of this month with 250,000 rations.
>
> I certainly lament the necessity which obliges me to halt at present, and will oblige me to withdraw from Spain, if it should continue. There is no man that does not acknowledge, even Gen. Cuesta himself acknowledges, the justice and propriety of my conduct in halting now, or in eventually withdrawing; and I can only say, that I have never seen an army so ill-treated in any country ...[7]

At least for some members of the British army there was good news on return to their bivouacs. Lieutenant Leslie wrote:

> We were shortly afterwards counter-marched and moved back to our bivouac in the olive-groves, in the vicinity of Talavera. That of my regiment was close on the left side of the main road to Madrid, and only about a quarter of a mile in front of the town. On arriving there we found our baggage waiting for us. Our paymaster and his coadjutor, the clerk, were likewise on the *qui vive* awaiting our arrival, it being the 24th – muster-day [payday]. He said with a gracious smile, 'Gentlemen, I shall

The Westphalian light horse were a part of General Merlin's brigade of IV Corps.

now have the pleasure of mustering you all, which is more than I expected.'

Given their privations, the soldiers were soon heading to the town to pay inflated prices for bread. Commissary Schaumann, who himself that morning had paid a small fortune for bread and onions, recalled the scenes in Talavera:

> On the marketplace in the town things went on in the same extraordinary way, for the moment the peasants had taken up their position with their bread, wine, onions, melons, red pepper, or loins of pork, they would be besieged, stormed and hustled this way and that by thousands of customers. Everybody wanted to be served at once, and held out his money, crying: 'Me first! I want bread, I want this, I want that, here's the money!' until the poor peasants were overturned with all their goods, and then trampled upon and plundered. In fact, the wretched devils thought themselves lucky if they escaped alive.

While the army rested and scraped together such food as they could, information was still arriving at Wellesley's headquarters, in this case from a pair of KGL Hussar squadrons sent east to confirm the French withdrawal and report on Cuesta's progress. Brigadier General Stewart rode with the hussars:

> On the morning of the 24th, it was my fortune to go on with two squadrons of cavalry, in front of Cuesta's army, as far at St. Olalla; we had there a smart skirmish with the rear-guard of the enemy, just as they were quitting the town; and I was enabled to ascertain that the main body had fallen back to Torrejos, on the Toledo road.

Based on information received from the KGL Hussars, Wellesley wrote to Frere for a second time, telling him that:

> They [the French] had their rear guard in St Olalla this day; and I have just heard that Gen. Cuesta was marching to that place instead of to Cevolla. I am only afraid that he will get himself into a scrape: any movement by me to his assistance is quite out of the question. I advised him to secure his communications with Venegas and the course of the Tagus, while measures should be taken to supply the British army with means of transport. If the enemy should discover that we are not with him, he will be beaten, or must retire. In either case he may lose all the advantages which might have been derived from our joint operations, and much valuable time, by his eager desire to enter Madrid on an early day. The enemy will make this discovery to-day, if Cuesta should risk any attempt upon their rear guard at St Olalla.

Far from being able to secure his communications with General Venegas as Wellesley recommended, Cuesta was actually marching east and was

An officer of the 1st Hussars of the King's German Legion. The hussar fashion was sweeping across the armies of Europe from the east.

consequently increasingly isolated. The Army of La Manche was still well to the south of Madrid, with about 30 miles separating the two Spanish armies. Not only that, Venegas's march out of contact with General Sébastiani had failed to either draw the IV Corps away from Victor or fix the King's attention south of Madrid. Thus, Sébastiani was able to march to Toledo, where he would rendezvous with the King's reserve and support Marshal Victor. The situation as it was developing was far from that envisaged by Wellesley and Cuesta when they formulated their campaign plans.

The situation the allies found themselves in was obvious even to a junior officer. Ensign Aitcheson of the 3rd Guards wrote in a letter home on 25 July:

> Our prospect is now unhappy in that the enemy will now either come upon us with superiority of force or, if it suits him better, he will retire behind the Ebro – how we are to follow him God knows, we are destitute of means of transport and already short of bread.

General Francisco Venegas, commander of the Army of La Mancha.

The Loyal Lusitania Legion on the Left Flank

While Cuesta had delayed before the Alberche, the reinforced Legion under Colonel Sir Robert Wilson had made a rapid advance and had worked its way to the north of the Alberche.[8] Major Scott Lillie wrote that this manoeuvre:

> brought us round the right flank of the enemy's corps which had taken post at Talavera ... where it was expected a general engagement would take place, which promised a most successful result to the British arms. However, the enemy finding his rear threatened by our corps, which had by this time got round his right flank, foresaw the imminent danger he was in of being cut off, should he come to an engagement with the allies on that day, consequently he abandoned his camp on the night of the 23rd, and fled in the direction of Toledo.

The French account confirms that it was not just the disparity in numbers between himself and the combined armies that induced Victor to retire towards Madrid. '... a corps of eight or ten thousand men, commanded by General Wilson, was advancing towards Escalona, along the right bank of the Alberche. The danger was imminent, and it was necessary to take decided measures.' A combination of judicious manoeuvre by Wilson and French inability to collect detailed intelligence enabled the Legion to again succeed in concealing it true strength from the enemy. Indeed, Victor is credited in French accounts for 'having affected his escape from being cut off by General Wilson's corps, which endeavoured to get in his rear'.

Wilson and the Legion marched on east, several days ahead of Cuesta, who was on the high road to Madrid. With King Joseph leaving Madrid to concentrate his force at Toledo to face the combined Anglo-Spanish army, the Legion approached the outskirts of his capital, which was garrisoned by a single brigade. A liberation of Madrid, however, was not to be. Scott Lillie recorded:

> The capital was at this time unprotected; for it appeared that the enemy had formed a junction of all the troops it was in his power to unite, for the purpose of engaging the allies, and had moved them in the direction of Talavera. Madrid must therefore have surrendered to our arms: but Sir Arthur Wellesley was not aware of this circumstance, and to strengthen his own army, had countermanded Sir Robert Wilson, and thus prevented our having sufficient force to occupy Madrid; and we returned by forced marches ...

25 and 26 July 1809

For the majority of the British army, the 25th was a quiet day in their bivouacs, but Wellesley was busy examining the ground astride the Rio Alberche. What he found was that the reasonably strong position that had been occupied by Victor facing west was lacking the same advantages to the east. The river itself was not a significant obstacle and there were few good positions on the open ground west of the Alberche. This was clearly not the place to offer battle. He did, however, in case of a need to assist a Spanish withdrawal, prudently deploy two of his divisions as an advance guard east of the Alberche. Still less than 3 miles beyond the river, Mackenzie's 3rd Division was positioned around Cazalegas and Sherbrooke's 1st covered the high road to Madrid at Casa Leguas, with patrols and vedettes provided by Anson's light cavalry deployed beyond.

The Spanish marched on towards their capital and by the evening of 25 July, Cuesta's headquarters had reached Torrijos, which unknown to him was less than 15 miles from the leading French formations. Rather than Victor being in full retreat as he imagined, I Corps was falling back to join the King and Sébastiani. The following morning the Captain General's error in making his vainglorious march east was quickly revealed. His army of 30,000 men was now facing a combined French force of 46,000; his only possible course of action was a hasty retreat back to the presumed safety of the Rio Alberche. To cover his withdrawal, Cuesta left Zayas's infantry division and a pair of cavalry regiments at Torrijos as a rearguard but the French, realising that they were facing Spanish troops, were quickly in action.

King Joseph had ordered General of Brigade Merlin forward to Torrijos with his light cavalry supported by La Tour-Maubourg's dragoons, while Victor's infantry turned to counter-march alongside IV Corps. The result was a sharp engagement in which two Spanish cavalry regiments were outnumbered, outclassed and overthrown. The Villaviciosa Regiment suffered particularly badly, as when retiring they became hemmed in by the high stone walls of some enclosures from which exit was difficult. Zayas fell back quickly on Alburquerque's cavalry division, which Cuesta had hastily sent to his assistance.

The French cavalry had scattered, hunting down the Spanish horsemen and, consequently, took some time to re-form for a second advance. The presence of Zayas's infantry alongside a more equal number of Spanish cavalry, however, seemed to take the urgency out of the pursuit. Other factors in the subsequent lacklustre pursuit may have been the length of the approach march and the fact that their own infantry was some distance behind. If they had known of the disorderly retirement of Cuesta's main body and the opportunity to disperse the Army of Extremadura, events may have turned out very differently. Consequently, covered by Alburquerque's cavalry, Zayas was able to fall back on the rest of Cuesta's army, which was withdrawing to the Alberche at speed and in increasing confusion. They reached the river without being caught by the French and Victor halted his corps having reached Santa Olalla.

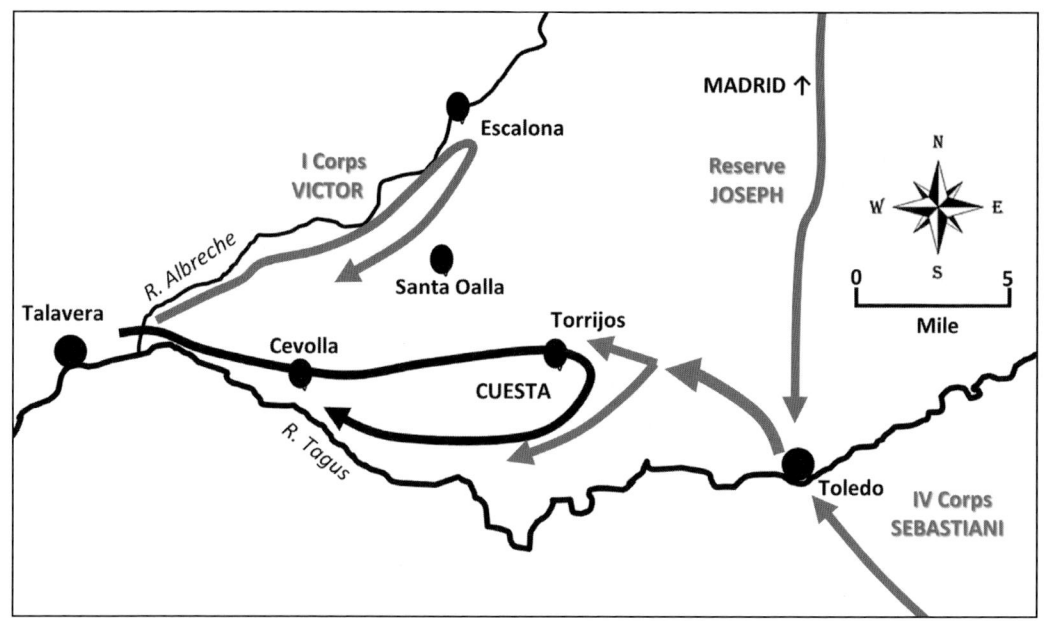

The Army of Extremadura's advance.

For the British the 26th was another day of relative inactivity, including one Lieutenant Leith Hay, who spent his time in 2nd Division's bivouac near Talavera. He wrote:

> During the 25th we heard nothing of the Spanish army, but on the following day the report of artillery announced its return – not unaccompanied. The cannonade was distant, but evidently becoming less so. Runaways and stragglers passed to the rear; the weather was very fine; from the vicinity of the Santa Olalla Road, we derived great amusement: it was covered by a succession of groups, habited in various costumes.

General Wellesley must have thought that General Cuesta would cross the Alberche to relative safety with his entire army, but the old Spanish general, with little sign of the French pursuit, halted his army short of the river, where it set about making fires and cooking. Despite now being behind the protective screen of General Sherbrooke's 1st Division, this was a dangerous situation with an obstacle behind him; a single bridge and several fords.

For most the 26th was a day of little activity but for the commissaries, orders had been given that all food collected was to be taken to a magazine established by Commissary General Dalrymple. Schaumann was scouring the country south of the Tagus:

> We had been riding about for an hour or two, and everything seemed deserted, abandoned and lifeless, when at last, feeling very tired, we halted in a narrow valley at the foot of a rather lofty chain of hills. We heard nothing, and there was no movement anywhere. Then suddenly it occurred to one of the dragoons, an Irishman, to climb to the top of a

Uniforms of the Spanish troopers of the 2nd Cavalry Division.

height, lay himself flat on the ground, and place one end of the ramrod of his pistol in the ground, and the other end to his ear, and listen. He had not lain there long, when suddenly he sprang to his feet, and swore by St. Patrick that he had heard the lowing of cattle and the clanging of cow bells on the other side of the hills.

The dragoon was not wrong. What they found was the livestock of the city of Talavera, which had been secreted away from the marauding armies in a:

> very narrow valley entirely surrounded by hills, and in the midst of it, to our great delight, a quantity of all kinds of cattle – bullocks, cows, calves,

An idealised image of Spanish soldiers of 1809.

pigs, about 6,000 sheep and goats, a wooden shed, a well, and also some dogs and a few herdsmen armed with long firelocks. As we approached the dogs attacked us savagely, and the herdsmen seemed thunderstruck. I got my dragoons to surround them, and then riding up to them alone, with pistol in my hand, told them that they must follow me with all their cattle to English headquarters, where they would be properly valued, and where they would be paid to the last penny in good money.

The gathering of rations as described above helped feed Wellesley's 20,000 for a day or so, but it was no replacement for a properly founded logistic system of the type developed later in the war. While on the subject of supplies, Schaumann also records that the commissaries were given orders to desist in attempting to appropriate convoys bound for the Spanish army.

At about 1700 hours Wellesley called at the Captain General's camp on the far bank of the Alberche, but Cuesta was still having his afternoon siesta and he was refused access. Eventually, hours later, Wellesley was received and put his case that the Spanish army should cross the river before the French advance guard arrived and occupy positions in the defensively advantageous country to the east and north of Talavera. Cuesta, however, steadfastly refused, until according to his own boastful correspondence, he agreed to cross the river only when: 'I had first made the Englishman go down on his knees.' Even if this was true, and allowing for the frustration of his failed advance on Madrid, no more needs to be said about the alliance or the Captain General's state of mind and his military character.

The French did not appear that night and as a result, had lost another golden opportunity to disperse one of the allied armies.

Regimental Baggage

French soldiers that saw the British Peninsular army on the march recorded their amazement at the sight of the ragged cavalcade of animals, men women and children that followed the marching columns. General Foy wrote:

> To look at the mass of impedimenta and camp-followers trailing behind the British you would think you were beholding the army of Darius. Only when you meet them in the field do you realise that you have to do with the soldiers of Alexander.

The French, of course primarily living by foraging off the land, had a much smaller baggage train and generally fewer followers.

As depicted in the picture on the following page, baggage was almost exclusively carried by mules or asses in the Peninsular, with carts of any description being at a premium and often unsuitable for following the route taken by battalions and brigades. General Wellesley also repeatedly issued orders that private baggage was not to be carried in the army's carts.

Company mules typically carried some or all of the following: company books, tents (if available), biscuit (again if available) and the heavy iron Flanders kettles.

At the time of the Talavera Campaign an allocation of baggage animals was also made at Government expense at the rate of a mule between two subaltern officers, a whole mule for a captain and two for field officers and so on up the chain of command. Official beasts were supplemented by officers' privately

An extract of a print made from one of Thomas Staunton St Clair's paintings showing a battalion's baggage on the march. St Clair served in the Peninsular in the 5th Caçadore battalion of the Portuguese army with the rank of captain.

purchased riding horses, mules and donkeys. These animals were collectively referred to as 'bat-horse/mules' and the men that looked after them – soldier servants or civilian employees – as 'batmen'.*

Officially an infantry company was entitled to be accompanied by up to six wives and not uncommonly their children as well. This number was, however, often increased by unofficial wives who joined the army during the campaigns. Wives who were entitled to a half ration would in return be expected to help with duties such as cooking, washing and mending.

On the march, each battalion would nominate a subaltern to take charge of its baggage for a day and a captain provided by units in turn would oversee the combined baggage of the brigade. Overseeing the unruly column of batmen, locally employed servants, women and animals was understandably not a popular duty.

Ensign Bell provides a vivid picture of one part of the cavalcade, the camp follower, that:

> became the subject of a General Order, for their own special guidance. They were under no control, and were always first mounted up and away, blocking up narrow passes and checking the advance of the army with their donkeys, after repeated orders to follow in rear of their respective corps, or their donkeys would be shot. On the retreat from Burgos I remember Mrs. Biddy Flyn remarking, 'I would like to see the man that wud shoot my donkey: faith, I'll be too early away for any of 'em to catch me. Will you come wid me, girls?' Aye, indeed, every one of us.' And away they started at early dawn, cracking their jokes about divisional orders, Wellington, commanding officers, and their next bivouac. Alas the Provost Marshal was in advance – a man in authority, and a terror to evil

A popular image of camp followers. The reality was that the battalions' wives and women would follow behind the columns with the baggage.

doers: he was waiting a mile or two on, in a narrow turn of the road, for the ladies, with a party all loaded. He gave orders to shoot the first two donkeys *pour exempie*. There was a wild, fierce and furious yell struck up, with more weeping and lamentation than one usually hears at an Irish funeral, with sundry prayers for the *vagabone* that had murdered the lives of the poor darling innocent *crathers* ... The victims picked up what they could carry, and marched along with the regiment, crying and lamenting their bitter fate. It was wonderful what they endured – but in spite of this warning they were foremost on the line of march next morning again. As Mrs. Skiddy, their leader, said, 'We must risk something to be in before the men, to have the fire and a *dhrop* of tay ready for them after their load and their labour: and sure if we went in the *rare* the French, bad luck to them, would pick me up, me and my donkey, and then Dan Skiddy would be lost entirely without me.'†

*From the medieval French 'bast', for 'pack horse'.
† Bell, George, *Rough Notes of an Old Soldier*, Vol. 1 (Day and Son, London, 1867).

An engineer officer questions an armed Spanish guerrilla.

Chapter Six

Talavera – the First Day of Battle

Even though General Cuesta had agreed the previous evening to withdraw across the Alberche, it was not until the early morning of the 27th that the Army of Extremadura crossed the river by the wooden bridge on the high road and by a couple of fords. Lieutenant Leith Hay was near the high road and witnessed the resulting scene:

> On the morning of the 27th we learnt that part of General Cuesta's Army had passed to the rear, while battalion after battalion formed a continuous line of march in the same direction. From amidst clouds of dust, disorderly chattering assemblages of half-clad, half-armed men, became occasionally visible; again, regiments marching in perfect order, cavalry, staff officers, bands of musicians, flocks of sheep, and bullocks; artillery, cars, carriages, and wagons, varied the animated, confused, and singular scene on which we gazed – forgetting for the time that all this was intimately connected with our very existence.

That 'very existence' was, however, to be tested later that day, not by the Spanish but by British inexperience.

Combat of Casa de Salinas

With the Spanish safely across the Alberche, Wellesley ordered both Sherbrooke's and Mackenzie's divisions to fall back as well, the former via the bridge and the latter across fords further north. As they retired across the river from Cazalegas, 3rd Division set fire to the French huts and furniture looted from Talavera, as they were about to be given over to the enemy who originally built them. The infantry's withdrawal was in turn covered by Anson's light cavalry, which began a controlled retrograde movement when the French horsemen started to appear around mid-day. They drove in Captain von Linsingen's squadron of KGL Hussars, which got into difficulty while crossing the river:

> ... for close by the ford was the French hut camp ... and this had been set on fire by the rear of the English division, as it marched through. The flaming huts scared the horses, and so impeded the march of the squadron that the rearguard were obliged to engage the enemy's advanced cavalry in the river, and these coming on in superior numbers, rendered

the contest unequal. The enemy would not, however venture to the right bank until their infantry had come up, and the squadron retired behind General Mackenzie's division ...

Once across the river, Mackenzie's division became the rearguard and halted on the edge of about half a mile of thick coppice and woodland beyond the Alberche. Being of little use in woodland, Anson's light cavalry had been sent on ahead to more open ground. The history of the 24th Foot records:

> The brigade [Mackenzie's] halted in a very thick wood; the piquets were told off and ordered to pile arms. The 24th Regiment was at this time on the right of the brigade. It was observed that the other regiments of the brigade were piling arms and taking off their packs and accoutrements, the order having been passed along from the left. The 24th did the same. Shortly afterwards an order came to cut down wood and bushes, and it was generally understood that the brigade was to bivouac for the night. The officers collected in small groups near their companies to discuss the numerous and extraordinary reports in circulation relative to the situation of the army, it being well known that there was a French army of near 50,000 men on the same ground with the British ... these facts created an extraordinary degree of excitement. The men dispersed among the trees, and were chopping off the boughs ...

Donkin's brigade was similarly employed preparing bivouacs between the ruined Casa Salinas and the river, when French soldiers of the 16th Légèr burst into the scene. The smoke from the burning huts and surrounding grass had allowed General Lapisse's 2nd Division to approach and cross the Alberche unseen by the 3rd Division's sentries, who in the thick country also had limited arcs of observation forward to the banks of the river. The piquets may also have believed that the covering cavalry was still out in front of them.

The French advanced in two columns and fell on Donkin's Brigade and the left of Mackenzie's. Fortunately for the 3rd Division, General Lapisse, having realised that he had the unexpected benefit of surprise and rather than waiting for the rest of his division to close up, launched the three battalions of the 16th Légère, which were leading his columns, onto the attack. What should have happened is that the piquets, that is the sentries, the sergeant's and outlying piquets, plus the inlying piquet, would be deployed sufficiently far forward to provide warning of the enemy's approach, even if the enemy fell on them unexpectedly. It is clear that the distance from the sentries to the reposing battalions was too short and, according to the 24th Foot:

> before the men could get on their packs and accoutrements the French light troops were in the wood. The piquets fortunately had not taken off their packs, and therefore had time to run to the front, and join some of

The Casa de Salinas photographed in the late nineteenth century. The tower is thought to be Wellesley's observation point.

the 60th [Rifles] who were keeping up a running fire and skirmishing with the advance troops of the enemy.

Lieutenant FitzClarence later commented that: 'We were by no means such good soldiers as in succeeding campaigns made us, and sufficient precautions had not been taken to ascertain what was passing in the wood (on the skirt of which the division was posted) and between it and the ford below Caselaguas [Cazalegas].'

Donkin's Brigade was not so lucky. Such was the speed of the *tirailleur*'s advance, some of the 2nd 87th's soldiers were shot while still lying down and both they and the 1st 88th Connaught Rangers broke and ran. In Mackenzie's Brigade the 2nd 31st were also broken and in the confusion of flight all three battalions fired at one another and the skirmish line of the 5th 60th Rifles. The French pursued the fleeing British, and they were soon swarming around the Casa de Salinas. On hearing the firing, Wellesley had climbed to a vantage point on the ruined building with his telescope and only just managed to escape by jumping down, mounting his horse and joining the throng of soldiers. He rode up to the veteran 1st 45th and gave orders to Colonel Guard. With musket balls flying thickly about them, the 45th fortunately had time to form and was standing their ground despite men fleeing past

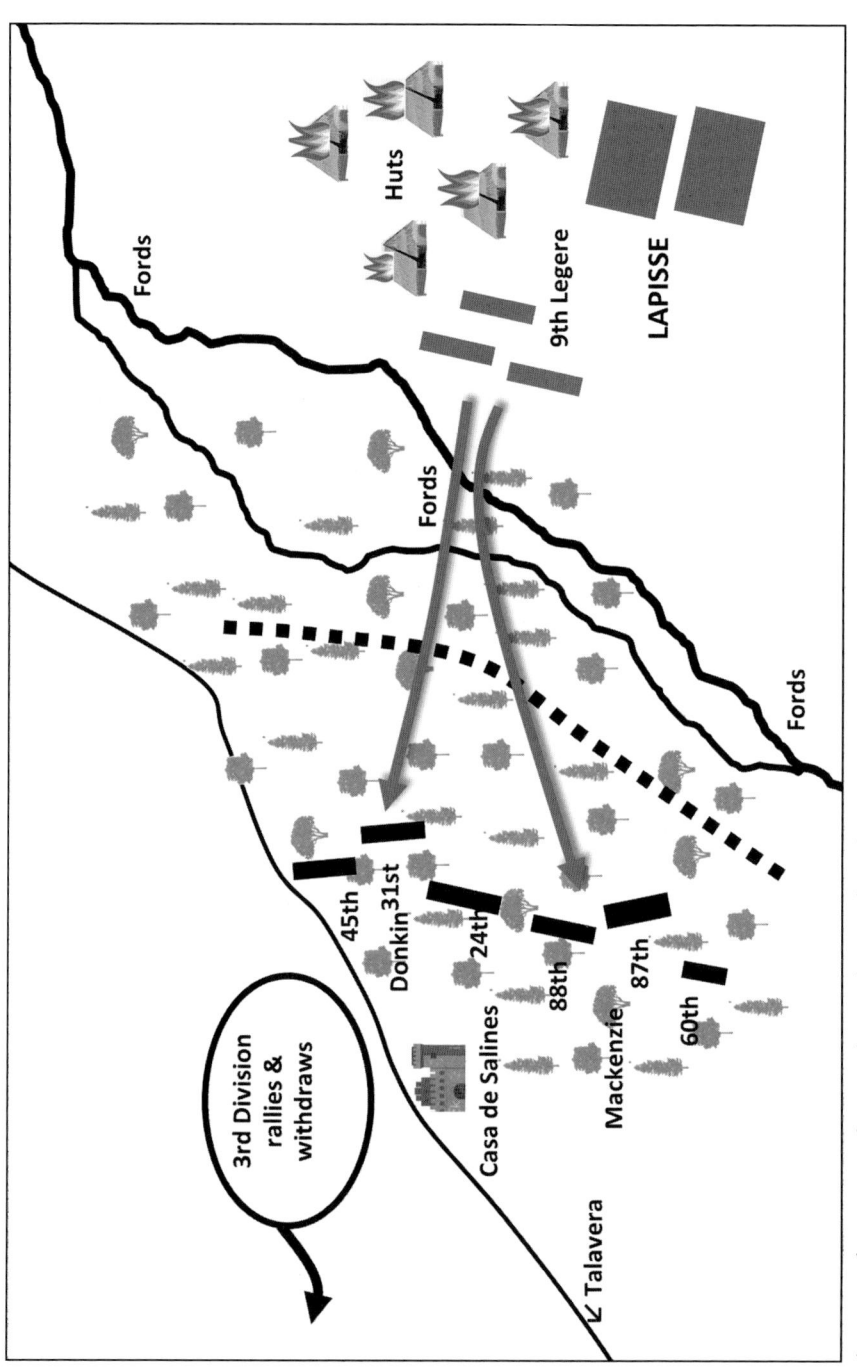

A supposed sequence of events during the Combat of Casa de Salinas.

them. So heavy was the fire that two musket balls hit Colonel Guard's sword while he conferred with Wellesley. Meanwhile, the five companies of the 5th 60th Rifles had been left with their flank open by the precipitate departure of the three battalions but also stood firm and were able to 'fire and retire', maintaining their order and keeping the French at a respectable distance. Halting, the riflemen bought time and space for the 87th and 88th to be rallied. The advance of the, by now disordered, 16th Légère was checked by the 45th, enabling the 3rd Division to re-form beyond the scrub for a withdrawal westward across 3 miles of largely open country. The 23rd Light Dragoons and the 1st Hussars KGL covered Mackenzie's flanks and the 45th provided the infantry rearguard. Their regimental history records that:

> The retirement ... was made by wings and companies so far as the nature of the ground permitted; and Colonel Guard being wounded, the command passed into the hands of Major Gwyn. It became necessary to separate the regiment into two parts; six companies under the Major retired upon the centre of the allied line, while four companies under Captain Smith, covering the retreat of some other portion of the forces, fell back upon the Spanish lines.

The French followed, bringing up artillery to gall the retiring column, which marched back to the Portina Brook in good order. FitzClarence recalled that the enemy came on:

> with vast bodies of troops, accompanied with quantities of artillery. These crossed at the various fords on the Alberche, to the plain west of it; while some of their cavalry, in the loosest order, came in crowds through the woods, following our advanced corps as they gradually withdrew to our position, of which, as we approached the chosen ground ... Their horse artillery soon overtook us in our retreat, and opened a heavy and constant fire, particularly of shells, under which the troops formed on their ground.

The Combat of Casa de Salinas cost the 3rd Division 422 casualties, with the 87th, which was caught by the first rush of the enemy, losing 198 men or a third of their strength, of which about half were taken prisoner. Of French losses, Oman estimates them at 100. The whole unfortunate episode was a salutary lesson for the 3rd Division.

The Talavera Battlefield and Allied Deployment

With the Spanish withdrawing across the Alberche and the arrival of the French, the British 2nd and 4th divisions marched to occupy their positions for the forthcoming battle, with the Spanish heading directly to their agreed defences. Having decided not to fight on the Alberche, during 26 July,

Piquets and Outposts

In any age of warfare, it has always been essential for an army to have a system of piquets and sentries to prevent a surprise attack. The action on the Alberche demonstrates that Wellesley's army was not as sufficiently practised or experienced in the deployment of sentries and their supports as it later became. The Light Division, which often provided the army's outposts, became the acknowledged experts in this important campaign skill. Writing under the pseudonym of 'Green Feather' in *United Services Journal* (c.1830s), an officer then of junior rank describes the deployment of an outlying piquet, as laid down by General Craufurd in his standing orders (the diagram opposite reflects those orders):

> One of the most important services of an army in the field is that of the outlying piquet, particularly when in the presence of the enemy. It is then interesting from its peculiar importance, as not only the repose and tranquillity, but the honour and even the safety of a whole army are dependent upon the manner in which it is performed. When the outlying piquet is first posted it is done with a view that with small detached outposts from it, and double sentries, the whole of the front of the position of the division from which it is detached should be covered, and every possible approach so watched that nothing can attempt to pass the line of demarcation between two armies without its being seen and reported. There are certain theoretical rules laid down for posting piquets, both with regard to detached outposts as well as sentries, which may be learned at home; but the continual practice of them in the field, when not before the enemy, will shortly render the outpost Officer competent; and soon, before the enemy, put him on a chess-board of defence to which his operations must be entirely confined. The active officer in charge of an outlying piquet must study all day what he will do all night; for as then his division sleeps under his protection, he should exercise every combination of mind and body to that end. Surprise would be dishonour under any circumstances; but the surprise of his division would be eternal shame. The disposition of the posts of an outlying piquet by day, as well as its sentries, in general vary from those of the night; these are either pushed forward or retired as the nature of the ground may favour, particularly as to the horizon of it; for although, in the day-time, a vidette or sentry should be posted on an eminence for the purpose of seeing far, and all around him, at night he should be invariably posted under the eminence, as he can then, from the light and shade, even in the darkest night, more easily discover any one approaching his post. The sentries should be relieved every hour under such circumstances: – in bad weather, which is the time chosen for surprise, more often; and by patrols, either or the Subalterns or Serjeants, their attention and vigilance should be continually excited, – not a word should escape – a precomposed sound of a 'hem!' or a whistle suffices.

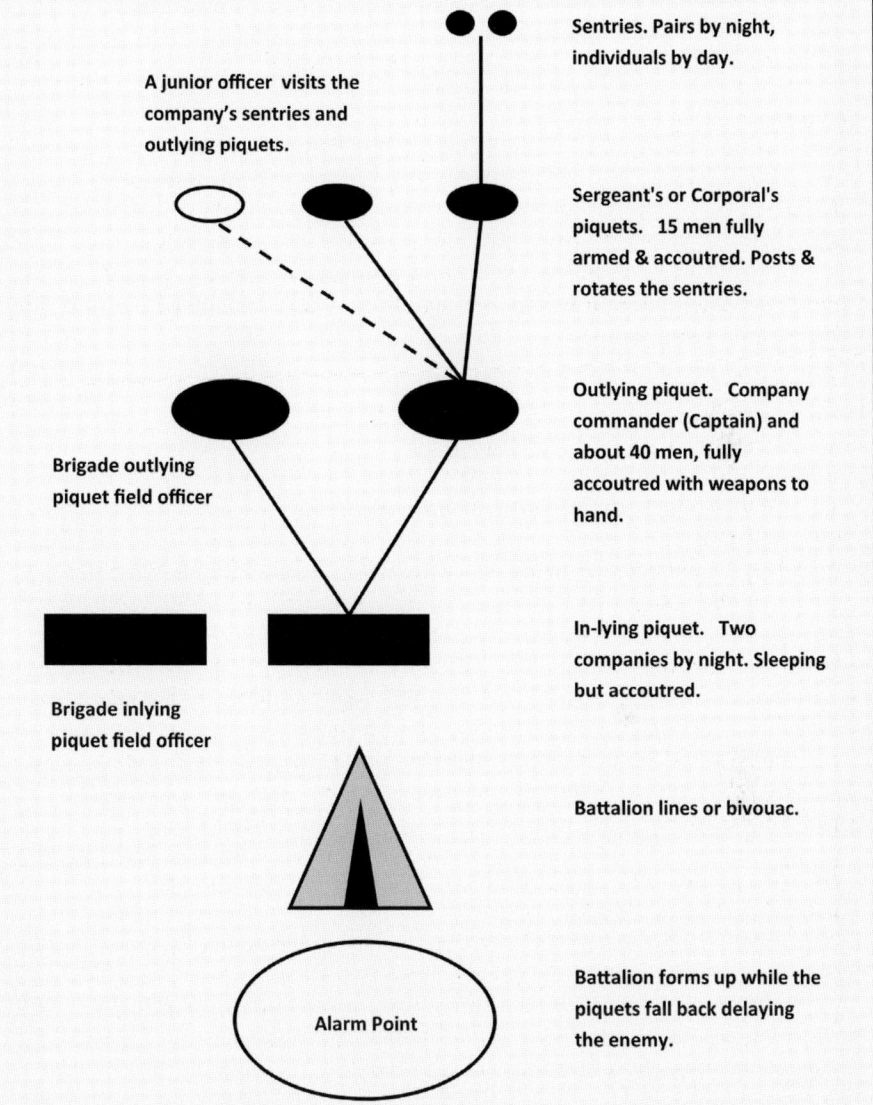

As at Casa de Salines an inexperienced force, or one deployed with a lack of caution, were often subject to a surprise attack, especially when facing a veteran enemy formation. Add to this, difficult ground, smoke covering the enemy's approach, and there was plenty of scope for disaster. Deploying piquets, however, was only a part of the equation. Warning of the enemy's approach had to be passed quickly and the main body of the troops capable of reacting in time. Hence Craufurd's insistence on the Light Brigade being packed up and assembled in just seven minutes.

Wellesley, with his keen eye for ground, spotted a better position from which to offer battle 4 miles further back, based on the Portina Brook north of Talavera, where the ground was favourable for a defensive action. Here the Tagus plain also narrowed significantly, with the distance from the northern outskirts of the city to the steeply rising hills of Sierra de Segurilla foothills being just 3 miles. Across the front lay the Portina Brook, which for most of its length was dry and its banks were significantly less of an obstacle than those of the Alberche.

In what was to become the centre of the battlefield, the ground offered few such defensive opportunities, being largely open and flat for a distance of 2½ miles. Further north lay the key position of the Medellín feature. This was a distinct east–west ridge that was cleaved into two by the Portina Brook, creating to the west the Cerro de Medellín and to the east the slightly lower Cerro de Cascajal. The Portina here had dug a steep-sided valley, which though not a major obstacle to infantry, would create delay and a need to re-form columns, thus providing a degree of protection to the defenders of the Medellín. To the north of the Medellín there was an open plain some 800 yards wide before the foothills of the Sierra de Segurilla rose sharply.

Wellesley dispatched ADCs with orders for the army's deployment. To the east of the city a small rise crowned with a chapel provided a position for a heavy battery of Spanish artillery, which was sited to cover the approach to Talavera via the Madrid road. One of the main attractions of the ground, however, just to the north of the city, was a strong defensive position in an area of embanked roads, enclosures, vegetable gardens and olive groves. It was obvious to both Wellesley and Cuesta that in this area the Spanish stood a chance of success. The Army of Extremadura was deployed on a frontage of about a mile in two lines, with the reserve forming a third.

In what was to become the centre of the battlefield, the ground offered few such defensive opportunities. From the low rise of the Pajar de Vergara where Lawson's battery of 3-pounder guns was established in a partly entrenched redoubt, there was a stretch of largely flat open country measuring a good half mile. This was the weak spot in Wellesley's chosen ground for the forthcoming battle. The two brigades of 4th Division, Campbell's and Kemmis's, were immediately north of the battery but due to a staff error Sherbrooke's four brigades were also in this area rather than at the key terrain on and around the Medellín feature. Here General Hill's two brigades of 2nd Division were deployed on the reverse or western slopes of the feature.

As the 1st Division had taken their intended ground in the centre, the brigades of 3rd Division effectively became Wellesley's reserves. At the southern end of the line, Mackenzie took position behind the 4th Division and the Guards, while Donkin was in the Medellín area but behind Stewart's brigades, which had been mal-deployed south of their proper position.

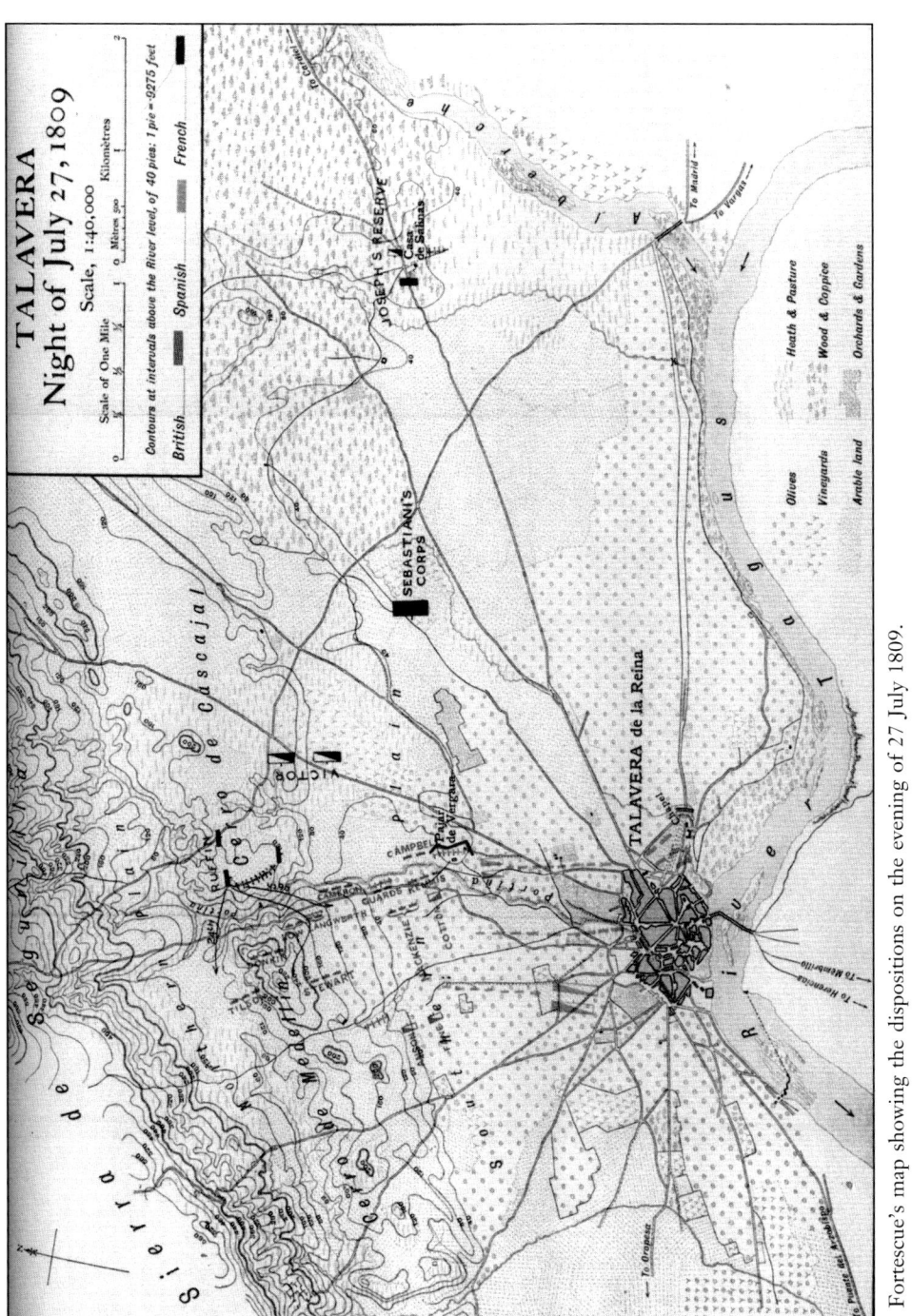

Fortescue's map showing the dispositions on the evening of 27 July 1809.

114   *The Talavera Campaign, 1809*

In addition, the two KGL brigades had been led by a staff officer a full hour's march west beyond Talavera before the error was discovered and they had to march back to the Portina in haste. They had, however, crucially taken up positions to the south of the Medellín by dusk.

The allied cavalry were in positions to the rear, less Cotton's light cavalry brigade, which was forward in the centre to the rear of Kemiss's brigade.

The sundry errors in deploying into their order of battle during the 26th, on top of the incident at Casa de Salinas, are examples of the lack of experience across the Peninsular army in 1809. The necessary creation of new formations headquarters at a time when there was a dearth of trained and/or experienced staff officers led to a poor passage of information and a lack of a detailed understanding of what was required of the various divisions. The British still had much to learn, but in the meantime, would the more experienced French be able to profit from their mistakes?

The Battle Begins

Lieutenant Leslie of the 29th Foot, a part of Stewart's brigade of 2nd Division, had seen the Spanish come back and had listened through the day to the sound of the approaching musket and cannon fire until about 1600 hours, when:

> We now had certain intelligence that the enemy was pressing on in force. Wounded men from our advanced guard began to come in, and the report of cannon announced to us that a battle was at hand. We ordered our dinner to be cooked in all haste and lost no time in despatching it. We then had our tent and baggage packed. This foresight was well-timed, for shortly afterwards the drums beat to arms, the bugles sounded the alarm, and we got orders to move to our left. The Spanish army began to take up their position on the ground we were quitting, forming in two lines with reserves in the rear ... Between four and five o'clock in the afternoon our brigade moved off, left in front, between the Spanish lines. The Spaniards appeared very valiant, and cried out, '*Rompez los Franceses.*'
>
> We could now hear smart musketry firing going on between our advanced guard and the enemy. The sound of cannon and small arms seemed to be approaching very rapidly. On getting clear of the enclosures and gaining the lower slope of the hill, our brigade, the 29th Regiment, one battalion of detachments, and one battalion of the 48th Regiment, was drawn up in rear of the front line.

According to Leith Hay, 'to the accompaniment of a heavy and incessant fire' from the east, the 2nd Division marched to its position on the slopes of the Medellín with Tilson's brigade on the northern flank of the feature and

Lieutenant Andrew Leith Hay. He is wearing a pelisse coat following his transfer to 12th Light Dragoons.

Stewart's on the southern. From his vantage point on the hill Leslie recalled that:

> We could now see our advanced guard retiring across the plain, closely pursued by the enemy. A portion of the advanced guard [Donkin's Brigade] moved directly towards us, and passed through our line, and proceeded to the different places in position. During this the French kept up a continued fire against them of shot and shell, which were now falling thick and fast amongst us. While this cannonade continued, we were ordered to lie down. As the evening was now closing, and darkness began to prevail, we could discern the shells and time their course from

the moment they left the mouth of the howitzers by their fuses burning like brilliant stars as they rose in the air, then rapidly descending right down upon us, or breaking over our heads. Many of us made narrow escapes, but on the whole no very serious loss was occasioned. The firing ceased, and all seemed hushed and quiet.

The first action by the French against the allied defensive position was a probing attack launched against the Spanish infantry of General Portago's division. It was a small affair by some French dragoons, which had been following the four companies of the 45th Foot's rearguard. The approach of enemy cavalry caused a small amount of nervous fire from several Spanish battalions that prompted others to fire volleys that had no chance of hitting the still distant French dragoons. In addition, some battalions of inexperienced Spanish troops ran and had to be rallied. For the French this had the satisfactory effect of fully revealing Cuesta's forward positions.

Lieutenant Leslie commented on 'the extraordinary battle' that was developing rapidly on the Spanish flank:

It was not confined to one spot, for it spread right and left, and they opened a running fire along their whole, which lasted for some time, until many corps, scared by they knew not what, fled to the rear, and it was only with great difficulty, we were told, that they were brought back into their places in line, again.

General Wellesley was with Colonel Samuel Whittingham, one of the British officers serving in Cuesta's headquarters. He remarked: 'If they will but fire as well tomorrow, the day will be ours; but as there seems to be nobody to fire at just now, I wish you would stop it.' Some 2,000 men, including four whole battalions, shouting 'treason' threw down their muskets and ran from the field, plundered the British baggage and spread rumours of disaster in the rear area. The resulting gap in the line needed filling and Wellesley again instructed Colonel Whittingham: 'Only look at the ugly hole those fellows have left. I wish you would go to the second line and try to fill it up.' The firing along the front started to die down at around 1900 hours and as the day was well advanced, the assumption was that the battle would take place the following day. General Hill confirmed this in a letter to his sister: 'As night was coming on, we did not expect any serious attack till next morning.' The armies started to settle down for the night.

Attack on the Medellín

On the evening of 27 July, Marshal Victor occupied the Cerro de Cascajal and correctly estimated that the Medellín was the allies' key terrain, but he had also seen that the area was barely defended thanks to the British errors in

Colonel Whittingham wearing a staff officer's dress uniform with its distinctive embroidered front.

deployment. What would have been a key factor was that when he decided to attack the two KGL brigades were still on their counter-march and not to be seen. An opportunity presented itself and not unjustifiably following the combat at Casa de Salinas, Victor's opinion of the British army was probably low. Of the troops defending the Medellín, there is considerable doubt as to the location of the two battalions of Donkin's brigade; some place them on the crest of the feature but given that they marched through Stewart's brigade, they were probably further back on the southern flank of the feature. Accounts from the five companies of riflemen of the 5th 60th with Donkin's

Canton Woodville's fanciful painting of Spanish troops fleeing from the field. Several observers claim to have seen Cuesta's coach among those running away, but it is not known if the general was aboard.

brigade recall confusion and being deployed forward they were shot at by both sides in the darkness.

Victor knew that one of the best times to launch an attack is at dusk, when there is sufficient light for the attack to prosper but leaves the enemy having to launch his counter-attacks with all the disadvantages of darkness. Therefore, on his own initiative, with no reference to King Joseph, he ordered the nine battalions of Ruffin's division to attack and seize the Medellín feature. To create surprise, while the attack was being prepared, he ordered his artillery on the Cascajal to cease fire and seemingly bring the affairs of the day to a halt.

The plan was that Ruffin's two regiments of line infantry were to attack in column of battalions and envelop the Medellín from the north and south, while Colonel Meunier's 9th Légère, in the centre, avoiding the steeper eastern face of the hill, were to clear the crest of the feature via the south-east

Ruffin's plan for the attack on the Medellín at sunset on 27 July 1809.

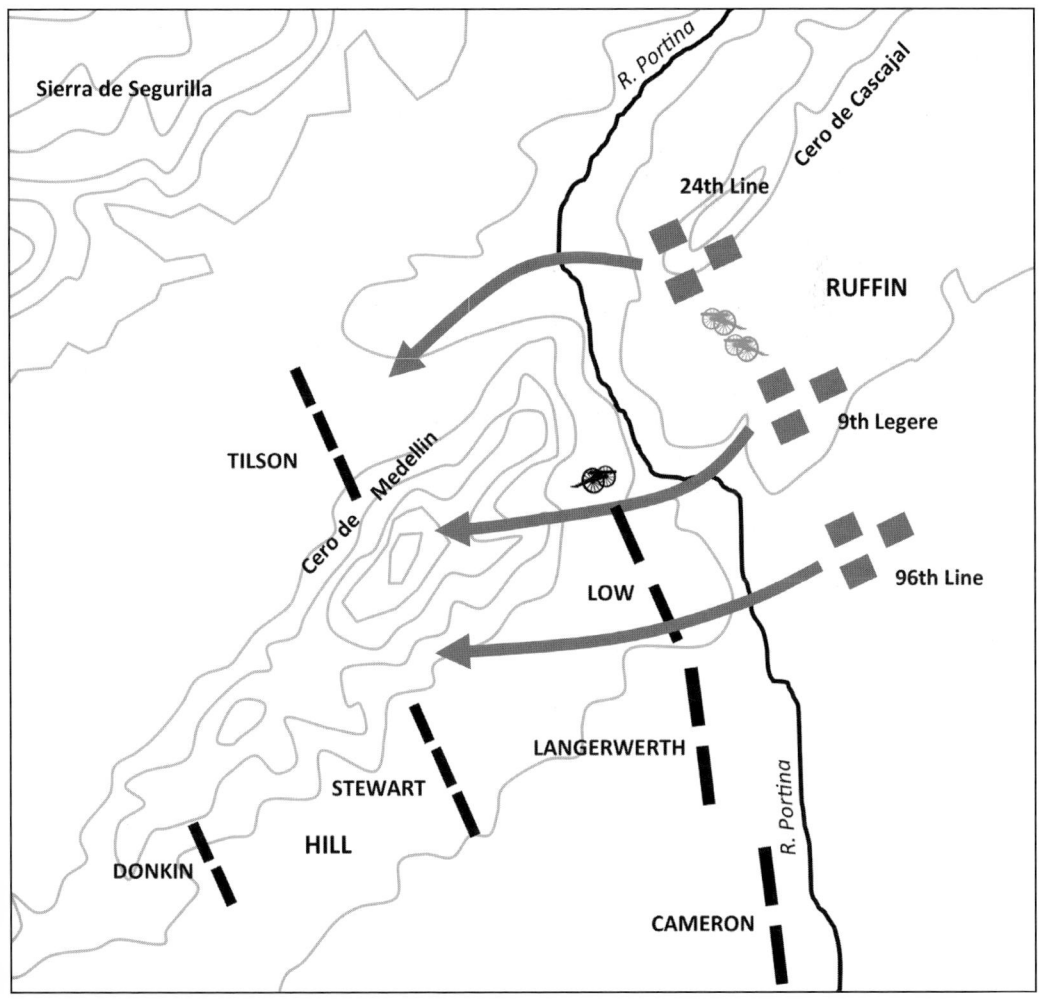

shoulder. The artillery already deployed on the Cerro de Cascajal would remain silent until musket fire was opened and then would sweep the crest of the hill with fire and enfilade any counter-attack from the south.

As dusk fell and with the aid of smoke from smouldering crops and dry grass helping to conceal them, the French advanced to the Portina Brook. The two leading battalions of 9th Légère crossed the largely dry bed and scrambled up the steep bank opposite. With the benefit of surprise, and having swung to the left, they fell on Low's Brigade of the King's German Legion. Low's and Langwerth's exhausted soldiers had just completed their counter-march and, believing themselves to be behind Hill's division, were beginning to settle down to rest. Piquets were still being posted and as described by Ludlow Beamish:

> Captain von Ompteda, of the first light battalion, had been sent up the hill with a party of riflemen to plant outposts: upon part of this detachment, consisting of the skirmishers of the first line battalion under Lieutenant von Hölle, the enemy's column fell, and charging, obliged them to retire, and Lieutenant von Hölle was severely wounded. In retreating, the skirmishers received the fire of the seventh line battalion, which regiment and part of the fifth being thrown into confusion by the suddenness of the attack, were charged by the French column, and gave way; they were, however, rallied.

With the KGL brushed aside, a couple of Captain Heise's heavy 6-pound guns were temporarily lost, and some eighty prisoners dispatched back to the Cascajal, while the leading battalion of the 9th Légère headed for the crest of the Cerro de Medellín. On their left, however, the 96th Line had in the gathering gloom, and more than probably on an un-recced route, become disordered on some steep ground. By the time they had crossed the brook, the KGL battalions had rallied, and a firefight developed between the 96th Line and the 2nd Light and 5th KGL battalions, without either side gaining advantage. Similarly, on the northern flank of the Medellín the 24th Regiment became disorientated in the growing darkness and failed to advance and contribute to the fight. If the KGL brigades had not returned in time and if the flanking French regiments had been more determined or fortunate in their choice of route down to the Portina, the story of Ruffin's attack could have been very different, along with the outcome of the battle.

Lieutenant Leslie, with the 29th Foot on the southern slope of the Medellín, describes how the quiet of the evening was broken:

> We had continued in this way nearly an hour, when in a moment, about nine o'clock, there opened a tremendous fire on the top of the hill on our left, and which seemed to have been taken up and ran down the first line

A heavy 6-pound gun as used by 4th Battery KGL. (*Royal Artillery Museum*)

in our front [the KGL brigades]. It was now evident that the enemy had made a dash at this, the key of our position, and were in possession of the top, as we could, by the blaze of firearms and the flashes of light, distinguish the faces of the French and those of our own troops returning the fire.

Having been away from his division, General Hill on his return, just before the French attack began:

> found it deploying in line and was shown by somebody where the right was to rest. I pointed out the hill on the line of direction we were to take up. I found, however, I had not sufficient troops to occupy the ground without leaving considerable intervals between the regiments. During this operation I recollect perfectly well that I was with the 48th Regiment, in conversation with Colonel Donellan, when, it being nearly dark, I observed some men on the hill-top fire a few shots amongst us. Not having an idea that the enemy were so near, I said at the moment, I desired Donellan to get into line, and I would ride up the hill and stop their firing. On reaching the hilltop, I found the mistake I had made. I immediately turned round to ride off; when they fired and killed poor Fordyce [Major of Brigade] and shot my mare through the body. She did

not fall, but carried me to the 29th Regiment, which corps, by my orders, instantly charged the French ...[1]

The general and his staff were lucky not to be all killed or captured in this incident, particularly Hill who had a French infantryman holding his arm and attempting to pull him off his horse, which fortunately leapt forward and released him. The general was able to make his escape – with musket balls flying around him. Hill was, however, wounded and went to the rear to be patched up, leaving Brigadier General Tilson in command.

Probably at the same time, Brigadier General Stewart ordered the 1st Battalion of Detachments into open column of companies to counter-attack up onto the Medellín, with left in front and a company of 95th rifles leading.[2] Of Stewart's brigade it would seem that the Battalion of Detachments reached the hill first. Sergeant Nichol of a company of Gordon Highlanders in the battalion described the desperate and confused fighting:

> At this time our brigade got a biscuit each man served out, when a cry was heard, 'The hill! the hill!' General Stewart called out for the

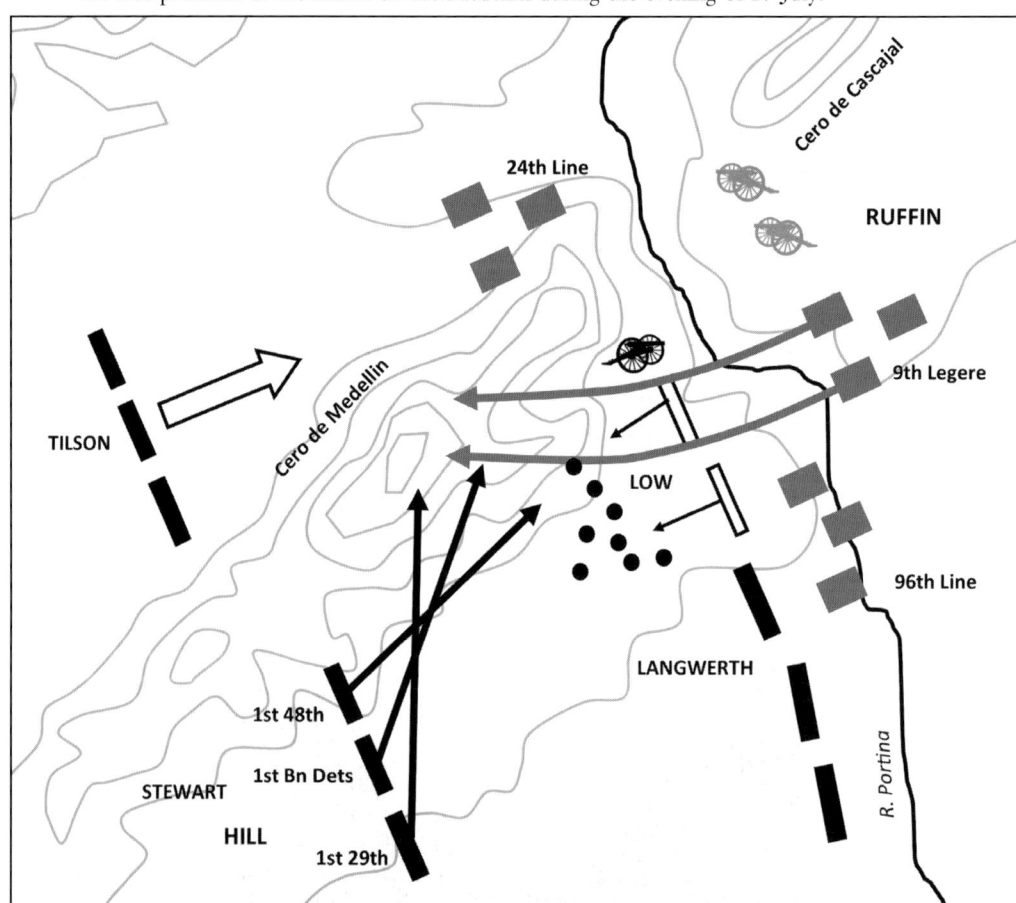

An interpretation of the action on the Medellín during the evening of 27 July.

detachments to make for the top of the hill, for he was certain that no regiment could be there so soon as we. Off we ran in the dark, and very dark it was, but the French got on top of the hill before us, and some of them ran through the battalion, calling out, 'Espanioles, Espanioles', and others calling 'Allemands'.

Their momentum carried the two battalions of the 9th Légère forward into the Battalion of Detachments. Sergeant Nicholl continued his account:

Our officer cried out 'Don't fire on the Spaniards.' I and many others jumped to the side to let them pass down the hill, where they [the French] were either killed or taken prisoners in our rear. I saw those on the top of the hill by the flashes of their pieces; then we knew who they were; but I and many more of our company were actually in rear of the French for a few moments and did not know it until they seized some of our men by the collar and were dragging them away prisoners. This opened our eyes, and bayonets and the butts of our firelocks were used with great dexterity – a dreadful melee.

As more of the 9th Légère arrived they became too numerous and the 1st Battalion of Detachments who '... disputed every inch of ground ... but outnumbered by their assailants, were gradually giving way and being driven off the hill'. Lieutenant Girod recalled that: 'We found and took captive approximately 200 Scots in kilts (these were the first we had ever seen) ...'[3]

Coming up the hill to their left were Lieutenant Leslie and his battalion. 'The 29th Regiment was immediately thrown into open column, left in front, and instantly moved up the hill to attack the enemy, directing our march

The colour of the 9th Légère. Unlike British colours, the eagle carried by the 1st Battalion was venerated by the regiment and the colour was rarely fixed to the eagle except on parades.

A carbineer (elite company) and a chasseur of the 9th Légère.

between the fire of both parties.' As the battalion reached the crest they came up to the Battalion of Detachments:

> ... who appeared to have got into confusion, and we pushed our way through them to rush at the enemy. The gallant soldiers of the battalion seemed much vexed; they were bravely calling out, 'There is nobody to command us! Only tell us what to do, and we are ready to dare anything.'
>
> Without halting, our left made a dashing charge, and after a short but desperate struggle drove the French off the summit of the position. We then wheeled into line, advanced obliquely to our left, and opened our fire on the French reserves which were pushing up in support of their discomfited comrades ... we formed into line, our right companies were some way down the slope of the hill. We could see the French [reserve?] column moving up across our front, their drums beating the charge, and we could hear their officers giving orders and encouraging their men, calling out, *'En avant, Francais! En avant, mes enfants!'* but our well-directed volleys and cheers of victory stopped their progress, and their shattered columns returned in dismay.

Lieutenant Girod, probably with the reserve battalion, recalls the 29th's fire:

> We had already reached two thirds up the height without meeting any enemy when suddenly we received a terrible discharge of musketry, that in an instant caused us to suffer a heavy loss: nearly 300 men and 13 officers ... in a nutshell, the principal commanders of our two columns were put *hors de combat*.[4]

Despite being ordered to go up first, the 1st 48th was the last of Stewart's three battalions in action. Lieutenant Close was marching with them:

> We were put in motion to support the defence of the position. Before we encountered the enemy, owing to the darkness of the night, the 2nd [*sic*] Battalion of Detachments, taking our left wing for the enemy, poured in two or three volleys, which was at last obstructed by Colonel Donellan riding in front of their line and telling them they were killing their own men. Little harm was, very fortunately, done [the 1/48th had eight men wounded] ... We advanced obliquely to our left, had scarcely formed line when a blaze of fire from a body of grenadiers, whose bayonets almost met ours, gave us the first information of the situation of the enemy. It was so dark we could hardly see, when the musketry proclaimed the firers. The firing however was soon terminated. The enemy called out with consternation *'Anglais, Anglais!'*, and down the hill they went.

The rapid and controlled volley fire of the British companies of Stewart's brigade as they arrived on the Medellín had swept away whole ranks of the

French and Lieutenant Girod commented that his battalion commander was soon convinced that it was impossible to hold this position; indeed, 'masses of enemy infantry advanced in the darkness threatening to surround us'. The 9th Légère withdrew down to the Portina, leaving among others their commander, Colonel Meunier, who was wounded having been struck in the head and the leg and was taken prisoner by the KGL. According to the regimental history, the 2nd Battalion lost its commanding officer, all its adjutant majors and the two carabiner (flank) company commanders, along with 300 men.[5]

General Hill, at the head of his division, had charged up the hill and driven the enemy off the Cerro de Medellín. If, however, the Battalion of Detachments had not counter-attacked so promptly, the French may have been able to organise a defence of the feature and bring up more troops, which would have altered the balance of the battle the following day. Sergeant Nichol of the Gordons concluded:

> Order was restored, and a deathlike silence reigned among us. The French kindled great fires in rear of their lines. I had a sound sleep for a short time ... When daylight appeared, each army gazed on the other and viewed the operations of last night. Round the top of the hill many a red coat lay dead; about thirty yards on the other side the red and blue lay mixed, and a few yards farther, and down in the valley below, they were all blue.

The Light Brigade's Forced March

While events were unfolding around Talavera during 27 July, Brigadier General Craufurd's Light Brigade was on its way east from Lisbon to join the army. Lieutenant Leith Hay, himself having just arrived in Lisbon, had seen them march to join the army:

> The brigade of General Robert Crawford, composed of the 43d, 52nd, and 95th regiments, left Lisbon to join the army. Three finer battalions never took the field; nor did their conduct upon any occasion ever belie the promise held out by their discipline, their robust healthy appearance, brilliant equipment, or distinguishedly military air.

Having marched by relatively easy stages, the brigade rested for two days at Castelo Branco before crossing into Spain on 20 July near 'the wretched village of Zebreirta'. During this march of up to 15 miles a day, Craufurd had written and issued what at the time were considered by the brigade his 'infamous' standing orders. These prescriptive and detailed instructions for the conduct of operations were strictly implemented by the brigadier and were bitterly resented, particularly by the officers of the 95th Rifles who regarded them as an obstruction to their use of their initiative and freedom of

General Hill, commander of the 2nd Division, suffered a wound to his head during the fighting on the Medellín.

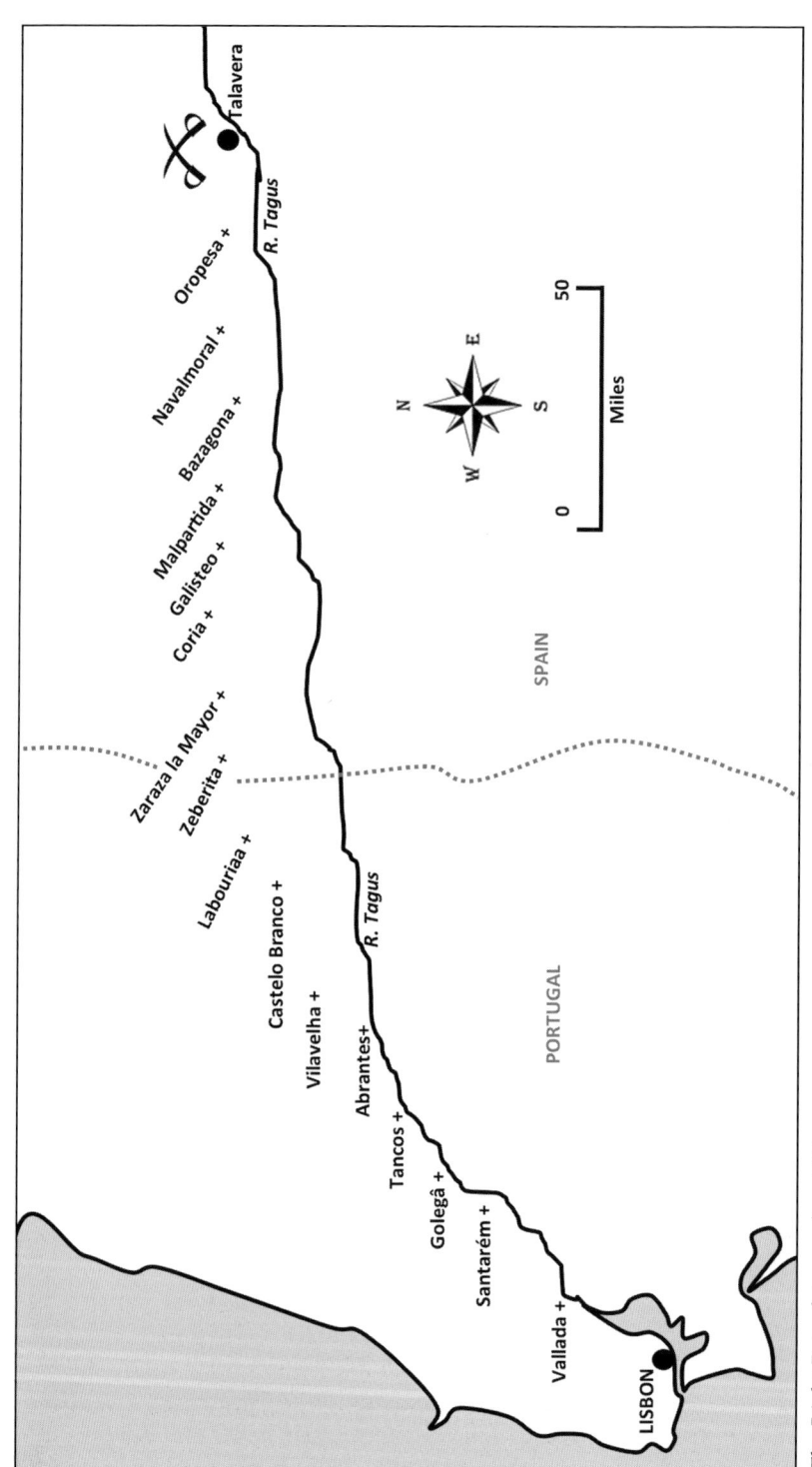

The Light Brigade's march to Talavera.

action. They would, however, later acknowledge that Craufurd's orders and the way he enforced them was 'the making of the division'.⁶

The brigade reached Navalmoral during 27 July with 'rumours circulating from those comings and goings as is normal in the rear of the army' that a 'general action might be expected daily'. The following morning, however, no special orders had been received, camp routine continued and, as usual, the two light and one rifle battalions fell in and marched at 0200 hours or 'before dawn' (according to some sources) on the 28th.

Craufurd's battalions had almost finished their normal day's march when during a routine halt an aide de camp arrived with an urgent message that Wellesley wanted Craufurd's brigade up with the army, as a general action was indeed imminent. The day's march was promptly extended until 1100 hours, at which time, the brigade had reached Oropesa, having covered over 20 miles. Craufurd ordered a halt as a lack of water and the heat of the day was terrible, with several men according to Captain Leach dying and others collapsing insensible. At 1700 hours, when the temperature had dropped somewhat, the march was resumed to the now continuous sound of distant cannon fire. Leach recalled that Craufurd:

> … then directed the commanding officers of regiments to select and leave at Orapeza such men as were thought incapable of enduring the forced march which he determined to make, and not to halt until he reached the British army, which was known to be engaged in our front, as the distant but unceasing cannonade plainly announced. Having rested his brigade in this burning plain, where water was not to be procured, General Crawford put it in motion towards Talavera de la Reina. It may well be conceived it was a march productive of the highest degree of feverish anxiety and excitement. The one only feeling was to push forward, to throw our mite into the scale, and to lend a helping hand to our brothers in arms.
>
> We soon met wounded Spanish soldiers, and Spanish soldiers not wounded, bending their course in a direction from the field of battle. I wish I could assert with equal truth that this retrogression was confined to our Spanish allies; but the truth must be told; and I regret to say, that stragglers from the ranks of the British army, some without a wound, were also taking a similar direction to the rear. As they passed our column, they circulated all sorts and kinds of reports of a most disheartening nature: 'The British army was utterly defeated, and in full retreat'; 'Sir Arthur Wellesley was wounded'; and, by others, 'he was killed'. In short, all was suspense and uncertainty. One thing, was, nevertheless, certain – that the cannonade continued without cessation. We pressed forward until ten o'clock at night, when, having reached a pool of

stagnant water near the road, in which cattle had been watered during the summer, and where they had constantly wallowed, a halt was ordered for an hour or two. Those who have never been in similar situations may be inclined to doubt my veracity when I state that the whole brigade, officers and soldiers, rushed into this muddy water, and drank with an eagerness and avidity impossible to describe ...

At the opening of the campaign the men of the Light Brigade were heavily laden, with their equipment and weapons weighing almost 60lb. Leach recalled that in the light and rifle battalions:

... each soldier carried from sixty to eighty rounds of ammunition, a musket or rifle, a great coat, and (if I recollect rightly) a blanket, a knapsack complete, with shoes, shirts, &c. &c.; a canteen and haversack,

The contents of a soldier's knapsack – according to regulation. Seasoned campaigners disposed of many 'surplus' items to reduce weight.

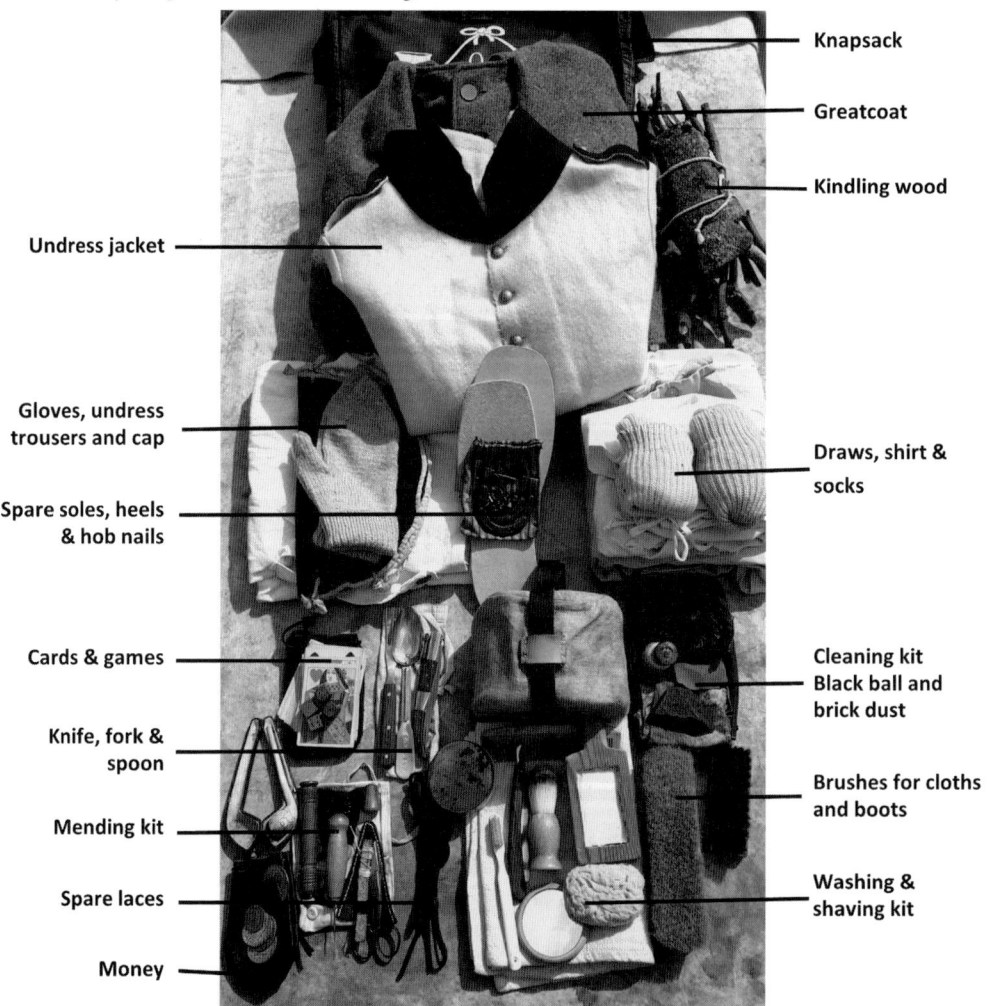

A Carbanier officer of the elite company of a French Légèere regiment in full dress.

bayonet, belts, &c. &c. Such a load, carried so great a distance, would be considered a hard day's work for a horse.

This last stage of the forced march to Talavera was again about 20 miles. There are several references to this being conducted in the manner that Sir John Moore had taught them, that is to say three paces walking and three running. Accounts claim that as few as fifty men fell out and straggled behind the columns but equally it is recorded that all carts encountered on the road were taken into service for the transportation of the footsore and there was only a two-hour halt during the night. Estimations of the distance marched in somewhat over twenty-four hours range between 49 miles (Napier) and 38 miles (Verner). While not a record-breaking achievement in terms of distance, given the Iberian summer heat, poor roads, inadequate shoes and a paucity of water and food, it does rank among the great testing marches in the history of the British army.[7]

A rifleman's equipment carried in full or heavy marching order.

Chapter Seven

The Day of Battle, 28 July 1809

In the short hours of darkness, with the armies at close proximity and their sentries within musket shot of each other astride the Portina Brook, it was a tense night with little rest. Noise and movement as enemy sentries were rotated and, in the darkness, 'moving bushes' playing tricks on sentries' eyes, all contributed to a disturbed night. Lieutenant FitzClarence recalled that with piquets deployed and:

> with the inexperience of our troops, principally [newly recruited former] militiamen, produced a heavy loss, from the jealousy they felt of all in their front, after the night attack [on the Medellín]. This was increased by the constant word 'stand up' being passed along the line, and on more than one occasion it led to an individual soldier firing at some object in his front, which was taken up by the next, and so passed, like, and to appearance being a running wildfire, down the front of one or more regiments, till stopped by the officers. In this, the troops unfortunately forgot their light infantry in front, and many brave officers and men fell a sacrifice to the fire of their comrades.

A sergeant deployed with a piquet mounted by the Light Company of the 1st Battalion 2nd Foot Guards realised what was happening: 'The left section of the light infantry were not more than twenty-five yards from the muzzles of the fire locks, and I who was one of them seeing what was likely to happen, ordered the whole of my section to lay down on their faces and thus probably preserve my life.' The result of these alarms was the repeated standing to arms by men who dozed fitfully on the ground fully accoutred, in their ranks, with weapons to hand. The blazing away by the British was matched by the Spanish again standing to arms and firing into the night.

The allied armies were not the only one panicked by the outbreaks of firing. The historian of the 9th Légère recorded that Captain Girod and his company were awoken by the sudden musketry along the Portina:

> All around him, his men leapt up, cast their muskets aside, abandoned their packs and began fleeing in panic. Using the last of his willpower Girod forced himself to snap out of his stupor and began rallying his men. He ran forward to his chain of sentinels and asked what had been going on. His men were perfectly tranquil, they had also heard some gunfire and had seen some muzzle flashes in the distance but were unable to explain it.

Having ridden north from the scene of the Spanish panic to the Medellín when Ruffin's attack was launched, General Wellesley slept on its rocky slopes surrounded by his staff wrapped in their cloaks. Brigadier Stewart noted that: 'We lay all night on our arms in momentary expectation ... but no attack was made.' Throughout the night on the Cerro de Cascajal opposite burning torches marking battery positions and the rumble of gun carriages being moved forward was a sure sign that an attack would come in the morning. This was readily confirmed by a number of mostly German deserters principally from Leval's division, which was marching forward from the Alberche.

The night was tense in General Wellesley's bivouac. FitzClarence continued his account:

> Our glances were constantly directed upon that point whence the sun was to rise for the last time on many hundreds who were here assembled within a mile around, while Sir Arthur, occasionally asking the hour, showed he looked for daylight with as much anxiety as any of us.

Needing to justify his unauthorised attack on the Medellín, Marshal Victor sent dispatches to King Joseph's headquarters, which had been established at Casa de Salinas. He reported his failure but went on to confidently announce that his corps was already assembling on the Portina to renew his attack at dawn on what was obviously the strongest and key point of the allied line.

A black powder being fired at night.

Marshal Jourdan disagreed with this course, probably preferring not to risk a general action when he knew of a threat to the British line of communication that would soon have them heading back to Portugal.[1] His hand, however, was forced by Victor's deployment so far forward and by anticipating Napoleon's predictably angry response if they waited for Marshal Soult to concentrate and march south, rather than attacking the enemy when an opportunity was presented. Consequently, Joseph and his chief of staff stayed their hands and Victor, who knew that the emperor would already find plenty to criticise in his conduct of operations so far, was allowed to continue his preparations.[2] Joseph, however, rather than throwing in the weight of his army as Napoleon would have wished, chose to regard the attack on the Medellín as a preliminary necessity and ordered Sébastiani's IV Corps not to advance to attack until ordered.

Meanwhile, back on the slopes of the Medellín, Wellesley was in the saddle as dawn broke at around 0400 hours and rode up to the crest and its views of the battlefield:

> Just before day, we quietly mounted our horses and rode slowly towards the height, where we arrived just as the light allowed us to see the opposite side of the ravine beneath us covered with black indistinct masses. Every instant rendered them more visible, and the first rays of the sun.

As it grew light what Wellesley and his staff saw cannot have been unexpected: a grand battery of I Corps' guns, numbering about thirty pieces, was arrayed on the Cerro de Cascajal in true Napoleonic style at a range of between 600 and 800 yards from his position. It was clear that, combined with Ruffin's division well forward, the battle would be renewed with a ferocious bombardment at the point of attack followed by a heavy assault on the Medellín. The block of troops to be seen behind and to Ruffin's left was Villatte's division. To the left, deployed in another dozen battalion columns, was Lapisse's division. Behind Victor's infantry divisions were his light cavalry brigade, commanded by General Beaumont and La Tour-Maubourg's division of dragoons. Further south the divisions of Sébastiani's corps were still moving forward towards Wellesley's centre but facing the Spanish to the south of the Pajar de Vergara redoubt, only a division of cavalry, Milhaud's 2nd Dragoons, could be seen. Out of sight at the Casa de Salinas was the enemy reserve of 5,700 men of Joseph's guard. This concentration of force had 40,000 French facing the 20,000 British and was distinctly in favour of King Joseph. Wellesley's staff's attention, as FitzClarence recalled, was focused on the immediate threat:

> Our eyes were, however, principally attracted by an immense solid column opposite but rather to the left of the hill, evidently intended for

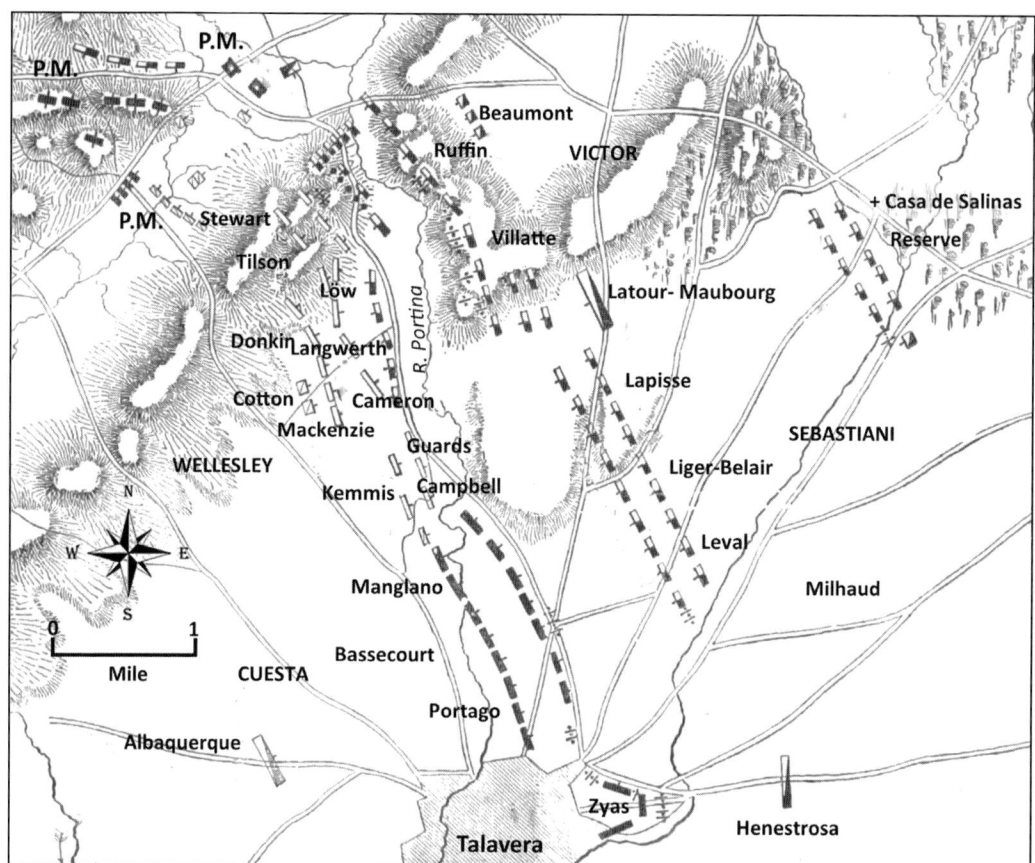

The general deployment of the armies at Talavera on 28 July 1809.

attack. Its front was already covered with *tirailleurs*, ready to advance at the word, and who saw before them the dead bodies of their comrades, who had fallen the night before, strewing the ground. The grey of the morning was not broken in upon by a single shot from either side, and we had time to observe our position (which had not been completely occupied before dark on the preceding eve) ...

Sergeant Cooper of the 7th Fusiliers, at the other end of the British line, remarked that: 'The dawn of the 28th saw more than 100,000 men standing ready to slay one another. None but those who have been in similar circumstances can even guess what is felt.'

The Bombardment

To the south of the Medellín, Sergeant Stevenson of the 3rd Guards wrote:

At daybreak all roused up; all eyes opened with the opening day, and ears too, expecting that as daylight appeared we should hear the roar of cannon and the balls whizzing through the air. The sun rose, and still all was quiet and silent, with that heavy foreboding stillness which presages the hurricane and the earthquake. In a little time four or five of the French infantry made their appearance in front of our brigade and passed along, placing themselves at the distance of about one hundred yards as sentinels before us. We began to say to each other, 'they are not fighting today,' when in a little time they showed us our mistake, by bellowing at us with twenty pieces of cannon. This was returned by ours; and so the battle began.

At 0500 hours the flash of a cannon from the centre of the Cerro de Cascajal batteries, followed by its boom a second later, announced the opening of the battle to both armies. The thirty guns massed in front of Victor's corps at a distance of twenty paces apart, covering a quarter mile front, opened fire and were joined by a similar number of cannon belonging to IV Corps targeting Wellesley's centre further south. Lieutenant Leith Hay, on the crest of the Medellín with the 29th, recalled:

> When it became perfectly light, a signal gun put the enemy's columns in motion, the whole of his artillery opening almost immediately after. The incessant and violent description of cannonade prevented the British infantry from interrupting the progress of the French columns; nor did they sustain any loss whatever in the early part of their advance, coming on with a resolute and rapid pace.

Wellesley, also on the Medellín, ordered both Stewart's and Tilson's brigades to retire behind a crest line and to lie down, which according to Lieutenant Leith Hay:

> the soldiers did with arms in their hands, ready to start up at a moment's warning. By this judicious arrangement, the regiment suffered little from the cannonade, although the enemy's practice appeared excellent, every shot either striking the ground immediately in front, or passing close over our heads.
>
> There is at all times something grand, imposing and terrific, in the sound of a cannonade. Here we had the astounding noise, with time to contemplate what was passing over us, without the attention being abstracted by great personal danger, or immediate effort at extrication. The effect was consequently very impressive. An old Scotch sergeant, crouching close to me, permitted his head to attain a very slight elevation, and, with a groan, said, 'Good God, sir, this is dreadful!' Without discussing the merits of our situation, I merely advised him to keep down his head, a hint instantly adopted, without any apparent reluctance, on his part, and, at the close of the affair, I was happy to find it was still upon his shoulders.

French foot artillerymen.

Lieutenant Leslie, with the 29th Foot on the Medellín, recalled that:

> The shot flew thick and fast about us, but it went principally over us, the guns being too much elevated [as the French were firing from lower ground]; but not so with the 48th Regiment below us on the right; we could see large gaps made at times in their ranks by the round shot.

The opening bombardment by the French artillery lasted up to forty-five minutes before Victor launched his attack. On the receiving end, the bombardment of the Medellín was one of the first recorded uses of a reverse slope position by Wellesley and no doubt heavily influenced his selection of his battlefields. In most subsequent battles he deployed the British and Portuguese infantry so that they would start the battle hidden as far as possible from the French artillery. The battalions of Sherbrooke's division were in the open centre of the position and were 'under a heavy fire of round shot and shell we sustained some loss'. On largely flat ground they could only lie down to reduce casualties.

With just four batteries of guns totalling thirty pieces, of which only a dozen 6-pounders were able to reply to the French 8- and 12-pounders, the British response to the bombardment did but little damage to the French columns that were soon crossing the Portina.

Attack on the Medellín

Ruffin's plan was for his three regiments to again attack in columns with two battalions forward and one in support. On this occasion, however, the 9th Légère was out on the division's right flank and the 24th Line were moved into the centre to deliver the frontal attack on the eastern face of the Medellín. The 96th Line was on the same ground it had attempted to fight across the

The Portina Brook and the first part of the slope up to the Medellín remains little changed.

previous evening. Both the 24th and 96th regiments attacked from positions behind the batteries on the forward edge of the Cascajal, which put them about 350 yards apart. According to Leith Hay, he saw the enemy battalions advancing in close column of double companies through gaps between the batteries.

Meanwhile, General Lapisse would mount a diversionary attack designed to fix Low's and Langwerth's brigades in position south of the Medellín.

Without effective British artillery fire and an easterly breeze, which filled the steep valley of the Portina with smoke, Ruffin's advance into the valley started well. Leith Hay wrote:

> When the French columns had mounted the ascent and were so near as to become endangered from the fire of their own artillery, a scene of great animation was exhibited. The summit, which had appeared deserted, now supported a regular line of infantry. Near the colours of the 29th stood Sir Arthur Wellesley, directing and animating the troops.

So thick was the smoke from the French artillery that blew across the Portina, despite the sound of musket fire and the rhythmic beating of the *pas de charge*, the battalions on the Medellín were surprised how close the French columns were when they could finally be discerned approaching through the smoke. Seeing their own skirmisher pairs steadily falling back 'firing and retiring', the defenders were ordered to 'stand' and 'dress' in two deep line with the soldiers standing shoulder to shoulder ready to receive the French.

However, so steady had the retirement of the light companies been and thanks to the smoke, they were already within effective musket range of the line, and therefore General Hill wanted the skirmishers out of the way for volley fire. He ordered the bugles to sound 'recall skirmishers' or the combined call of 'close and retire'. In only one of two recorded occasions, Hill was heard to swear in frustration at the light companies' leisurely withdrawal: 'Damn their filing, let them come in anyhow.'

In the case of the 2nd 66th of Foot in the centre of Tilson's Brigade, as described by Ensign Clarke they were lying down:

> behind the ridge until the enemy's column had reached the top, then [we were] to rise, deliver a volley, and charge. I was sent to the summit by the commanding officer to let him know where the enemy were and returned with the intelligence that a strong column was only fifty yards off.

Appearing out of the smoke still in close column of double companies, the French battalions were either not aware of the proximity of the British or they did not have sufficient time to attempt to deploy into line. Consequently, still in column they were greeted by British volley fire as they came up or over the

The allocated space for an infantryman in line was 22in, which had their shoulders lightly touching on either side. Dressing, forming a straight line from the right, centre or left, depending on the situation, was essential for manoeuvre, which required both distances and alignments to be strictly maintained.

crest line into range. Leslie recorded that the French were allowed 'to come up pretty close to us':

> When our brigadier general, Richard Stewart, said 'Now, 29th! Now is your time.' We instantly sprang forward to our feet, gave three tremendous cheers, and immediately opened fire, giving them several well directed volleys, which they gallantly returned ...

Having failed to deploy into line, the leading ranks of French column, fifty to sixty files wide, was significantly outgunned by the British two deep line and only managed a 'ragged' return. After a short firefight the moment came to go in with the bayonet. Clarke, of the 2nd Battalion 66th Foot, continued:

> The volley was delivered and we rushed on them with the bayonet. At first, they appeared as if they would stand the charge, but when we closed, they wavered, and then turned and ran down the hill in the wildest confusion.

Leith Hay also wrote of that crucial moment in the battle:

> General Ruffin had nearly surmounted all the difficulties of the ground, when a fire burst forth that checked his advance. His troops waivered. Sir Arthur ordered a charge. With one tremendous shout, the right wing

Charge of the 29th at the height of the fight for the Medellín.

of the 29th, and an entire battalion of the 48th, rushed like a torrent down, bayoneting and sweeping back the enemy to the brink of an insignificant muddy stream, nearly equidistant in the ravine which separated the two armies. In the pursuit, all order was speedily lost. The men advanced in small parties, destroying those of the enemy who had not ensured their safety by flight.

All six battalions of Hill's 2nd Division had charged down the hill at one point or another and were called back to the Medellín, while the French re-formed and tried again, with the same resulting volley fire, charge and pursuit. Leith Hay describes the arrival on the scene of a second line French battalions:

> At this moment, when the whole valley was filled with troops, in all the confusion attending the eagerness of pursuit, a column of French infantry appeared close upon our right flank, facing towards the irregular mass. It became necessary to collect the pursuers, to form a front, and to charge these fresh assailants.

This formed column was as the previous evening most likely to have been one of the supporting battalions, which through 'great exertion' was defeated:

> Broken as we were, an irresistible impetus had been given, and the enemy's column followed the example of those who had mounted the hill at the *pas de charge*. So completely were these attacks repelled, that the British infantry were quietly collected in the ravine, and marched back to the height, without being seriously assailed. The enemy now threw out light troops in front of his defeated 1st Corps.

Having endured the bombardment with only modest cover to shelter behind, Low's brigade also contributed to the defeat of Ruffin's columns, as Lapisse, who had been ordered to join Ruffin in the attack singularly failed to do so. No even vaguely credible explanation has ever been given for this failure to execute orders. Consequently, Brigadier General Low, observing that Ruffin's attacks on the Medellín had been 'renewed with vigour' and the result 'appeared for a time doubtful', directed one of his battalions into the exposed flank of the 96th:

> The 5th Line battalion of the [King's German] legion which formed the left of the German brigades, was ordered to ascend the height, and the corps of riflemen [two companies of the 1st Light Battalion, KGL,] became hotly engaged. The struggle was furious and obstinate. The inequalities of the ground not permitting the troops to retain their compact formation, separate contests of small bodies ensued. Major von Wurmb, gallantly leading on the German riflemen, was followed by Captain Langrehr bearing the regimental colours, at the head of the

General of Division François Amable Ruffin.

General of Division Pierre Lapisse.

5th Battalion; the skirmishers fell upon the enemy's left flank, while the battalion attacked him in front, and furiously assailing one of the French columns with the bayonet and butt-end of the musket, caused tremendous destruction around them.[3]

The casualties among Ruffin's men during this attack were, indeed, at 1,300, terrible, but losses were certainly not one sided. Lieutenant Leslie was one of the 850 British casualties on the Medellín:

In the midst of the exultation, about seven o'clock a.m., I received a ball in the side of my thigh, about three inches above the right knee. The sudden and violent concussion made me dance round, and I fell on my back. I immediately put my hand on the wound, which was bleeding profusely, to feel if the bone of my leg was broken, and, to my great satisfaction, I found that it was not. As I found myself unable to rise, I called for assistance, but from the noise and hurry of battle no one seemed to take notice of me. At length my friend, Andrew Leith Hay, perceived me. He raised me up, and then, taking the musket out of the hand of Corporal Sharp of my company, he directed him to conduct me out of action, and to find out the surgeons.

Of the wider situation General Hill, writing shortly after the battle, recorded:

During the attack on me the enemy did not allow the remainder of the line to be quiet, for, with their numerous artillery, they kept up a constant and destructive fire on it, not regarding the Spaniards at all. In about four or five hours, the enemy's fire slackened for a short time; they, however, afterwards began as serious an attack upon General Campbell as they had upon me …

Towards the end of the early morning action on the Medellín, General Hill was also wounded but fortunately not seriously. He later wrote:

My horse was wounded early in the action. I got another from an officer, shortly before the enemy gave up the conflict, and was struck by a musket ball near my left ear, and the back of my head. The blow was so violent that I was compelled to leave the field. I continued unwell during the whole of the next day, and the next; I am, however, thank God, much better to-day. My hat saved my life …[4]

As the wounded Lieutenant Leslie testified, the area to the flanks of the Medellín was still under fire, as he limped back with a wound to his thigh, accompanied by a soldier with a smashed arm:

I then passed through our second line, which, without, of course, being able to take any part in the action, was suffering much from round shot and shells falling amongst them. Indeed, I was nearly knocked over, and I made a narrow escape of being killed even at some distance in the rear. A shell came whizzing close to our heads, and alighted a few feet in front of us, throwing up the earth in our faces, but it fortunately bounded to the left down the slope of the hill, when it exploded. I soon afterwards reached my friend, Dr. Guthrie, who with his assistants were actively employed in amputating legs and arms.

After two to three hours of hard fighting, during which the French had reached the crest of the Medellín several times, Ruffin's regiments finally retired back to the Cerro de Cascajal admitting defeat. The 9th Légère, as the

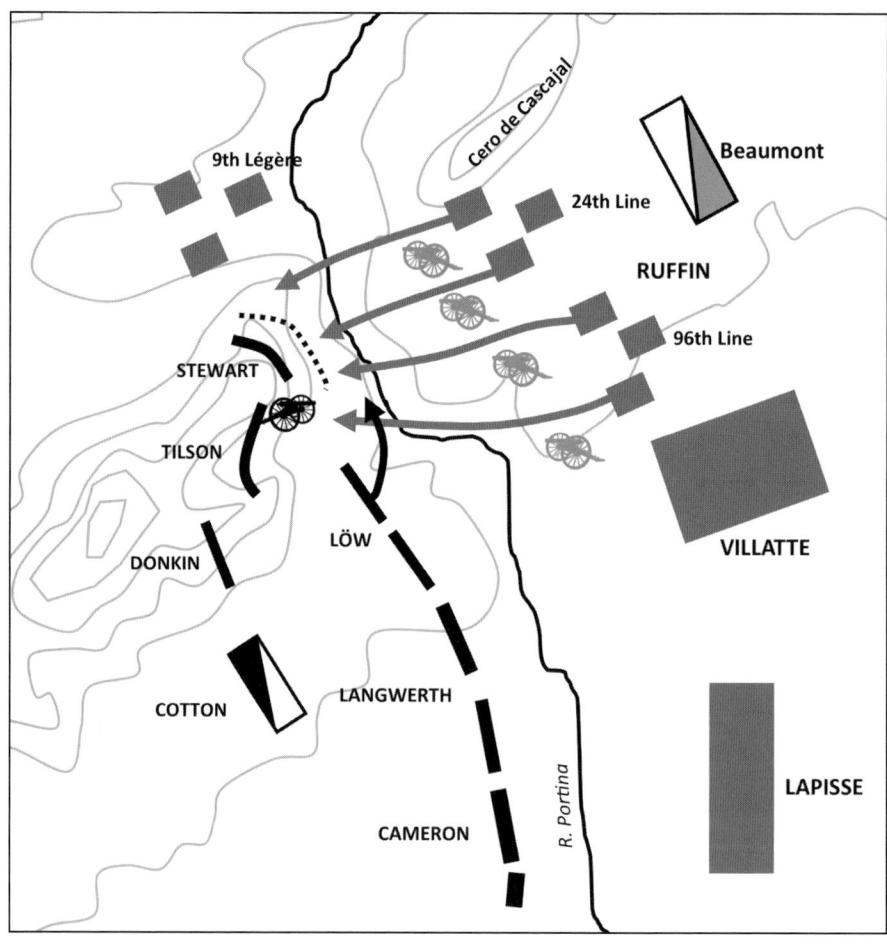

The third French attack on the Medellín, 28 July 1809.

24th had the previous evening, contributed little around the northern flank of the Medellín where there were no British battalions to extend the line northwards. With his troops having returned to the Cascajal, Victor deployed skirmishers into the valley and eventually over their heads resumed a bombardment of the Medellín.

Hill's 2nd Division line, which included some 2nd battalions that had been hastily brought up to strength with soldiers who volunteered from the militia, had now twice beaten back attacks by some of Napoleon's veteran units. This was some achievement, as Ruffin's regiments all had long distinguished records of success, including the highly regarded 9th Légère, which had been nicknamed 'The Incomparable' by Napoleon himself after delivering him victory at Marengo.

King Joseph and Marshal Jourdan have been criticised for not launching an attack on the Spanish right to distract attention and to march columns around the allied left via the largely unguarded plain. It is argued that such a move either overnight on the 27th–28th or early on the 28th would have turned Wellesley's flank and at least forced the British to fight on two fronts if not withdraw. After the second attack on the Medellín, it was too late for a redeployment and an envelopment to be successful.

In a letter home, Lieutenant Colonel Ellis, one of the Assistant Adjutant Generals with the staff up on the Medellín, wrote two days after the battle: 'They thrice came on with great Resolution and were as often Repulsed with immense Slaughter, a favorite Reg't of Buonaparte's the 24th had scarce a man left out of Twelve Hundred.'[5]

The 'Pause'

As Victor's men fell back to the Cerro de Cascajal sometime after 0800 hours, the artillery fire ebbed away and silence fell across the battlefield. Sergeant William Lawrence, of the 48th Foot, wrote in his memoirs:

> ... a period of truce was allowed for both armies to collect their wounded and convey them to the rear, where they lay often intermixed, a friendly intercourse sprang up between them, the Allies and French often going as far as to shake hands with each other.

This was the pause in the fighting most diarists refer to and other commentators mention an unofficial truce agreed by officers for a duration of two hours between the Cascajal and the slopes of the Medellín for the clearance of the dead and wounded. Elsewhere, the fire may have slackened but as FitzClarence remarked 'the cannonade continued; our centre and right suffering considerably ...'. He wrote:

> As the weather was dreadfully hot, and it was impossible to know how long we should occupy this ground, orders were given to bury the men who had fallen the night before and in the morning attack, lying around the hill interspersed with the living.
>
> We were occupied after this attack in carrying away our wounded in blankets, by four or five soldiers, and within a short time the number of unfortunate men assembled round our field hospital, a small house and enclosure behind our centre, barely out of cannon shot, proved our heavy loss.
>
> The dead of the enemy lay in vast numbers on the face of the hill, and had been tall, healthy, fine young men, well-limbed, with good countenances; and as proof of their courage (the head of their column having reached within a few yards of the top of the bill before being arrested),

A portrayal of French officers' uniform.

The Day of Battle, 28 July 1809 149

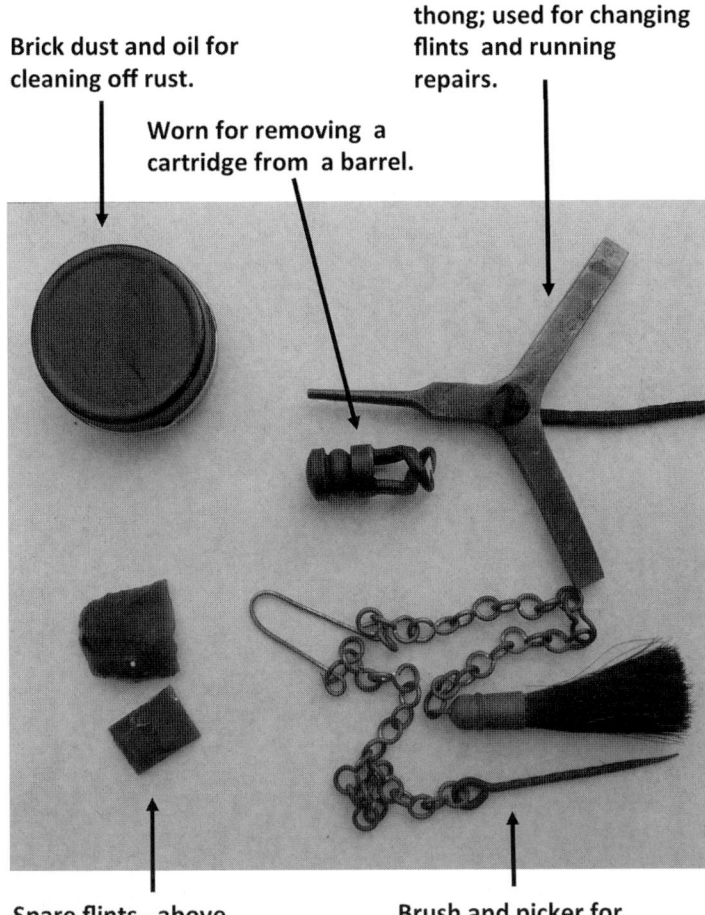

- Brick dust and oil for cleaning off rust.
- Worn for removing a cartridge from a barrel.
- Musket tool on a leather thong; used for changing flints and running repairs.
- Spare flints - above musket, below rifle.
- Brush and picker for cleaning the pan and clearing the touch hole.

Tools essential to keep muskets and rifles firing during a protracted action. For instance, flints broke or became rounded and would not spark, or touch holes became fouled with black powder residue.

the bodies lay close to our ranks. The face of the height was furrowed out into deep ravines by the water rushing down its steep sides during the rains, and the dead and wounded of both nations lay heaped in them.

The entrenching tools were thus employed, and it was curious to see the soldiers burying their fallen comrades, with the cannon shot falling around, and in the midst of them, leaving it probable that an individual might thus be employed digging his own grave! Gradually, however, the fire slackened, and at last wholly ceased, and war appeared as much suspended as before daylight and previously to the attack of the morning.

Meanwhile, in the centre the artillery fire of both sides slackened and the soldiers' need for water grew along with the heat of the day. Consequently, men of both sides went down to the Portina, nervously eying each other as they filled their canteens from the same pools of uninviting water, all that remained in the course of the nearly dry brook. Early on in the war this mutual tolerance was borne out of sheer necessity, in this case raging thirst, but as time progressed, fellow feeling for their sufferings prevailed and a system of live and let live often developed between the piquets.

Not just thirst tormented the British soldiers, as explained by FitzClarence:

> About nine it was evident that the enemy had no intention of disturbing us for some time, as their numerous fires proved they were not inclined to fight again on empty stomachs. This *was* a painful sight to us, who felt acutely for our starving soldiery, who began to experience the most pinching want. All the promises of the Spaniards had ended in nought. They had made no arrangements to act up to their word, and starvation began to stare us in the face. Generally, however, it was borne by our men with philosophy, but one hungry soldier became almost troublesome, and, close to Sir Arthur and his staff, said, 'It was very hard that they had nothing to eat,' and wished that they might be let to go down and fight, 'for when engaged, they forgot their hunger'. The poor fellow was, however, at last persuaded to retire.

Meanwhile, at about 1000 hours King Joseph and Marshal Jourdan, their glittering staff officers and escorting cavalry all making a considerable cavalcade, rode along the length of the Portina examining the ground and the allied dispositions. On reaching the Cerro de Cascajal they halted out of range of the KGL's 6-pound guns, the escort deployed, and the King held a disputatious council of war. The issue was whether to retire to the Alberche, without risking a general action and the possible loss of Madrid, where they could safely await the development of Soult's moves from the north, or to follow the strident Marshal Victor's wish to deliver a general attack on the allied army. The former course of action was strengthened by the now obvious reinforcement of the allied left flank beyond the Medellín but Victor's hectoring and repeated assertion that 'We should give up making war' if we do not attack, after an hour wore the King down. A decision hung in the balance when two pieces of information arrived. Most important was a report from Marshal Soult that his move south had been delayed by a slow concentration. The second was that General Venegas's Army of La Mancha had finally gained contact with the French at Toledo, presenting a threat to

The Day of Battle, 28 July 1809   151

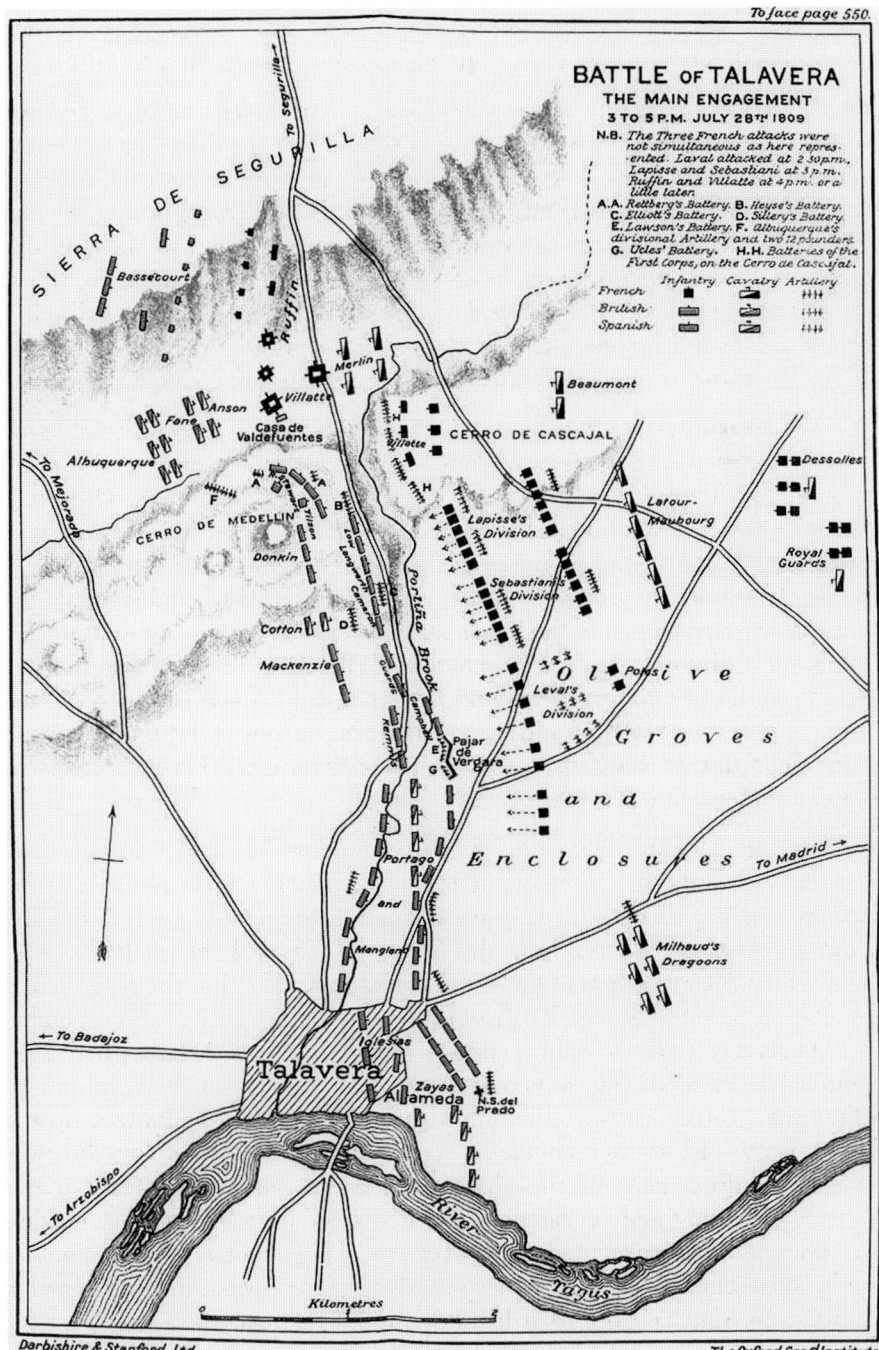

Oman's map of the battle on the afternoon of 28 July 1809.

Marshal Jourdan and King Joseph.

King Joseph's rear and possibly Madrid as well. In these circumstances, it would not be simply not be possible to stand for a week on the Alberche in close proximity to the combined allied army having detached sufficient troops to cover the approaches to Madrid from the south.

With a decision forced on Jourdan and the King by the change in the balance of risk, the plan for the renewed attack was based on the deployment that had already been made, namely an assault on the centre by Sébastiani's corps and a resumption of the attack on the British left by Victor. Milhaud's dragoons would continue to watch Cuesta in his defensive position and the King's reserve would remain over 3 miles to the rear at Casa de Salinas.

The death of General Mackenzie at Talavera.

Chapter Eight

The Main Attack

Having been forced to commit to a general action by Soult's delay and Venegas's advance on Madrid, the King and Marshal Jourdan made their plans to resume the attack. It was not to be a repeat of Victor's underwhelming attempts on the Medellín but one that would use the full resources of the army, still largely concentrated against the British. Consequently, the dissemination of orders and deployment for the renewed attack took the rest of the morning.

While they prepared their attack, French commanders could see that the Medellín was being reinforced by Wellesley. Consequently, there was to be no third attack on the feature but instead a belated attempt to turn the allied northern flank via the plain and hills beyond. Villatte's division was to replace Ruffin's battered battalions on the Cascajal; however, Ruffin was to remain engaged, this time on the northern plain. The deployment was as follows: the 9th Légère was work its way west through the foothills of the Sierra de Segurilla, while the rest of Ruffin's infantry was reinforced by the 3,000 men of one of Villatte's brigades and by Merlin's light cavalry division; together they marched towards the plain north of the Medellín. On seeing this movement, Wellesley made a corresponding deployment, reporting in his Talavera dispatch to Castlereagh that:

> In consequence of the repeated attempts upon the height upon our left, by the valley, I had placed 2 brigades of British cavalry in that valley, supported in the rear by the Duque de Alburquerque's division of Spanish cavalry. The enemy then placed light infantry in the range of mountains on the left of the valley, which were opposed by a division of Spanish infantry, under Lieut. Gen. Bassecourt.

With Villatte's division still coming forward to replace Ruffin's battered division on the Cerro de Cascajal, there was ample time for Wellesley to complete the reinforcement of his left flank described above. The British commander also appealed to Cuesta for more guns, which was answered by the dispatch of two batteries to reinforce his ally's centre and left. One heavy battery went to the Pajar de Vergara redoubt and the other accompanied Bassecourt's division and was sited to cover the plain north of the Medellín.

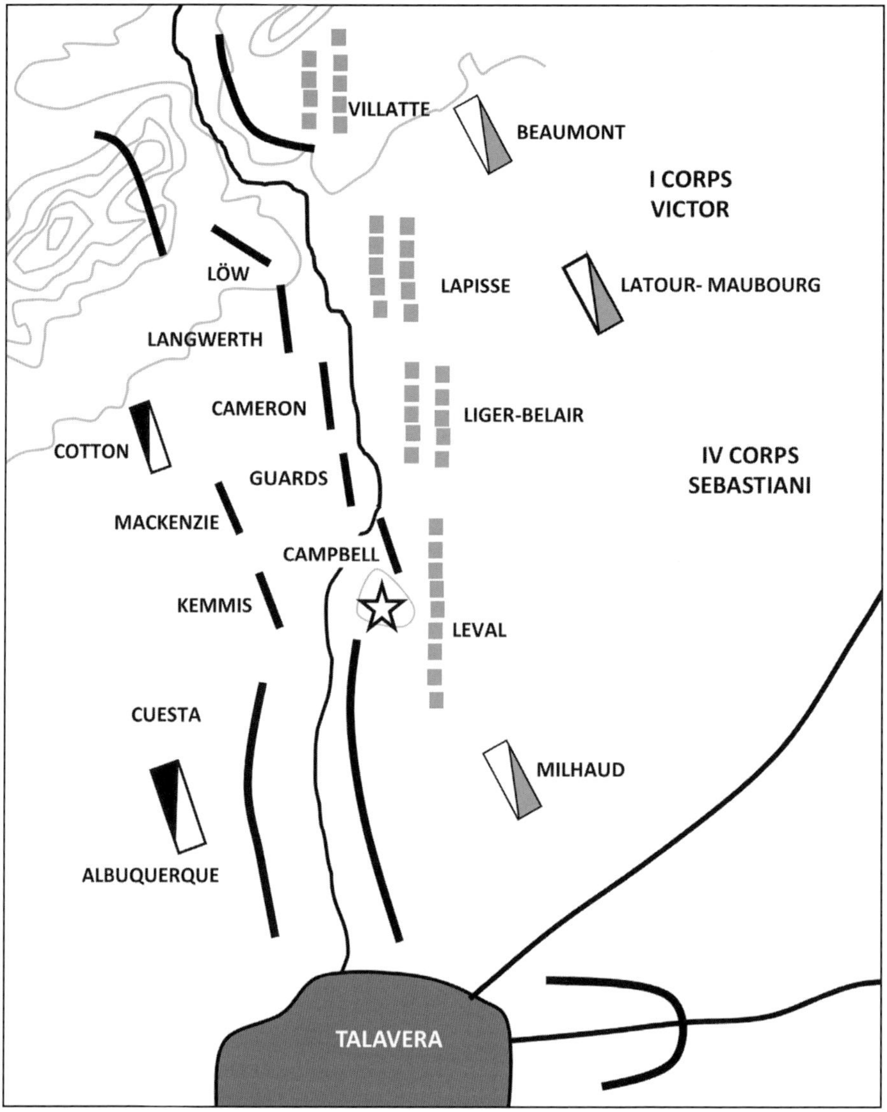

The main attack on the afternoon of 28 July 1809.

There had been little fire for two hours, with the dead and wounded being cleared, and canteens being filled from the Portina, but as recalled by Lieutenant FitzClarence:

> Till about eleven o'clock all remained quiet, but about that hour immense clouds of dust were seen rising above the woods towards the Alberche opposite the centre of the Allied army, implying movements of

large bodies of troops. This indicated the preparing for a general assault, and was occasioned by Sébastiani's corps forming a column of attack.

The second French attack, this time on the Allied centre, was to be made by the massed divisions of Generals Leval and Lapisse and General of Brigade Liger-Belair. The latter replacing Sébastiani while he was absent commanding IV Corps. The attack, supported by twenty-four guns of the corps plus the flanking fire from the grand battery on the Cascajal that raked the British centre, was made by some 19,500 men and began at around 1400 hours. General Leval's 2nd Division had, however, pressed forward too quickly through some close country towards the junction of the two allied armies and the Pajar de Vergara redoubt, which had by now been reinforced by the Spanish battery. Leval's attack should have been somewhat behind the other division's so as to present a refused flank to the Spanish, but it seems that in approaching the Portina Brook through some thick country, co-ordination with General Liger-Belair's 1st Division to his right broke down. Unable to see his flanking formation, Leval pressed on, not wishing to be late, and as a result was almost thirty minutes early in clashing with Brigadier General A. Campbell's piquets of 4th Division on the Portina.

Attack of Leval's Division

General Leval's regiments each consisted of two battalions of Dutch and soldiers from a variety of German states, plus a single battalion from Frankfurt. Unusually, he deployed all nine battalions of his division in a single line of close columns. Consequently, there were no battalions in support, just two small Polish battalions of Valence's division in distant reserve back at the deployment area. This formation was probably dictated by the broken ground and foliage that also deprived Leval of a field of fire for his artillery. Thanks to this difficulty and lack of an elevated position, Leval's artillery was unable to contribute to the softening up of the British line, so his guns followed behind the infantry battalions.

The ground in front of Campbell's position consisted of an open field of some 50 yards, a ditch and bank and what is described as a 'light wood', which given contemporary maps was probably an olive grove. The thicker country beyond the Portina was, however, a disadvantage to the two battalions of Brigadier A. Campbell's Brigade, as it allowed the French to approach and take the piquets by surprise, again pointing to a lack of British experience in the outposts. Sergeant Cooper of the 2nd Battalion, 7th Fusiliers' Light Company was with the piquets and almost fell victim to a *ruse de guerre* by the six battalions of the Nassau, Dutch and Baden regiments:

> One of these, after threading its way among the trees and grape vines, came up directly in our front, and while deploying, called out *Espanholas*,

wishing us to believe they were Spaniards. Our captain thought they were Spaniards and ordered us not to fire.[1]

This was an easy error to make as many of the Spanish regiments wore blue coats as well, but as Cooper recalled 'they soon convinced us who they were by a rattling volley. We instantly retired upon our regiment ...'

Having been surprised in the close country and promptly driven in, the sight of the Light Company coming back at the gallop unsettled the rest of the Fusiliers and the adjacent 2nd Battalion 53rd (Shropshire) Regiment. Cooper continued:

[our regiment] sprung up and met the enemy on the rising ground, but our men being all raw soldiers, staggered for a moment under such a rolling fire. Our colonel Sir William Meyers seeing this, sprang from his horse and snatching one of the colours [the King's], cried 'Come on Fusiliers.' 'Twas enough.

Lieutenant Colonel Sir George Bingham, commanding officer of the 53rd Foot, recalled that the Fusiliers 'immediately rallied, aided by the second right company of the 53rd'.

Having pushed the light companies of Campbell's brigade back as described above, the centre and right French columns had advanced into more open ground in front of the redoubt. Adjacent to this stood the shaken two deep line of the 7th Fusiliers and two companies of the 53rd of Foot, supported by the hastily redeployed 2nd 24th. Leval's columns were, however, quickly brought to a halt by volley fire from the muskets and grape shot from the redoubt at a range of 200 yards. Oberst von Porbeck, commander of the Baden Regiment, was killed and his regiment was the first to break and retire in confusion. In Leval's centre, the Dutch battalions withered away under artillery fire and also fell back.

With further attempts to advance by the Nassau battalions being thwarted by Cameron's brigade, Leval ordered forward his divisional artillery in order to swing the balance of firepower in his favour against the well-drilled British volley fire and redoubt. However, while the battery was still negotiating the vines and olive groves, eight companies of the 2nd 53rd were brought up from reserve and counter-attacked into the flank of the French division and Leval's guns were, however, unable to get into a sufficiently good position to be effective. Lieutenant John Carss, of the 53rd, explained:

During this charge their cannon had got close up to this bank which prevented the shot from hurting us, as they went over our heads. They were pulling down part of the bank to get the guns up to our right for the purpose of raking our line, but when we ran our charge to the bank, we commenced a very brisk fire and almost killed every man at the guns in half an hour ...

Meanwhile, Leval's infantry wavered. Lieutenant Colonel Meyers seized the moment and led the Fusiliers forward, as Cooper described:

> On rushed the Fusiliers and 53rd Regiment and delivered such a fire, that in a few minutes the enemy melted away, leaving 6 pieces of cannon behind, which they had not had time to discharge. The 6 pieces were immediately rendered unfit for use, as our balls were too large for their bore.[2]
>
> While charging the enemy, a Frenchman [sic] fell in his hurry, and was collared by a brutal serjeant of ours, who exclaimed 'I'll kill a Frenchman for once,' and then deliberately shot the poor fellow dead ...

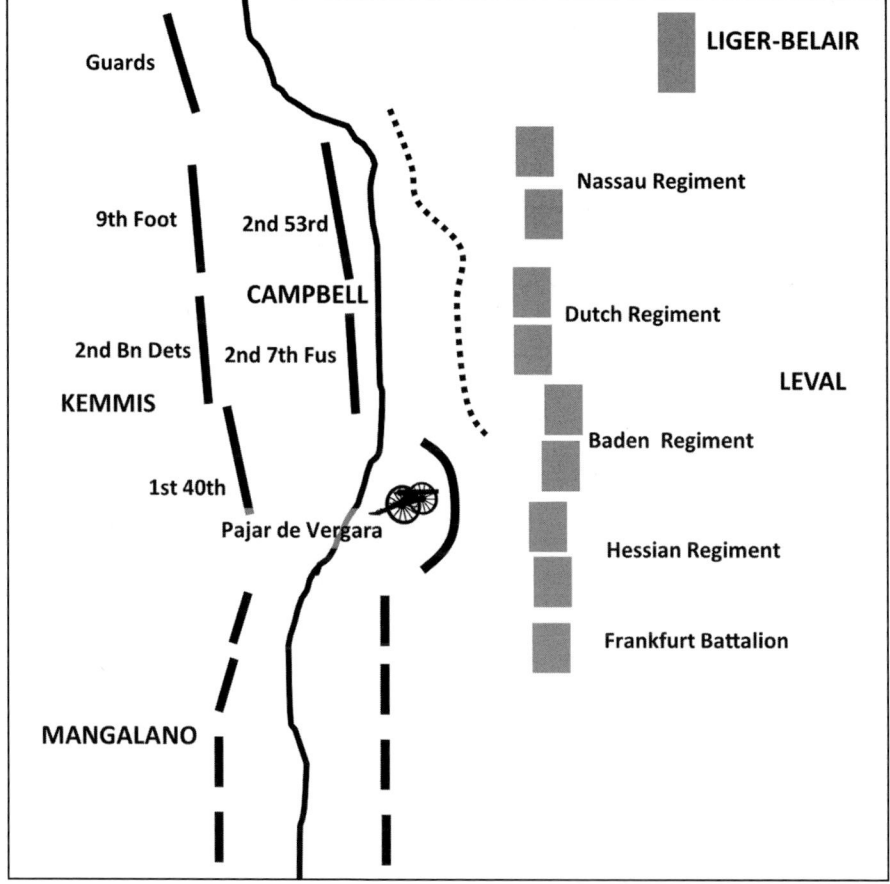

The attack of Leval's division at 1400 hours on 28 July 1809.

158 The Talavera Campaign, 1809

Light grape shot was normally the size of a musket ball and in the example above it is contained in a metal case. For longer ranges heavy grape was used; in the example below the lead grape shot is of 2in diameter and could be cast and made up into canvas bags in the field.

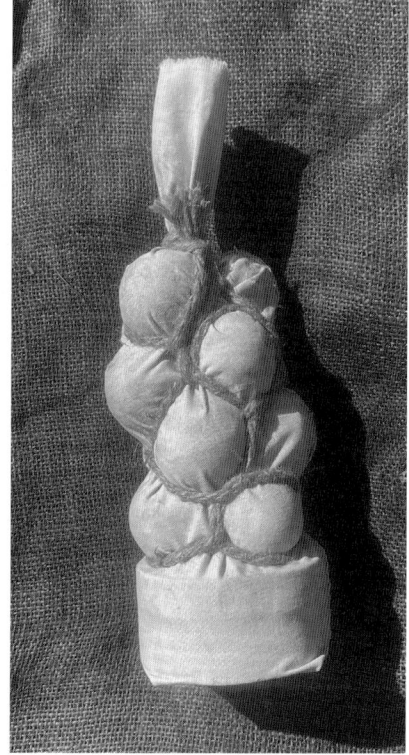

The Main Attack 159

Lieutenant Colonel Sir William Meyers, commanding officer of the 7th Fusiliers.

Colonel Bingham, of the 53rd, reported that:

> In this charge, we passed at first the outmost of the two enclosures in front of the work [the Pajar de Vergara redoubt], and in the retreat of the enemy they left a brigade of ten guns³ and some tumbrels of musket ammunition. The Brigade [Campbell's] then lined the ditches of the enclosures, and thus formed a flanking fire on the column that attacked our line more to the left, by which means the Nassau Regiment suffered badly.

A combination of the unnerving stillness of the red-coated line, a volley or two, followed by a charge with the bayonet while the French column was reeling from the impact of the lead balls that smashed into its ranks, was now established as the signature tactic of the British infantry. The disparity between the casualties suffered by Cameron at Talavera and Laval's division confirms the effectiveness of the line versus the column in such encounters in the Peninsular.

Meanwhile, on Leval's left flank, the Hesse-Darmstadt Regiment and the Frankfurt Battalion overlapped the front of the Spanish, which with oft-unrecognised steadiness, opened fire with musket and artillery from the redoubt and adjacent banks and held the attack. For a time matters here had degenerated into a firefight with no clear advantage to either side but on seeing the Dutch and Baden regiments falling back on their right flank the Hessian and Frankfurt battalions also withdrew.

Having defeated what would be Leval's first attack, Brigadier Campbell, though wounded in the thigh, rallied and re-formed the battalions of 4th Division back in their original positions just north of the Pajar redoubt, before going to the rear for treatment. As Campbell was helped back, according to Lieutenant Carss: 'Sir Arthur sent down to General Alexander Campbell commanding our brigade to say we were the bravest fellows in the world, and he had no words to express how highly pleased he was with us.'

The Attack on Sherbrooke's Division

While the protracted fight was still going on, to the left, the four brigades of Sherbrooke's 1st Division were still steady and holding Wellesley's centre, despite having been under artillery fire for much of the morning. The renewed artillery bombardment again had them lying down. Ensign John Aitchison, of the 1st Battalion 3rd Guards, wrote:

> A tremendous cannonade – shots and shells were falling in every direction – but none of the enemy were to be seen – the men were all the while lying in the ranks, and except at the very spot where a shot or shell fell, there was not the least motion – I have seen men killed in the ranks by cannon shots – those immediately round the spot would remove the mutilated corpse to the rear, they would then lie down as if nothing had occurred and remain in the ranks, steady as before. That common men could be brought to face with the greatest danger, there is a spirit which tells me it is possible, but I could not believe that they could be brought to remain without emotion, when attacked, not knowing from whence. Such, however, was the conduct of our men (I speak particularly of the [Guards] Brigade) on 28 July, and from this steadiness so few suffered as by remaining quiet the shots bounded over their heads.

Initially deployed behind the Guards, Mackenzie's brigade was also subject to the bombardment. According to the regimental history of the 24th of Foot,

General Sherbrooke.

among the 2nd Battalion, 'the men fell fast from shot and shell. The brigade was therefore ordered to lie down, and then the round shot did little damage, but the shells annoyed the men much.'

Approaching Sherbrooke's division under cover of the billowing gun smoke were the veteran divisions of General of Brigade Liger-Belair and General of Division Lapisse. Fortescue described the deployment of their heavy columns:

> Both of the French generals had drawn up their troops in two lines: Lapisse placing his second brigade in rear of the first, while Sébastiani drew up his two brigades side by side: but in each case the first line consisted of six battalions, each battalion in column of double companies, and each group of three battalions closed up to within six paces of interval, so as to present a massive front of one hundred and fifty to

one hundred and eighty men, nine ranks deep. (The first line of Lapisse therefore consisted of the 16th Light and 45th of the Line: his second of the 8th and 54th of the Line. Sébastiani's first line consisted of the 28th and 58th: his second of the 32nd and 75th. Each regiment had three battalions.)

The columns described above were so closely deployed that it is obvious that with no room to deploy, Sébastiani had no intent to fight in line but for his forces to attempt to bludgeon their way through as they had hitherto on the battlefields of central Europe. Of the deployment of the following line of battalions (see diagram opposite), Fortescue wrote:

> The second line was of even denser formation than the first, each group of three battalions being drawn up either in line of company-columns, with a front of about one hundred men and a depth of eighteen ranks, or in close column of double companies with a front of fifty to sixty men and a depth of twenty-seven ranks.

Proceeded by clouds of *tirailleurs* deployed in a skirmish screen, the pair of French divisions with their drums beating the *pas de charge* crossed the Portina Brook in twenty-four columns and advanced on Sherbrooke's eight battalions deployed in two deep line.

On the right of this division and adjacent to Campbell's brigade, the Guards Brigade were soon also under attack and its light companies and No. 5 Company of the 5th 60th Rifles were driven in by General Liger-Belair's columns. The French attack developed across more open ground; Sergeant Stevenson of the 1st Battalion, 3rd Guards, later wrote: 'We had been lying down for some time under a heavy fire of round shot and shell, and

The flat and now largely coverless ground astride the Portina Brook in the centre of Wellesley's deployment.

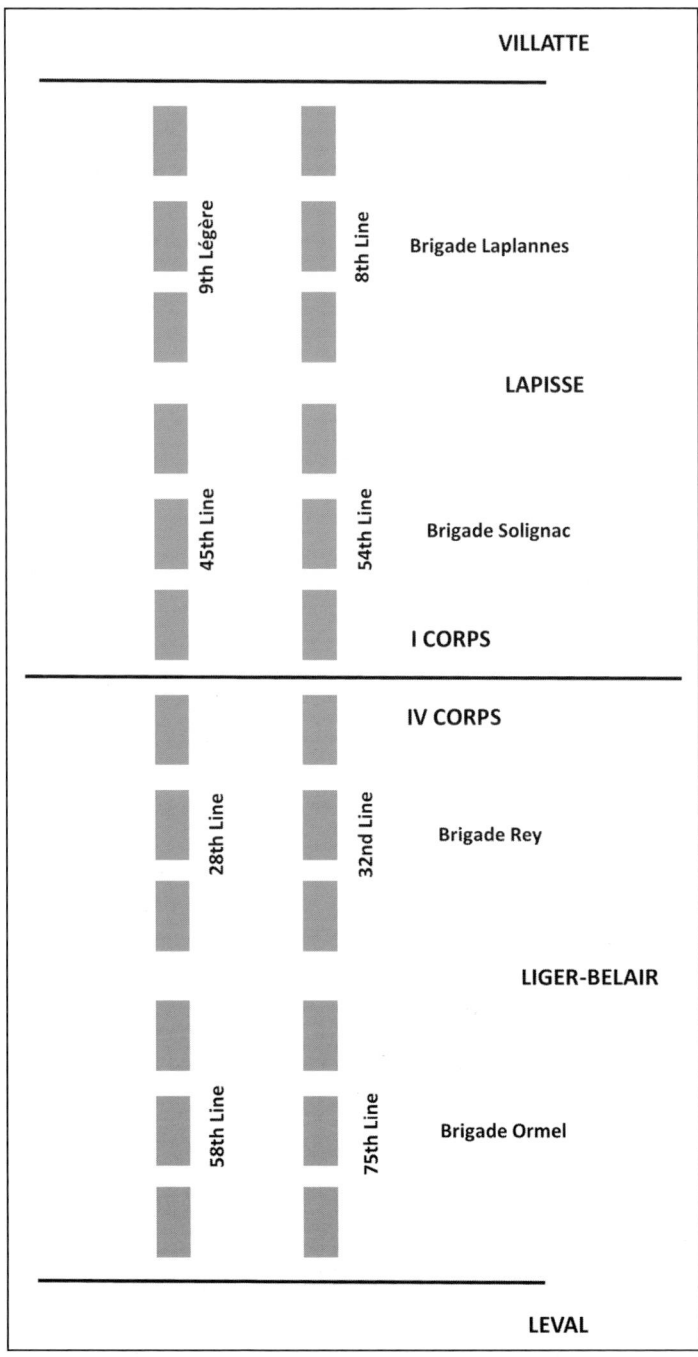

A diagram after Fortescue of the formations adopted by Liger-Belair and Lapisse.

164   *The Talavera Campaign, 1809*

sustained some loss but now we started up, and there were the two lines [of columns] within musket-shot.' Sergeant Cooper was still fighting and recorded that:

> ... the battle raged with great fury, and the struggle was continued on nearly the same ground, with the utmost fierceness on both sides. For a considerable time, the combatants were enveloped in a mighty cloud of smoke. This, with the thunder of artillery, the roll of musketry, and the huzzas of our men as they pushed back the masses of the foe, constituted one vast continuous uproar. At this time the British guards were brought up.

In Sherbrooke's centre, to the left of the Guards, was Cameron's brigade of two weak battalions and No. 9 Company of the 5th 60th. They were also facing the advancing columns of Liger-Belair, in this case his right-flank regiments, the 28th and 32nd Ligne, which were again deployed in two lines each of three battalions. Cameron had been reinforced by another hasty redeployment of the 2nd 24th Foot to the left. Unlike the Guards Brigade, the rest of 1st Division had crucially lacked a second line of infantry in support behind them, hence the 2nd 24th filing to their left at the double. Further back was Cotton's light cavalry brigade.

Lieutenants Close of the 1st Battalion, 48th Foot, and Leith Hay of the 29th, up on the Medellín near Wellesley and his staff, described watching the attack develop:

> The staff at this time wore very long faces, The enemy's shot were flying in all directions. Lifting their telescopes, they peered through the rising dust clouds to take in the sobering spectacle ... To those who, elevated as we were, saw every movement, this was the most anxious moment of the whole battle. Heavy columns of French infantry seemed following in succession to press upon the weakest part of the line; nor did it appear ... the centre could successfully resist the overwhelming force.

Writing in the third person after the war, one of the artillery commanders, General Marquis de Georges Chambray, described the attack from the French perspective:

> The French advanced with their muskets at the shoulder according to their use. When they arrived at a short distance from them the English line remained motionless, and there was some hesitation in the march. The officers and NCOs shouted to the soldiers, '*En avant, marchez, ne tirez pas*'. Some even cried, '*Ils se rendent*' ['They are surrendering']. The forward movement was therefore resumed; but a very short distance from the English line, it began to fire in two ranks, which carried

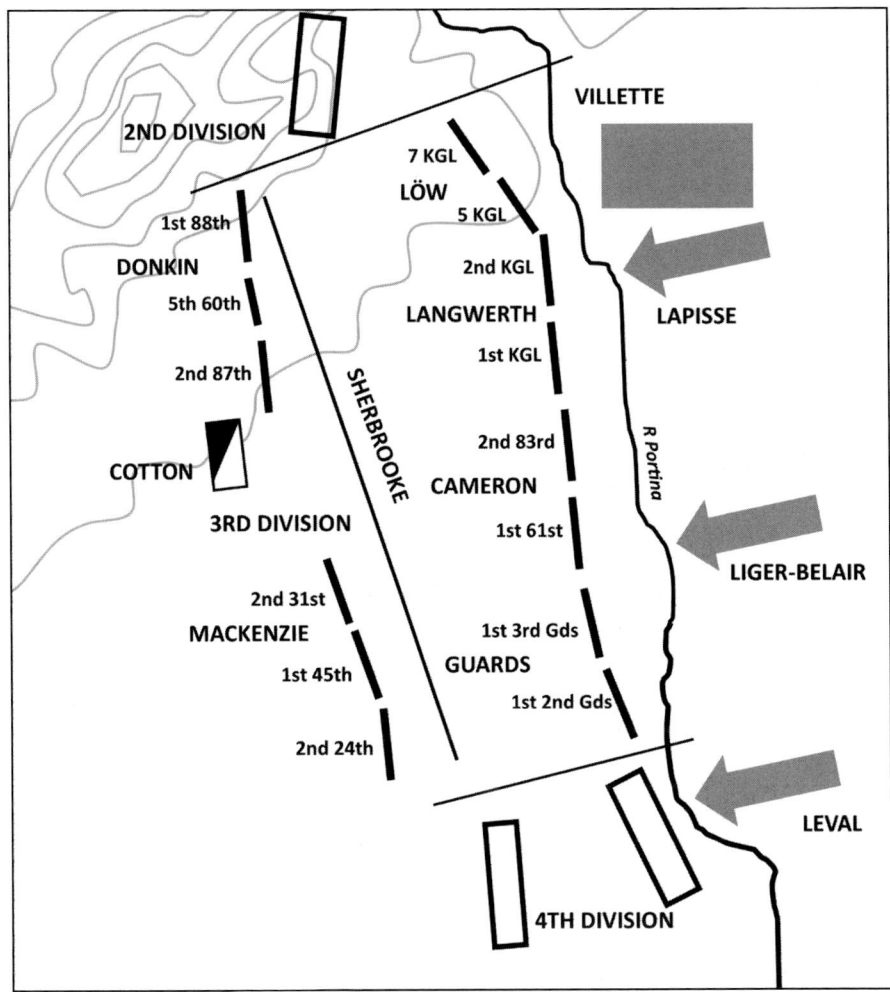

The deployment of Sherbrooke's 1st Division and supporting formations.

destruction into the bosom of the French line, checked its movement, and produced some disorder.[4]

Two of those battalions that 'remained motionless' were the 1st Battalion, The Coldstream Guards, and the 3rd Guards. The British line, 'Awaiting the enemy with ported arms, having been instructed to hold their fire until the French column was within 50 paces ...' had clearly unnerved the French veterans with their silence and stillness. Sergeant Stevenson continued:

> ... at length Sir Arthur came along close to us and told the general of our division in our hearing, that when they attacked us, we were to charge

The head of a heavy French battalion column.

without firing, and in a little time General Sherbrooke called out 'Get ready, Guards! They are coming upon you in two lines!'[5]

The word of command was given, and we advanced to the charge. As soon as we came near them, they gave us a few shots and turned about: we continued our advance in line, but they fell back so rapidly that we could not come up with them. We halted on disadvantageous ground, and almost as soon as our general had called 'halt!' they returned upon us with reinforcements, and a tremendous fire on both sides commenced, I had often heard of shot flying like hailstones, but I never was in such a shower as that either before or since.

The conflict continued until the enemy's ranks got so thin that the rest turned about and fled with all speed beyond the reach of musket-shot, and then opened a fire of cannon with grape-shot.[6]

General de Chambray recalled that, despite orders to the contrary, some French infantrymen returned the fire but:

the English suddenly ceasing theirs, charged with bayonets. Everything was favourable to them, the order, the impulse given, the resolution to fight with the bayonet: among the French, on the contrary, no impulse; the surprise caused by the unexpected determination of the enemy, the disorder, it was necessary to flee.

General Marquis de Georges Chambray from the frontispiece of his memoirs.

Of the Guards' advance and subsequent disorder when they pursued the enemy's 58th Line Regiment, Ensign Aitcheson, as is often the case in personal accounts, blames the loss of cohesion on the two brigades on the division's left flank for what was, in fact, an equal failure. He wrote:

> On their approaching within 200 yards, we were ordered to advance without firing a shot and afterwards to charge this *we* did as became British officers. The enemy did not wait for us, we carried everything before us, but unfortunately the infantry of the German Legion, which formed the left of our division, gave way and this made it necessary for our brigade to retire. When we faced about, the enemy that were flying rallied and opened a heavy fire and we were taken in our left flank by that part of the enemy which ought to have been driven back by the Germans.

The Guards had pursued the enemy too far and hadbecame disordered. Meanwhile, the French battalions rallied and delivered a well-timed attack that was joined by the second line of battalions belonging to General of Brigade Liger-Belair's division. Atchison, in a letter written in September while convalescing, provides more detail:

> In the centre where at last the enemy made his grand push we charged when he was within 100 yards, and our fire was reserved until they were flying. The eagerness of our men in advancing without support, beyond the distance intended, had nearly proved fatal, for we had no sooner passed the ravine [the Portina] in our front than the enemy perceived the troops on our left halted, took us in our left flank by his retiring columns and the [second line of] columns which were posted in our front in a wood behind the bank of a vineyard. Thus gaining confidence, nearly turned our right, they stood till the grenadiers were actually within double musket length, but they then retired in great confusion. At this point of the action our numbers were diminishing very fast, and it being impossible to maintain this advance position we were ordered to be withdrawn. Accordingly, we faced about, retired to the ravine, slower and in better order than we advanced. Here we made a stand and did considerable execution, but the enemy having come on with all those troops that had been flying, supported by strong columns which concealed in the wood, it was deemed necessary to order another retirement, and we once again faced about – the enemy by this time having advanced within a few yards, the havoc was great, and we were thrown into momentary confusion.

On Sherbrooke's left flank, Langwerth's and Low's KGL brigades faced the advance of General Lapisse's division of a dozen battalions also deployed in two lines of battalions. According to Beamish, the KGL were:

> Reserving their fire until the French had crossed the ravine, these regiments received the enemy with a volley, and then rushing forward with the bayonet drove the assailants in disorder the other side; from hence the fire of a second line [of French battalions] opening up on them and being also exposed to a murderous discharge of grape, the Legion brigades were ordered to retire and fell back, leaving general von Langwerth amongst the slain.

Captain James Somers Cocks, with the 16th Light Dragoons, a part of Cotton's cavalry brigade to the rear of the KGL, reported that: 'Poor Langwerth seized the colours [of the 1st Line Bn, KGL], planting them, called to the men to form. He was killed attempting to rally them.'

The Main Attack   169

The KGL battalions had pursued the first wave of broken French battalions and not only crossed the Portina but 'with reckless energy' started to climb the slope up to the Cascajal, from where they were hotly engaged by the French artillery. Lieutenant FitzClarence, looking down from the Medellín, saw what happened to the KGL battalions:

> The flying enemy led [them] on till they [the French] opened a battery on their flank, which occasioned so heavy a loss that the ranks could not be formed after the disorder of the pursuit and, on being ordered to resume their ground, produced confusion.

It was now the turn of the fleeing British and KGL troops to taste the fresh French bayonets of the second line, having been checked by French musket fire.

In contrast to the rest of the division, Brigadier Cameron in the centre had halted the pursuit by his brigade just beyond the Portina, before it got beyond control of the officers of the 1st 61st and 2nd 83rd Foot. With the brigades on both flanks falling back in disorder, driven in by the battalions of the second French line, they were in danger of being enveloped and were in turn forced

The 3rd Foot Guards at the crisis of Talavera.

Relatively light black powder smoke from a French musket volley.

to withdraw but did so in goon order. Despite Cameron's caution, the situation in Wellesley's centre was becoming critical, with Sherbrooke's division 'sorely pressed'.

Most of the 1st Division's battalions had been thrown back and with the second line of French battalions advancing, with their first wave rallying behind them, it looked as if the line would crumble and the way would be open for La Tour-Maubourg's six regiments of dragoons, numbering 3,200 sabres, to rip Wellesley's centre asunder, brushing aside Cotton's 1,000 troopers. Facing a total of 8,000 French cavalry, the allies would be hard put to cover what would surely be a pursuit. Two actions, however, changed the course of the battle: a battalion advance below the Medellín and, at the other end of the British line, when General Mackenzie ordered a brigade of 3rd Division forward.

Wellesley sent an ADC spurring to the 29th Foot ordering them down from the Medellín to form a line, behind which the KGL could rally. According to Lieutenant Leith Hay, seeing just how weakened in numbers the 29th were, instead he instructed Colonel Donellan of Stewart's brigade to take his battalion, the 1st 48th, to stabilise the situation. The battalion marched down from the top of the hill in open column of companies at quarter distance, and Major William Napier explained that:

> At this moment, although Hill's and Campbell's divisions, on the extremities of the line, held fast, the centre of the British was absolutely

broken, and the fortune of the day seemed to incline in favour of the French, when, suddenly, Colonel Donellan, with the forty-eighth regiment, was seen advancing through the midst of the disordered masses. At first, it seemed as if this regiment must be carried away by the retiring crowds, but, wheeling back by companies, it let them pass through the intervals, and then, resuming its proud and beautiful line, marched against the right of the pursuing columns, and plied them with such a destructive musketry, and closed upon them with such a firm and regular pace, that the forward movement of the French was checked. The guards and the Germans immediately rallied, a brigade of light cavalry came up from the second line at a trot, the artillery battered the enemy's flanks without intermission, the French wavered, lost their advantage, and the battle was restored.[7]

The 1st 48th, with admirable steadiness, marched 600 yards down from the crest of the Medellín and deployed into line. Lieutenant Close reported 'two columns were advancing with rapid stride, following the broken troops ...' and the 1st were forced to confront them. He continued, making it plain that their action was far from as straightforward as Napier suggests:

> We fired a volley and ported arms. We advanced, and fired another volley ... for a considerable time we had the fight entirely to ourselves, not a single regiment was near us. A very destructive fire was opened on us at this time from their guns. All the shot and shell was directed at us. A squadron of [16th] Dragoons came to our aid at this juncture. They were no sooner perceived than all the artillery was levelled at them, and they were obliged to retire from the shower; but, before they did so, our men fell fast from the shot directed at them ... When Ensign Vander Meulen was wounded, I went to take the colour from the Sergeant who held it. When I arrived at the centre a shell fell. We lay down till it had burst. My head was between the legs of a soldier, and a soldier was on my right and left side close against me. The shell burst; the man whose legs my head was protected by had half his head carried off; the other two were dreadfully mangled: the body of one was laid bare from his loins to his breast, and both the legs of the other were carried off near the knee. We were ordered to shorten our front by doubling our right wing in front of our left ... the aspect of things at this period was somewhat disheartening. The right wing suffered very much, nearly half the Grenadier Company were *hors de combat*.

Despite the dreadful casualties, one of the battalion's officers wrote: 'A close and well-directed fire from us arrested the progress of the French ...' While urging his men to advance, General Lapisse was killed and in the return of fire

172 *The Talavera Campaign, 1809*

Colonel Donellan also received what proved to be a mortal wound to his leg. Still aboard his horse, as the French wavered, he addressed: 'Major Middlemore, you will have the honour of leading the 48th to the charge.' Lieutenant Close describes the battalion's action, led by the second in command, against battalions of the 8th and 54th line regiments: 'under his command our charges were made. They would not stand our charge ... the French eventually retreated close under their guns.' Another officer of the battalion makes it clear that while the 48th may have facilitated the rallying of the German

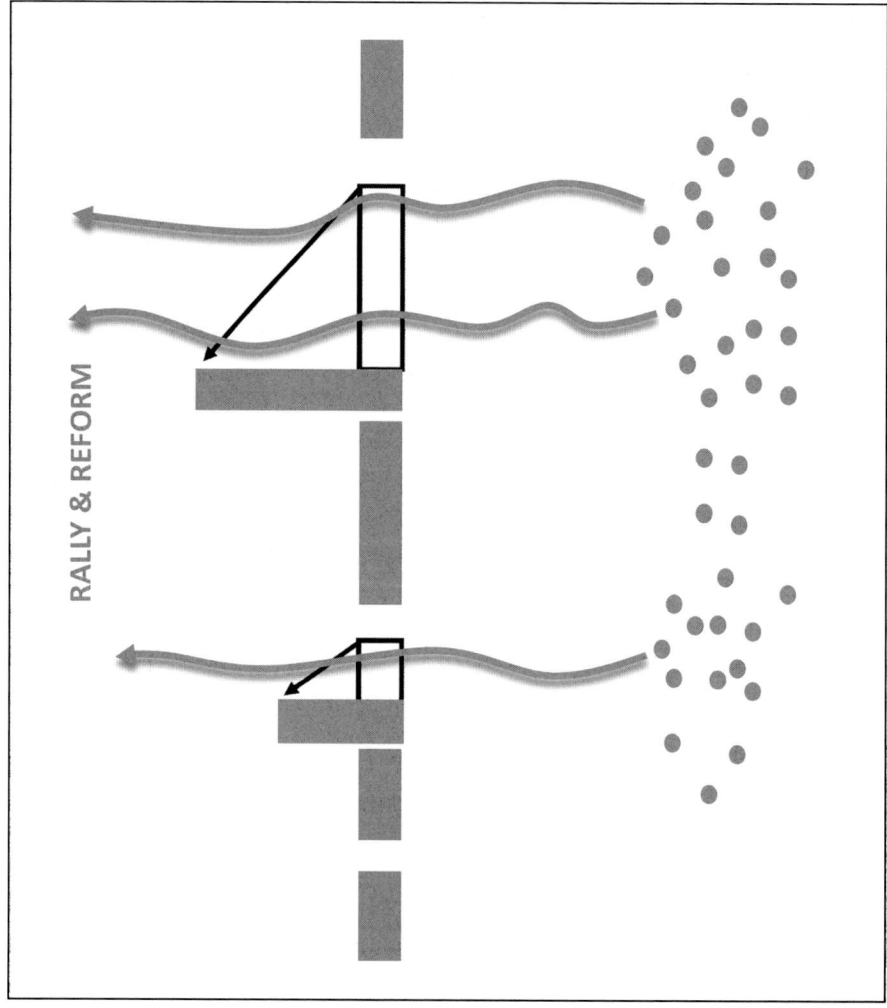

A diagram of two of the ways a line could open to allow withdrawing troops through. In this case by wheeling back by company and platoons (half company). Such a manoeuvre also reduced the likelihood of the line being carried away by fleeing men.

Colonel Donellan of the 48th, wounded in the leg, tells Major Middlemore to lead the charge.

battalions, throwing the six disorganised French battalions back across the Portina was not a solo effort but involved at least one steady battalion of Cameron's brigade:

> As the enemy came on the men gave a loud huzza; an Irish regiment to the right [the 2nd 83rd] answered it with a thrilling cheer. It was taken up from regiment to regiment and passed along the whole British line. The leading files of the French halted, turned, and fled back and never made another effort.

With the KGL rallying and the British having thrown the disordered ranks of Lapisse's battalions back across the Portina, the situation beneath the Medellín was stabilised.

Meanwhile, on the other flank, Brigadier Mackenzie, having seen the Guards Brigade being thrown back, had ordered his brigade forward, in a similar manner to the 1st 48th Foot, into the position vacated by the Guards and recalled the 24th Foot back to its position on the right flank of his brigade.

Thus, the two battalions of guards were also able to fall back to safety through the gaps opened by companies of the 24th, 31st and 45th wheeling back and then re-forming their line to open fire. This is an often unrecognised manoeuvre (by Wellesley included) that brought the French second line to a halt and arguably plugged a hole that otherwise would have probably delivered victory to King Joseph.[8] Brigadier General Mackenzie was, however, killed at the head of his brigade as it engaged the enemy in a protracted

An imagined view of the 'Death of Colonel Donellan' of the 48th Foot.

firefight that cost 632 casualties out of the 2,084 men who took to the field that day. Now in relative safety behind Mackenzie's brigade, the Guards re-formed. Lieutenant Aitcheson, of the 3rd Guards, wrote that:

> the same ardent spirit which had urged our men to advance beyond the point originally intended still operated – they rallied with astonishing

rapidity and their exertions keeping pace with the exigencies, success crowned their efforts in the complete rout of the enemy.

Aitchison remarked, however, that: 'It was in this retrograde movement that I was wounded, and I was shortly after obliged to quit the field. It was not, however, until our men had formed round their colours in a drill.'

It is worth recalling that King Joseph had a not inconsiderable reserve of nearly 6,000 men, made up of his Royal Guard, some line infantry and a couple of cavalry regiments. This force under General Dessolles was, however, between 2 and 3 miles to the rear, having started the battle at Casa de Salinas, and was not on hand to be thrown into battle at the crucial moment of allied vulnerability.

Leval's Second Attack

Having attacked somewhat earlier than Sébastiani's other divisions, by around 1600 hours while the fighting was still in the balance to his right, General Leval had rallied and reorganised his regiments, and was again

A miniature of an unknown British field officer. Such portraits were often painted before loved ones sailed to the Peninsular.

advancing, now reinforced by two fresh Polish battalions. Sergeant Cooper recalled that 'many voices' in the ranks of the 7th Fusiliers called out: 'Here they come again and so they did, but we were ready and gave them such a warm reception that they speedily went to the right about.' Campbell's Brigade of 4th Division had been reinforced in the firing line by the three fresh battalions of Kemmis's brigade, including the 2nd Battalion of Detachments. Lieutenant Carrs, of the 53rd, provides more detail:

> The enemy sent down a much larger body of infantry to engage us again and to retake their cannon which we had got over the bank. When they got within forty yards of this bank, which we took for a breastwork, we let fly at them ... they gave way and left the ground almost covered with their killed and wounded.

This, however, is not the complete story: the British volley fire against the German, Dutch and Polish regiments was complemented by a well-timed Spanish Cavalry charge. Amidst the banks, groves and gardens, the three battalions of Hessians and Frankfurters on the flank saw the approaching

General Sébastiani was temporarily in command of IV Corps.

horsemen of the Regiment del Rey only at the last moment and were caught in the process of forming square. On difficult ground the cavalry was unable to develop the momentum of a full charge or completely deploy. This allowed the German infantry to form an untidy but effective clump bristling with bayonets. Thus, they were able to edge their way back to the safety of the thicker cover. The Spanish, however, were able to capture another artillery battery that had been sent forward to support the attack.[9]

It is clear that in Leval's second attack the morale of his infantry, from a mixed bag of states, was not good thanks to their previous experience at the hands of the British and Spanish, combined with the more formidable line of redcoats in front of them as they appeared once again from the thick country. Even so, they advanced bravely but volley fire and the cavalry soon had them retiring. It would appear from the testimony of Captain Józef Rudnicki of the 2nd 4th Polish Regiment that the Poles did not move forward to join the action:

> After receiving our provisions, we began to ascend the heights in columns and from there we encountered the English troops and artillery and observed the flight of the German division, the remains of which fell back in our direction. We maintained our position on the heights, and here, under arms, held firm until nightfall.[10]

The enemy briefly recaptured the six guns they had lost earlier but had to give them up again as they fell back. The Dutch regiment abandoned two cannon and a howitzer as they fell back, which were added to the tally of guns captured by the British.

Brigadier General Alexander Campbell was praised by Wellesley in his dispatch for his careful and effective handling of the 4th Division deployed right of the centre of the allied position.

Sergeant Stevenson, of the 1st 3rd Guards, recalled that, having beaten back the main French attack, the battle was certainly not over:

> The conflict continued until the enemy's ranks got so thin that the rest turned about and fled with all speed beyond the reach of musket-shot, and then opened a fire of cannon with grape-shot. It was now near sunset: so, they continued the fire of the cannon while their infantry was retreating, and at dusk they all retired, leaving us masters of the field. Our loss was severe: the company that I was in, commanded that day by Captain Bowater, (now Major-General Sir Edward Bowater) lost thirty-five killed and wounded out of eighty-nine.

The Brown Bess and the Charleville Musket

The British Land Pattern Musket and the French *Modèle* 1777 Musket had both been in use by their respective armies since the first half of the eighteenth century. They became more or less standard, but with numerous modifications and derivatives being produced. Both used flintlock technology, had a smooth bore and fired a lead ball propelled by black powder. There were, however, differences, not least of these was the calibre of .75 inch for the Brown Bess and .69 for the Charleville, the latter reducing the burden for the infantryman without effecting the musket's hitting power.

The Charleville was significantly more standardised than the Brown Bess as it was manufactured at a handful of government arsenals in France, while production of British muskets had a distinct cottage industry feel about it. Not only were muskets produced in India to different patterns, but in the UK much work was contracted out to gunsmiths, with assembly at armament factories. The result of this was that the Charleville was easier to repair with a greater commonality of parts and was, in addition, simpler for the French soldier to strip for cleaning and routine maintenance.

The big difference between the two muskets was how they were used. With the demands of continental war on a wholly different scale to the British, the need for a constant supply of fresh soldiers for Napoleon's armies led to a very different training regime for French conscripts. In contrast to the British recruit, who spent days and weeks over the basics of drill and firing the musket at depots in the UK, the French recruit did much of his training on the march, with inevitable differences in performance on the battlefield. The elan of the French soldier that was carried forward into the armies of the Empire met their match when pitted against the steadiness possessed by the British infantry and the fire power of the two-deep line.

The British Short Land Pattern 'Brown Bess' Musket and the French *Modèle* 1777 Musket. (*SASC Weapons Collection*)

Chapter Nine

The Final Phase and the Aftermath of Battle

A part of King Joseph's plan for the main attack was an attempt to belatedly turn Wellesley's left flank via the open grass plain to the north of the Medellín. This was trusted to Ruffin's division of Victor's corps, with General Villette's in reserve on the Cascajal behind the grand battery. Neither of these commanders relished the task; Ruffin's regiments were battered, having twice failed to take the Medellín feature, which was still held by the British as a well-defended pivot. Not only that, both generals could see that the plain and the Sierra de Segurilla now had British and Spanish infantry, cavalry and guns marching to its defence. As a result they only assembled and moved forward slowly and thus, co-ordination with the main attack was lost and the advance onto the plain only just getting under way by the time the crisis in Wellesley's centre had all but passed.

To check the advance of the 9th Légère along the southern foothills of the Sierra de Segurilla, Bassecourt's Spanish division had been deployed in a blocking position. Down on the 800-yard-wide plain itself, with the British infantry already thinly spread and committed to action, the majority of the allied cavalry, the brigades of Anson and Fane and Alburquerque's Spanish division, had been moved to the north of the Medellín. On the feature itself, Rettburg's KGL battery, reinforced by a pair of Spanish 12-pounders, was sited to cover the low ground and the companies of riflemen with the First Battalion of detachments from Stewart's brigade could cover the ground around the Valdefuentes farm.

The French plan was simple. Ruffin's three regiments, joined by Villette's 27th Line, was to advance west down the valley supported by Merlin's light cavalry brigade, numbering 1,100 sabres, with as already mentioned the 9th Légère advancing through the foothills to their right.

Lieutenant Leith Hay, of the 29th Foot, was on the crest of the Medellín when Wellesley's attention was dragged away from the unfolding crisis in the centre of his army by events beginning to develop north of the Medellín:

> The movements of the divisions Ruffin and Villatte had, during the contest just described, been vacillating and uncertain. Formed to all appearance determined again to attack the height, they had even advanced some distance towards its base. Their light troops skirmished closely and

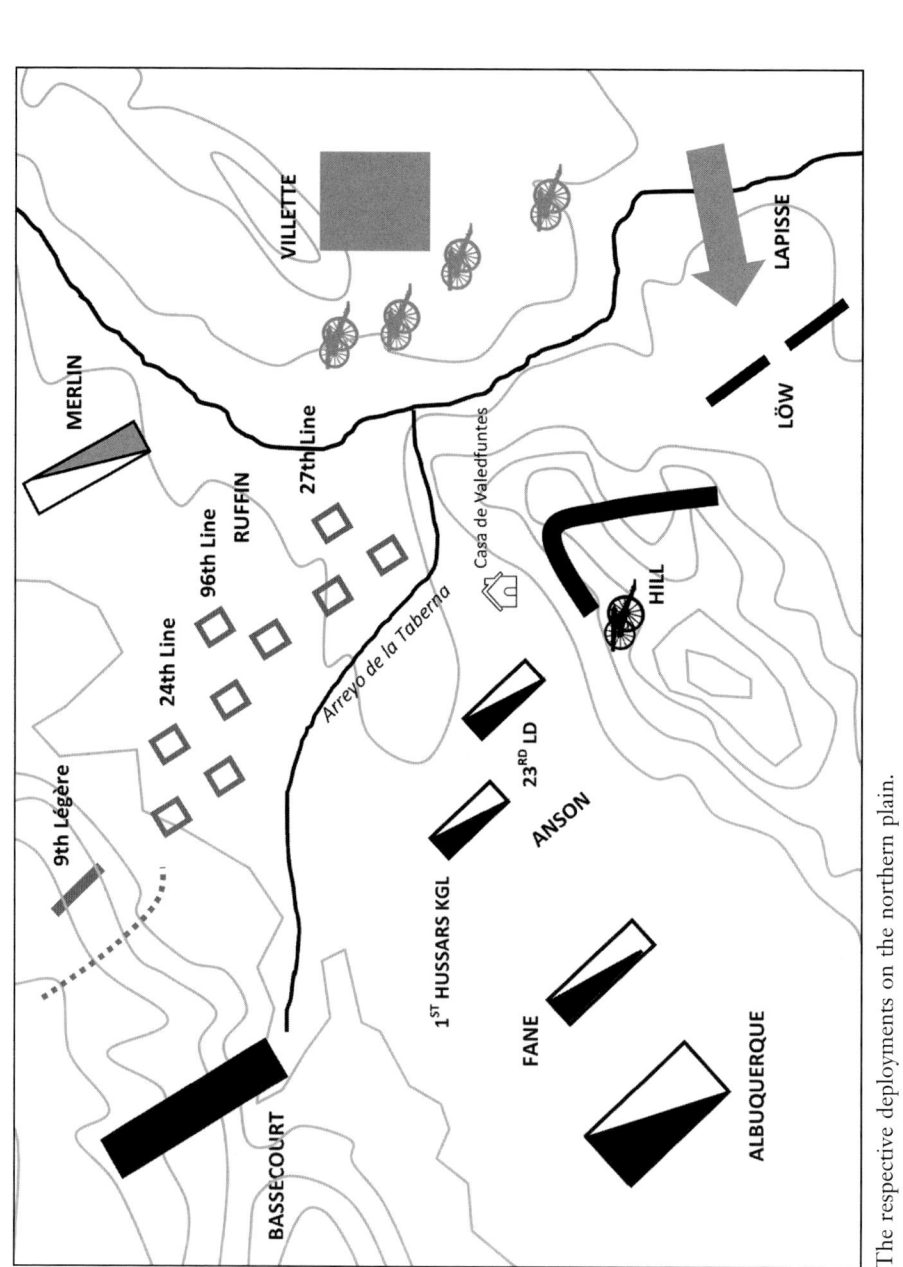

The respective deployments on the northern plain.

seriously; but nothing like the attack of the morning was again attempted. Still the right of the French army had a very imposing appearance. In columns of attack, and supported by numerous cavalry, a serious effort was every moment to be expected. Sir Arthur Wellesley crossed with rapid step from the right of the 29th to the part of the hill looking directly down upon General Anson's brigade of cavalry, which mounted on the instant. It was immediately known that a charge would take place.

To preserve their horses the British cavalry spent as much time on foot as they did in the saddle. On this occasion, seeing the dust thrown up by enemy movement, Anson's two regiments, the 23rd Light Dragoons and 1st Hussars KGL, mounted and prepared for action. This action was, however, to be against unbroken French infantry but in the absence of infantry, it was necessary to check the French advance down the northern plain. According to Commissary Schaumann, the action was initiated by the arrival of an ADC with orders from Lieutenant General Payne, commander of the British cavalry.

Leith Hay added that: 'The ground upon which this brigade [Anson's] was in line is perfectly level; nor did any visible obstruction appear between it and the columns opposed. The grass was long, dry, and waving …' Across this ground the brigade steadily gained speed and momentum as it progressed from a walk through a trot to a canter as they distance closed on the enemy

British light dragoons wearing the pre-1812 uniform and the Tarleton helmet.

infantry. Ahead of the brigade rode, Lieutenant Colone Elley, Anson's assistant quarter master, who could be easily discerned on a grey horse. Leith Hay was watching:

> For some time, the brigade advanced at a rapid pace, without receiving any obstruction from *the enemy's* fire. The line cheered. It *was* answered from the hill with the greatest enthusiasm; never was anything more exhilarating or more beautiful than the commencement of this advance.

According to Lieutenant Colonel Decken of the 1st Hussars: 'After the first order to trot, no further word of command was made known to the squadron officers.' The French, however, seeing the British and German horsemen approaching with clear intent to charge them, had each regiment form three battalion squares,[1] with Merlin's light cavalry providing a backstop. In front of the 23rd, near the Valdefuentes farm, were the squares of the 27th Line and ahead of the KGL Hussars stood the 96th Line, and to their right were the 24th. As the cavalry regiments advanced east down the valley, they came into the arc of fire of the right-hand cannon of the grand battery on the Cascajal. With French shot and shell pitching among them, the horsemen started to edge to their left but the 23rd reached the gallop ready to deliver their charge within 100 yards of the squares' bristling bayonets, when disaster struck. Concealed in the tall grass was the dried-up course of the Arreyo de la Taberna,[2] which is described as a 'hollow cleft ... six to eight feet deep and twelve to eighteen feet in breadth'. Colonel Elley, probably because he was riding ahead of the ranks on a good horse, managed to jump the Arreyo. Not so, however, the crowded ranks of the regiment's right division behind him:

> With some difficulty he cleared it at a bound, and on gaining the opposite bank, endeavoured by gesture to warn the 23rd of the dangerous ground they had to pass; but advancing with such velocity, the line was on the verge of the stream before his signs could be either understood or attended to.

Even allowing for the slightly looser formation, unlike the heavy cavalry that rode boot to boot, there was little most of the 23rd's troopers of the worst-placed squadron could do in the front rank, let alone those following, to avoid piling into the watercourse at speed. The result was a tangle of men and horses in the cleft, most with broken bones.

Most of the 23rd's left division and the KGL Hussars, the latter being to the left rear of the 23rd, were able to pull up in time but, as Leith Hay wrote, the cleft was not the only hazard. Even at the extremity of a volley's effective range the French opened fire to add to the chaos astride the Arreyo:

> At this moment the enemy, formed in squares, opened his tremendous fire. A change immediately took place. Horses rolled on the earth; others

The Final Phase and the Aftermath of Battle   183

Colonel Sir John Elley as an officer of the Household Cavalry after the war.

were seen flying back dragging their unhorsed riders with them; the German hussars coolly reined up; the line of the 23d was broken. Still the regiment galloped forward. The confusion was increased; but no hesitation took place in the individuals of this gallant corps. The survivors rushed forward with, if possible, accelerated pace, passing between the flank of the square, now one general blaze of fire, and the building on its left.

Colonels Elley and Ponsonby led the surviving troopers between the checkerboard layout of the squares, where that 'blaze of fire' took a terrible toll on both horses and riders.

Looking down from the Medellín, Lieutenant FitzClarence could not see what had happened 'the whole country was instantly covered with horses galloping back without riders, and men straggling to the rear without horses, while a dense spot seen from the hill marked where the slaughtered lay'. The 'dense spot' was presumably the squadron that had borne the brunt of both the disaster at the Arreyo and the enemy square's fire.

The fight was, however, not totally in favour of the French. Bombardier Dierking, of Rettberg's battery, sited near Wellesley on the Medellín, was engaging the enemy squares 'against which the charge was directed'. So accurate was his fire that the general reputedly 'clapped him on the back, and said, "Very well, my boy".'

Of those horsemen of the 23rd that either managed to jump the Taberna or scrambled across avoiding collision or falling in the watercourse, it would seem that a higher proportion of officers got across. Presumably this was because most of them were either riding in front or to a flank and had better-quality horses. The second rank of the 1st Hussars and the left division of the 23rd were able to cross the Arreyo and assembled in a rough line. The KGL Hussars re-formed under their commander, Colonel Arentschildt, and resumed a circumspect advance on the squares of the 24th, described as 'a disorderly and ineffective charge'. 'Few of them arrived at the bayonets ... no impression was made upon the square', which duly knocked over men and horses with their musket fire.

Colonel Elley led the remains of the regiment, estimated to be 160 men of the squadrons of Captains Allen and Drake, between the Valdefuentes farm and the squares of the 27th Line, which fired on them as they passed. Once through or amidst the French infantry's squares, with all cohesion lost, the 10th Chasseurs of the front rank of Merlin's light cavalry brigade wheeled back and allowed the 23rd to pass and face the Westphalian Chevaux Légère in the second line, which halted them. The 10th Chasseurs then wheeled back surrounding Colonel Elley and the 23rd. In a couple of Polish sources[3] there

The Arreyo de la Taberna that the squadron plus of the 23rd Light Dragoons rode into is today under the surface of the reservoir, but this photograph of the northern plain looking east between the Medellín rising on the right and the Sierra de Segurilla on the left provides a sense of the scene of the action.

is mention of the part played by the 1st Regiment of Vistula Lancers in a counter-charge by Merlin's brigade, which they claim was ordered personally by Marshal Victor. Outnumbering the 23rd by almost eight to one, on surrounding them, they 'routed and nearly annihilated English Dragoons'.[4] Only Colonel Elley and a handful of men fought their way out of the melee and made it back to safety.

The threat of cavalry action had, however, been enough to halt the French and force them into squares under the battery on the Medellín but it can hardly have been Wellesley's desire for his cavalry to charge unbroken squares. With Colonel Elley gallantly leading the survivors across the Arreyo, it is easy to see how the British cavalry's reputation for 'galloping at everything' developed and endures.

The 23rd lost 207 out of 458 men listed in returns before the battle, with the French claiming to have captured 100 cavalrymen on the afternoon of 28 July, clearly most of them from the 23rd, as the KGL returned with only thirty-seven men lost. Thus, the charge of Anson's brigade on the northern plain was costly and certainly not a tactical success. However, the brigade had shown rare determination, and with Fane's heavies and Alburquerque's division drawn up behind them, Ruffin after his previous rough handling during the previous twenty-four hours, did not venture to continue his advance.

The guidon of 23rd Light Dragoons bearing the campaign honour 'Peninsular' and the single battle honour 'Talavera'. The regiment returned home to recruit but its next active service was not until the Low Countries and Waterloo.

There were no more French attacks during the late afternoon of the 28th, leaving the allies holding the approximate line they had at dawn, while the French were back east of the Portina. With the centre of the British line only just holding and Lieutenant FitzClarence reporting that 'the gaps in our lines, which now forcibly showed themselves, by the regiments not covering one-third of their former ground', few could have hoped that the fighting was over for the day. Cannon fire, however, continued, with vegetation being set on fire by burning wadding and cartridge paper. Smoke from burning brushwood combined with that of black powder now obscured much of the view of the respective armies astride the Portina.

One of the factors that prevented the French from renewing the attack on the afternoon of the 28th was the possibility of an allied reinforcement. The heavy British casualties had meant that there was a steady stream of men being carried to the rear throughout the attacks and now soldiers, having dropped off their comrades, were returning to their battalions. Viewed through the smoke and burning grass, this throng of men was interpreted as being Sir Robert Wilson's Lusitania Legion arriving to join the battle, having in true Napoleonic style marched to the sound of the guns. Sir Robert was at this stage actually still some distance to the north-east.

As the flames spread, Sergeant Bostelmann, with his battery on the Medellín, saw the fire approaching his battery's ammunition waggons:

> Bostelmann ... considering that the loss of the ammunition might have a material effect on the result of the battle, as the battery to which it belonged was posted on the key of the allied position, against which the enemy's main efforts were directed, determined to attempt the preservation of the wagons, regardless of the personal danger with which the effort would evidently be attended. Of his assistants, the four gunners only were available, the workmen, expecting every moment an explosion, having run away; and with the aid of these four men, Luttermann, Zingreve, Warnecke, and Lind, the gallant sergeant succeeded in removing the heavily loaded ammunition wagons through the burning heath, and placing them on a spot in the rear, which a little trench had yet preserved from the flames.

French Indecision

An officer of French hussars, Lieutenant Rocca, commented that following the last attack on the British line:

> ... one other effort was necessary to break through onto the plain and do battle on equal terms [He complained that the ground astride the Portina was unfavourable]. But King Joseph thought it was too late to advance with the reserve, and the attack was delayed till the following day.

Eventually, as the evening wore on, peering through the smoke and haze, FitzClarence noted that:

> it was no unpleasing sight to see them begin gradually to draw off their infantry, and bring forward, to cover their retreat, their cavalry, which had been all day in numerous *echelons*, extending back to the woods. They formed several lines, and must have numbered not less than 9 or 10,000 cavalry, dressed in all the colours of the rainbow.

King Joseph, supported by Marshal Jourdan, even though they had the Royal Guard and the majority of Villette's division intact, wavered, lacking the confidence to throw these 5,000 men into the fight with several hours of daylight remaining on the 28th. They saw the British as a firm defence rather than the thin battered line of some hours earlier, but a decisive factor was a report from General Milhaud's dragoon division that General Cuesta's Spanish army was showing signs of movement. Consequently, the prospect of being attacked in the flank was sufficient to induce the King to stay his hand and by the time that it was reported that the Spanish were not in fact moving it was too late to launch another attack in daylight. Another minor factor was that General Venegas, whose timidity and lack of activity had already undermined Wellesley's and Cuesta's plans, after glacial movement over almost a

The 1806 Pattern shako plate of the French 27th Line Regiment.

week had finally advanced to the Tagus. Rather than being a significant threat to Joseph's rear and Madrid, the King and Jourdan had the measure of Venegas and treated the threat with the contempt it deserved.

The British were relieved not to be attacked again late that afternoon but as evening lengthened into night, they remained prepared. As dawn rose on the 29th, however, the French had completely pulled back during the night.

A portrayal of the pre-1812 uniform of a British Light Dragoon.

Captain Cocks, of the 16th Light Dragoons, summed up the situation: 'We knew not that night the extent of our victory, we did not think it improbable we might have been attacked the following day and we were ill prepared for this.'

As the evening wore on, the bombardment from batteries on the Cascajal died down and the King's staff issued orders, as observed from the Medellín, for a withdrawal first of all to the site of the army's previous bivouacs. Marshal Victor was reluctant to accept these orders as it would be confirmation of his failure. He conformed to the withdrawal with bad grace at 0300 hours and joined the rest of the army marching back across the Alberche.

For the French, their withdrawal was a temporary expedient, as the King and Marshal Jourdan were well aware that Soult's march on Plasencia would threaten the rear of the allied army and transform the military situation. More of that anon.

The Night

The British army slept on the ground in their positions with their weapons to hand, with an expectation that if not attacked by night, the battle would be renewed the following morning. The ground in front of them was thick with the dead and wounded, the night was full of cries of pain and shouts for help. A sergeant of the Coldstream Guards recalled that: 'This was a dismal night, great numbers of wounded on both sides lying on the field, their cries & groans were most piercingly grievous ...' Battalions sent out parties to search for their wounded, while individuals hunted for fallen friends. Many of the wounded were found burned to death on the charred, still smoking ground. Sergeant Stevenson, of the 3rd Foot Guards, wrote in his memoirs that during the night:

> We lay on the ground on which the battle had been fought ... during which all our surgeons, and many soldiers were employed in attending to the wounded, and not withstanding their exertions, some of our own soldiers who were disabled in the action and very many of the enemy's lay on the field all night, without so much of as their wounds being bound up and nothing more than this could be done for any.
>
> In the evening I went out once or twice amongst the dead and wounded, and saw some of my comrade sergeants lying dead, as though they were only asleep, one in particular that paid the next company to mine, appeared as if he had laid down to take a little rest, with the colour in his face just as though he was alive. I came to two French soldiers of the 28th Regiment, who lay wounded: they asked for a little water, so I gave my canteen into the hand of one of them, and told him not to drink much, but give some to his comrade, and when they had taken a

little, their expressions of gratitude I shall never forget, 'merci, merci, comrade!' that is, 'thank you, thank you, comrade.' So we, that had just been furiously fighting against each other, having executed the commands of our generals, could lay aside every feeling of animosity, and exhibit some symptoms of returning humanity.

As dawn rose on the 29th, the French had completely pulled back during the night.

Colonel Bingham, of the 53rd, in a letter home, described the task that confronted the British army on the morning of the 29th, having remained in possession of the battlefield:

> The first work to be done, was to remove nine or ten thousand English and French wounded into Talavera; and to bury four or five thousand dead bodies. What a task for 16 or 17,000 hungry worn-out men to undertake! T'was impossible! We had but few tools, and the ground was hard and rocky, therefore the dead were either thrown into the dry beds of winter torrents, &c., and scantily covered with earth; or, together with dead horses, gathered into heaps and burned. The smell was intolerable. As for the wounded, they perished in great numbers while lying in the blazing sun, in want of water, dressing, and shelter.

Sergeant Stevenson described the fate of the dead that it was impractical to bury:

> So instead of being interred they were laid in heaps of forty or fifty together, clothed and accoutred as they were, and then they were covered over thickly with the boughs of olive trees, and the whole was then set on fire, and the wood being oily though green, the fire burnt very fiercely, and the heap of corpses was soon reduced to a mass of ashes, and thus hundreds of young men that one day were full of life and vigour were nothing but ashes strewed on the ground the next. Hopes of promotion, and anticipations of wealth and visions of glory that had outlived many a storm, and escaped many a danger, that had been flattered in many a victory, and cherished in many a defeat, here perished, and perished forever.

That morning Stevenson looked at the dead of the French 28th Ligne, which he thought to be:

> one of the finest regiments that ever we had seen stand before us, and no doubt they were the flower of the French army and selected to fight the British Guards. But I am of opinion that they did not fire with that coolness and precision which our men did. Numbers of our men went down

Lady Butler's picture of soldiers of the 43rd Light Infantry carrying out the dreadful task of clearing the dead from the field of Talavera.

on one knee every shot, and as appeared afterwards made sure of their mark. ... some of the officers from other parts of the line were walking over the field of battle, one of them came in and inquired what regiment we were. He was answered 'Foot Guards, sir.' 'Why,' said he, 'the enemy lie dead in front of you thicker than at any other part of the line'.

Stevenson was in the Light Company of his battalion and thus would be expected to aim and fire. He does, however, seem to indicate that in a protracted firefight that the Guards as a whole took aimed shots, presumably once they were permitted to prime, load and fire in their own time.

The British army had borne the brunt of the attacks by 26,000 French infantry and suffered a grievous loss of 5,365 men (801 killed, 3,915 wounded and 649 missing), but the French lost 7,263 (761 killed, 6,301 wounded and 206 missing). For the whole period Spanish losses were reported as being 1,201 men.

Arrival of the Light Brigade

The 3,000-strong Light Brigade, despite their epic march of the previous day to join Wellesley, arrived at Talavera after dawn on 29 July. Lieutenant Pollock, of the 43rd, recorded in his personal diary that:

> Great was the disappointment and disgust in the brigade at finding they were but a few hours too late to take part in the battle, but as in close column they passed over the field they were cheered by the whole army, and their arrival at this particular moment was hailed as an auspicious omen.

Brigadier General Robert Craufurd was ambitious and keen to make up for the perceived stain on his reputation as one of those surrendered by Whitlock at Buenos Aires several years earlier. There is, of course, no better place than on the battlefield to cement a reputation as a fighting general. Captain Jonathan Leach, of the 1st 95th Rifles, questioned the brigade's relatively leisurely progress up the Tagus valley from Lisbon:

> It is not my intention to question the propriety or necessity of the light brigade having been halted two days at Santarem, one day at Abrantes, two days at Castello Branco, and one day at Coria; on its march to Talavera; certain, however, it is, that one day's rest at Santarem instead of two, and one day's rest at Castello Branco instead of two, would have brought a reinforcement of more than three thousand light troops to Sir Arthur Wellesley, before the bloody battle of the 28th; and that such an addition to his force would have been highly acceptable, particularly as he was deficient in the number of his light troops. Could General Crawford [*sic*] have foreseen that by those halts his brigade would have arrived a *few hours too late* at Talavera, I feel thoroughly convinced that he would have pushed on, *pele-mele*, without a single halt between Santarem and the field of battle.

On the arrival of his brigade, Craufurd led it across the battlefield that had by now been abandoned by the French withdrawal, and across the Portina on to the Alberche stream. The experience of marching across the field of Talavera and seeing the wounded who had died in the grass fires was a horrifying introduction for the former militia men and volunteers that filled the ranks of the 43rd and 52nd Light Infantry, as well as the 95th Rifles on their return

A fully accoutred and laden rifleman courtesy of the 2nd 95th Living History Society. As the war progressed veteran soldiers dispensed with all but the essentials or shared them among a section.

from Vigo and la Corruna. Of the sights, sound and smells of the battlefield, one man commented:

> The horrid sights were beyond anything I could have imagined. Thousands of dead and dying in every direction ... and, I'm sorry to say, Spaniards butchering the wounded Frenchmen at every opportunity, and stripping them naked, which gave admission to myriads of pernicious flies and the heat of the burning sun.

The Light Brigade

The need for light infantry had been obvious during the far-flung wars of colonisation during the eighteenth century and there was a general reliance on European mercenaries and line infantry battalions' light companies. At home, however, the conservative military establishment was not convinced of their utility on the European battlefield. Consequently, the number of light troops steadily reduced, with the term 'light bob', which subsequently became something soldiers were happy to embrace, being at the turn of the century regarded as an insult.

The army's experience at the hands of the Revolutionary Armies started to change attitudes in Horse Guards. French infantry columns, preceded by clouds of *tirailleurs*, galled the lines of the armies of the *ancien regime* and, with few of their own skirmishers to protect them, they were half defeated before the columns closed. In response, Colonels Coote Manningham and Stewart proposed that the army should raise a unit of British rifle armed light infantrymen and, gaining the support of the Duke of York, the Experimental Rifle Corps was formed in 1800. The Corps was re-formed the following year as the Rifle Corps, later taking its place in the line as the 95th Rifles.

The short-lived Peace of Amiens brought developments to a halt but on resumption of hostilities in 1803, a series of brigade camps were formed along the southern and eastern coastline of England for coastal defence *and* to raise standards of training. The most famous and arguably effective of these camps was that established at Shorncliffe under Sir John Moore, a leading evangelist of light tactics. Along with the 95th Rifles, his own regiment the 52nd and the 43rd were both converted to light infantry.

A light infantryman, be he from a light battalion or light company, was expected to be able to be master of close-order tactics as laid down by General Dundas, as well as the less closely defined skirmishing drills.

Subsequent operational experience in, for example, South America and Denmark, proved the worth of the light battalions and rifles but it was during the Corunna Campaign, when they were formed into the Flank Brigade under Brigadier General Craufurd, that they truly earned their spurs. The two battalions of the 95th Rifles in particular emerged from the retreat with a very high reputation. So numerous were recruits and soldiers transferring from the militia to the Rifles that a third battalion of 95th was able to be raised.

The need for a complete refit and recruitment to bring the battalions of what was now known as Craufurd's Light Brigade up to strength, delayed the brigade's return to the Peninsular to join Wellesley's army.

Militiamen were favoured recruits as they at had at least been well drilled in accordance with Dundas' regulations and they only needed training in the appropriate manoeuvres required by light infantry and rifles, plus marksmanship.

The Final Phase and the Aftermath of Battle 195

Hamilton-Smith's representation of the uniform of the 5th, 60th and 95th Rifles.

Craufurd established his headquarters in the Casa de Salinas and deployed his brigade, replacing Campbell's in an outpost line on the banks of the Alberche, covering the front of the exhausted army. Yards away, on the other side of the river, stood the vedettes of the French cavalry, providing a similar screen for the enemy.

Over the following days those members of the brigade not on piquet assisted in the grim business of collecting the rapidly decomposing bodies for burial or burning. While on the Alberche the Light Brigade was joined by the Royal Horse Artillery troop that they were to serve with for most of the rest of

A 5in howitzer. Ross's troop had one of these of guns and five light 6-pounders.

the war, three days after the rest of the brigade. It had been a testing march for Captain Ross's troop. He wrote:

> During the first two days my troop were on the ground, I lost eight horses – that is to say, four dropped down on the march from Medellín and four died in the lines the following day. Both men and horses continue very unhealthy.[5]

On the arrival of Craufurd's Light Brigade, the soldiers of the Rifle Company, who had been serving in the 1st Battalion of Detachments in Stewart's brigade, left to join the 1st 95th Rifles, while the officers and soldiers of the 43rd and 52nd Light Infantry, who formed a sizeable percentage of the battalion, also subsequently re-joined their regiments. These moves were, however, not official until a General Order was issued on 14 September 1809, formally returning soldiers of Light Brigade regiments to their battalions.

After the Battle

In the days immediately after the battle hopes ran high that the army would now make a victorious march to Madrid and beyond. Captain Cocks wrote: 'The consequence of this victory cannot be calculated, the French will probably retreat towards the Ebro or perhaps not make a stand until they get

The Final Phase and the Aftermath of Battle 197

there,' but these expectations were to be shortly dashed. Even though they had defeated Joseph's army, Wellesley's divisions were in no immediate position to purse the enemy. Wellesley, as noted in a letter to Marshal Beresford, however, still intended to lead the army east 'as soon as it shall be a little rested and refreshed after two days of the hardest fighting that I have ever been a party to. We shall certainly, if not interrupted by some accident on our flank.' Wellesley, however, makes it clear in a note to Castlereagh that any advance was to be circumspect:

> I think the battle of the 28th is likely to be of great use to the Spaniards; but I do not think them yet in a state of discipline to contend with the French; and I prefer infinitely to endeavour to remove the enemy from this part of Spain by manoeuvre to the trial of another pitched battle.
>
> The French, in the last, threw their whole force upon us, and although it did not succeed, and will not succeed in future, we shall lose great numbers of men, which we can but ill afford. I dare not attempt to relieve ourselves from the weight of the attack by bringing forward the Spanish troops, owing to their miserable state of discipline, and their want of Officers properly qualified. These troops are entirely incapable of performing any manoeuvre, however simple. They would get into irretrievable confusion, and the result would probably be the loss of everything.

One immediate problem alongside rest was that supply, which as described by Colonel Bingham was in contrast to the French, was becoming critical:

> They [the French] had been well supplied with provisions previously. We had been half starved. They had dined on the field of battle, and liquor had been served out before they attacked us. This was proved by what we found in possession of the dead. On the contrary nothing was served out to us from 2 or 3 p.m. on the 27th, until about 10 a.m. on the 29th.

Cooper, of the 7th Fusiliers, however, noted that when rations did arrive it was meagre fare: 'At about 10 a.m. on the 29th, we were served with 4 ounces of bread, which was for the next 24 hours. This might be 6 or 8 decent mouthfuls.' Without food in the army's haversacks for the following days, Wellesley could not contemplate a pursuit of the enemy towards Madrid. Bingham continued:

> We are now without a day's provision in advance, without magazines (notwithstanding what you may have heard in England) with a population very lukewarm on our behalf. The whole day of the action our people were without provision, and we have been detained here ever since for the want of it.

Cuesta's army had been barely engaged during the battle but following his previous rebuttal on the road to Madrid, and with supplies running short, he flatly refused to advance across the Alberche, even though the enemy had this time been manifestly defeated.

A Review of the Battle

With hindsight, it is easy to list the errors made by commanders and their armies during a campaign or battle. Generals and their subordinate officers, of course, have to be able to understand the enemy's intent based on partial or simply incorrect information and they need their soldiers to perform their part in the battle as ordered or as the situation develops. At Talavera both the allied and French armies suffered from a lack of knowledge and human failings.

General Wellesley was without a doubt correct in not fighting on the Alberche, having appreciated the defensive qualities of the ground on the Portina north of Talavera, particularly the mile of enclosed ground that suited the Army of Extremadura. The withdrawal from the Alberche was, however, nearly a disaster with a combination of Mackenzie's poorly posted piquets and the French exploiting the smoke from the burning huts to surprise the British.

In another example of inexperience, British divisional and commanders were at fault in executing their orders. One brigade marched an hour west of the field, while the brigades of the 1st Division were badly mis-deployed and other brigades that believed themselves to be in the second line found themselves attacked in the front line. All this contributed to the crisis for Wellesley on the Medellín during the evening of 27 July, where the British commanders were saved from a disaster that would have been hard to recover from by the steadfast fighting of their battalions. Wellesley and his staff should have supervised the deployment of the army into its correct positions, which the coherence of the defence relied upon. Over the following two years, as the army expanded, Wellesley was forced to take an increasingly active role in overseeing his generals, their deployment and marches.

An equal failure by Victor, Joseph and Wellesley was ignoring or being unaware of the northern plain beyond the Medellín and Cascajal features. If the French at the earlier stages of the battle had exploited this line of manoeuvre, they could easily have turned Wellesley's left flank with some of their ample cavalry, let alone more infantry. Covering this eventuality with his own infantry would have stretched Wellesley's already thinly spread line to a point that it could be easily broken. It can, however, be argued that Napoleon's maxim 'He who defends everything, defends nothing' applies here.

One of the most egregious human failings was the fractured relations within the French command, with Marshal Victor ambitious and needing to make up for his earlier failings in the campaign. He forced on King Joseph

Marshal Victor, commander of I Corps.

most of the courses of action taken by the French during the battle. This behaviour was, of course, not confined to Talavera but a product of Napoleon's dictatorial style that set the marshals in competition, which bedevilled the French during the whole of the Peninsular War.

French confidence in their columns that had served them well against the continental armies and the British in the Low Countries and elsewhere since the Revolutionary Wars and was to take Napoleon to the apogee of his power in 1809 was misplaced. In facing Wellesley's army, the column had found an able adversary in the firepower of the British line that numbers and French *elan* could not easily defeat. The British infantry tactics at this stage were, however, far from fully formed, with some brigades taking the pursuit too far and themselves becoming vulnerable to defeat by counter-attacks. This lesson was learned but the French in one form or another persisted in confronting the British line without deploying from their columns.

In terms of trophies, the British captured seventeen French guns and the 29th several coloured flags. Lieutenant Leslie described them as 'banners or

The Military General Service medal with the clasp Talavera awarded to those that were still alive to receive it in 1848.

small silk standards, termed in French *fanions*, belonging to the defeated column'. By this period the 1st Battalion carried the only eagle of regiment and *fanions* were battalion flags for the more junior battalions.[6] As Fitz-Clarence points out, they were less than impressive trophies that were deposited at Wellesley's headquarters and:

> ... left in our possession several silk standards, but whether they had borne eagles or not it was difficult to say; as, besides being much broken and torn when brought into headquarters, the staff of one had been used as a poker to a bivouac fire.

The French captured a number of British camp colours. These 18-inch square cotton flags of the regimental facing colour were used, in addition to marking out company bivouac lines, as deployment markers and carried by a number of sergeants. Wellesley insisted that these be as plain as possible to avoid the enemy claiming to have captured regimental colours.

The dispatch sent by the King and Jourdan to Napoleon attempted to hide the truth from the emperor. An extract reads:

> Sire, yesterday the English army was forced into battle positions. Besides Wellesley's 25 to 30 thousand English, we had to deal with Cuesta's army, which amounted to 35 to 40 thousand men. The battlefield on which we are established is littered with their dead ... I set off to save Madrid, which was threatened by a corps of Portuguese arriving at Navalcarnero, and by the army of Venegas, which was trying to penetrate through Aranjuez ... I have one regret, sire, that it is of not having taken the whole English army prisoner.[7]

The emperor was, of course, to be not deceived by such weasel words.

An unusually detailed silhouette of an unknown officer of the 43rd Light Infantry.

An engineer officer and a soldier using signal flags.

Chapter Ten

The Withdrawal to Portugal

'No man could ever be more deceived or disappointed than I believe nearly the whole British army have been in the consequences of the battle of Talavera.' [Captain Cocks' letter, 17 August 1809][1]

So far only oblique references have been made to Marshal Soult concentrating and moving south to cut Wellesley's line of communication with Portugal. This reflects the British army's lack of accurate intelligence on events to the north around Salamanca during the advance into Spain and while it stood at Talavera. On so many occasions Napoleon gave detailed orders to his commanders in the Peninsular that were often based on out of date information that had often been overtaken by events. On this occasion, however, in the early summer of 1809 Napoleon anticipated the course of events with clarity and issued appropriate orders to Marshal Soult.

Following his expulsion from Oporto and his precipitate flight through the mountains to safety of Galicia, Soult subsequently took his badly battered corps east into León, leaving Marshal Ney's VI Corps mounting vain attempts to secure Galicia and destroy General La Romana's elusive army. Soult argued, quite correctly, that once his corps was reconstituted in León, he would be well placed to deter any incursion into Spain by Wellesley, forcing the British to stand on the defensive. It was at Salamanca that he received his orders from Napoleon, which brought a temporary halt to the feuding and bad faith between Soult and Ney regarding their divergent campaign aims.

Soult took being placed in command of a sizeable portion of the French armies in Spain as a green light to demand money, troops, rations and guns from the King for another attempt at an invasion of northern Portugal. These requests were quite impossible to deliver as resources would have to come from the other resource-starved armies in the Peninsular. Consequently, Marshal Jourdan wrote to Soult explaining the wider situation in Spain and telling him that he would have to make do with the 50,000 men and resources he already had under his command.

In accordance with the emperor's orders, Soult gave instructions for the assembly of his own II Corps of 18,000 men, Ney's VI Corps (12,000) and Mortiers V Corps (19,000) in the area north of Salamanca. However, with reports of isolated or strung-out French formations regularly being attacked

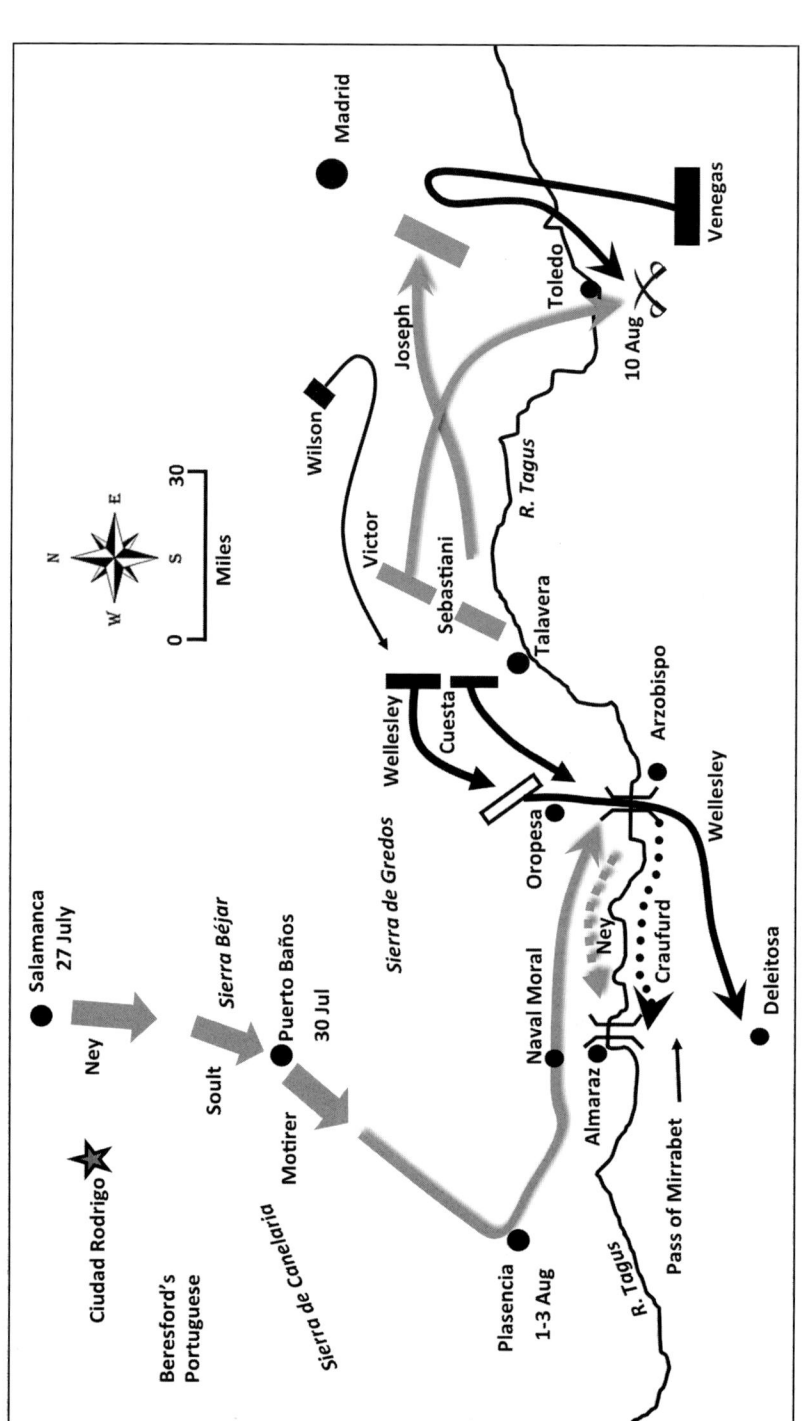

The situation after Talavera and Soult's threat to the allied armies in the Tagus valley.

by guerrillas and Spanish formations, Soult followed Napoleon's direction to only march with his formations well concentrated. Consequently, with assembly taking time, Soult could not move south towards the Tagus valley until VI Corps was within mutual supporting distance of the other two corps. The marshal also had to await the arrival of guns to replace those he had lost in his retreat from Oporto. These reasons, however, in the aftermath of the Battle of Talavera did not stop Joseph and Jourdan from severely criticising Soult's slowness in an attempt to offload some of the blame for their defeat.

Soult's move south only began on 27 July. The advance was led by Mortier's corps, followed at several days' interval by II Corps and finally Ney's corps. After three days' march Mortier brushed aside a small Spanish force in the Sierra Béjar at the Puerto de Baños pass. Word of the southerly movement of the French was quickly on its way to Plasencia and on to the commanders of the combined allied army.

Wellesley had, meanwhile, foreseen the possibility of a French strike south into the Tagus valley, but his calculations were based on intelligence that Soult could only assemble 12,000 to 15,000 men rather than the 50,000 that were actually marching to Salamanca. Consequently, he had deployed Beresford and the bulk of the active Portuguese army in the area of Almeida as a deterrent. The French, with a much larger force than expected, was not deterred by Beresford's presence at Almeida or Del Parque's Spanish division at the fortress of Ciudad Rodrigo. Consequently, Wellesley did not appreciate the scale of the threat posed to his line of communication by Soult's advance until it was almost too late.

Indications of the French movement south had, however, been reaching Wellesley's headquarters for some days before the battle, but with the expected small scale of French operations from the north, Soult was not a great source of concern. As the French march south got under way, he wrote to Beresford on the 29th stating that 'the enemy would not venture through the passes into Estremadura, having me on one side of him, and you and Romana upon the other'. Despite his lack of concern, Wellesley had over the previous days failed to persuade Cuesta to reinforce the garrison of just four battalions at the Puerto de Baños. He had recommended the whole of General Bassecourt's division be deployed to the pass as an insurance policy, and on favourable ground this would have at least forced Soult into a significant action.

On 30 July, information started to arrive at the British headquarters that the French intent was indeed an offensive south and that Beresford at Del Parque had not deterred Soult, but it was now already too late for Bassecourt's division to occupy the Puerto de Baños. The scale of Soult's force, however, had still not been appreciated, but even so, Wellesley wrote to Mr Frere, the British plenipotentiary to the Central Junta, explaining

Marshal Soult, commander of the French II Corps.

that: 'My first duty is to attend to the safety of Portugal: at all events if my flank and communications with Portugal are not secured for me, while I am operating in the general cause, I must take care of myself ...'

Over the following days, having crossed the Puerto de Baños, the French advanced guards reached Plasencia on the British lines of communication some 60 miles to Wellesley's rear during 1 August. In the hastily abandoned town, Marshal Mortier found that the only Britons still remaining were 334 men in hospital who were too sick to be moved. The French also secured the British commissariat's stock of grain that had been so painfully collected locally or brought up from Portugal; a major bonus for the French.

Still unaware of the true scale of the threat to his rear, later on 1 August Wellesley penned a second note to Viscount Castlereagh, Secretary of State, reporting an important development in front of the allied armies:

> When I addressed you this morning, I had not received the report from the outposts. It appears that the enemy withdrew the rear guard which

was posted on the heights on the left of the Alberche last night at 11 o'clock, and the whole army marched towards St Olalla, I conclude, with an intention of taking up a position in the neighbourhood of the Guadarama, with a view to be able to throw their whole force upon Venegas, or upon this army, if either should move towards Madrid.

A combination of his defeat, Soult's delay, and the threats to his rear and to Madrid posed by Venegas and Sir Robert Wilson's Loyal Lusitania Legion had prompted this move on King Joseph's part.

With the King having withdrawn, but with Soult on the allied line of communication and still believing his force to number just 15,000 men, on

Viscount Castlereagh was Secretary of State for War, 1804–09.

3 August Cuesta and Wellesley agreed to confront Soult with Bassecourt's division (5,000 men) and the British army, now numbering 18,000 effectives. Wellesley wrote to Beresford that: 'The movement of Soult through Puerto de Baños had deranged all our plans and I am obliged to return to drive him out,' but for once the French were better informed. Soult had in his hands an intercepted letter from Wellesley to General Erskine asking him to substantiate reports of the approach of a small French force from the north. Thus, Soult with 50,000 men, had a clear opportunity to spring the trap and destroy the allied armies.

Those officers and men in the divisions and brigades knew little of these developments in the situation, including Commissary Schaumann, who was serving with Anson's light cavalry brigade:

> On August 3rd the army began to move out of Talavera and we stood for about an hour under arms before we quite knew whether our direction lay forwards towards Madrid, or backwards. Very soon, however, all doubts were at an end, for debouching from the grove of olives we were marched along the road by which we had come, in the direction of Oropesa, where we bivouaced.

With the British turning to confront Soult at Plasencia, a decision had to be made regarding the 4,000 wounded and a rapidly increasing number of sick that were crowded into the churches and religious institutions in Talavera. Wellesley requested carts be supplied by the Spanish to evacuate the casualties, but only a handful of Spanish wagons and mules were available. Consequently, much of the army's baggage was offloaded and replaced by the wounded. The convoy marching on 3 August was joined by numerous walking wounded but 1,500 of the most serious casualties were left behind guarded by the Army of Extremadura. It was, however, intended to send the carts back to collect those left behind who could be moved. The suffering of the walking wounded, among whom Captain Charles Boothby of the Royal Engineers numbered, was terrible:

> The road to Oropesa was covered with our poor limping bloodless soldiers. On crutches or sticks, with blankets thrown over them, they hobbled woefully along. For the moment panic and terror lent them a force inconsistent with their debility and their fresh wounds. Some died by the road, others, unable to get further than Oropesa, afterwards fell into the hands of the enemy.

At this time another column of six British infantry battalions marching to join the army had entered Spain. Lieutenant Sherer, of the 34th Foot, wrote:

> On the fourth morning we marched to cross the Tagus at Villa Vella, and pursued our route to Zarza la Major, the first town on the Spanish

Few sprung waggons for the wounded were available and those that were could rarely cope with the roads away from the towns and cities. The jarring of the wounded in far more basic waggons must have been excruciating.

> frontier, in the road to Placentia. This movement was made, I believe, without any instruction from Sir Arthur Wellesley; and had for its objects the diversion of Soult's force, which was known to have arrived in the neighbourhood of Coria [20 miles distant] and Placentia [45 miles], and which, it was thought, might act offensively against the British, on their retreat from Talavera; which, encumbered as they were with wounded, could not have immediately followed the battle, or been effected with any extraordinary rapidity.[2]

This force, though significant in number, had no cavalry or artillery and in consultation made a short withdrawal back across the Portuguese border on hearing that a withdrawal had begun.

As explained by Lieutenant FitzClarence, ADC to Brigadier Stewart, the Adjutant General:

> We left Talavera on the 3rd, under the full expectation of fighting the forces coming from the north, concentrating about Naval Moral. On our arrival at Oropesa on the evening of that day, Bassecourt was pushed on towards that place, and orders were given out implying active and immediate operations, by directing the troops to hold themselves in readiness

to march by such orders as they might receive from the Quarter-master general.

But the course of the night changed all our prospects. Sir Arthur received a despatch from Cuesta stating that he had received information on which he could depend, that not only had Soult's corps moved from the north, but that it was accompanied by the two other corps, the 5th and 6th …

This time it was a French dispatch captured by the Spanish that revealed to Generals Cuesta and Wellesley the true enemy intent and that the force descending on their rear area from the north was at least twice the size reported so far. This news changed everything. With just his 18,000 men and the Spanish division, Wellesley had to recast his plan immediately as the French cavalry were just a day's march from Oropesa, driving back Cotton's cavalry patrols. Colonel Bingham summed up the situation:

We were now in a trap: the enemy we had beaten were still more than double our number and not far off in front: another army under General Soult, perhaps nearly as numerous as that before us, had come through a mountain pass in our rear, and taken possession of the large stores of bread that we had left at Placentia.

These two French armies, probably numbered about 70,000, well supplied with provisions, &c., while ours only amounted to 17,000 in want of nearly every necessary. We were actually reduced to a starvation point.

A French battalion on the march.

As Oman described, Wellesley had to decide 'On the morrow must fight or fly' but the former course of action would be doomed to failure. Heavily outnumbered, his only realistic option was to march to the safety of the left bank of the Tagus via the bridge at Arzobispo. As the army was already moving west towards Oropesa, doubling back across the Tagus bridge at Talavera would have both put the army further from the safety of the Portuguese border lands and into country already stripped of supplies.

General Cuesta, however, proposed an alternative course of action. When he met Wellesley at Oropesa, in the early hours of 4 August, the two generals were again at loggerheads, with the Spanish commander resuming his 'mania for fighting pitched battles', proposing that the allied armies should find a good defensive position north of the Tagus and 'defy Soult to attack them'. After protracted argument, Wellesley finally declared that his army would cross to the left bank of the Tagus that evening and the two angry generals returned to their armies. At 0600 hours the British army began its hot and toilsome 9-mile march to Arzobispo.

The Withdrawal Begins

'As day dawned on the 4th August, the infantry struck camp. At ten o'clock I halted in the van of the army, on the heights of Oropesa, with the whole of the cavalry, and every regiment ready to mount. A few rations were distributed. Sir Arthur and his staff also halted here, and with their telescopes scanned the plain. Eleven o'clock arrived. Nobody knew what the halt meant. At last we perceived huge clouds of dust beginning to rise above the Estrella hills and the Tietar, along the same road which we had taken from Plasencia. It was the French under Soult. "Mount!" was the command, and the cavalry marched away.'

[Commissary Schaumann]

The march to Arzobispo would be conducted by soldiers both British and Spanish with empty bellies and those who could help themselves did so, as described by Thomas Garrity of the 43rd Light Infantry. '... it was notorious that the Spanish cavalry intercepted the provisions and forage destined for the English army, and fired on foreigners, as if they had been enemies'.[3]

The army's withdrawal to the safety of the Tagus was made in a precipitate twelve-hour forced march, with the Light Brigade and some dragoons providing the rearguard, helping along some 700 wounded men who attempted to keep up with the column. The march was made in 'suffocating heat, with clouds of dust and not a drop of water to be got'. The scene at the bridge was described by Schumann:

> In the afternoon we reached the Tagus and the bridge of Arzobispo. Over this bridge there now began to pour a throng consisting of the

most motley assortment of infantry, artillery, baggage, wounded, mules, bullocks, donkeys, women, and vehicles of all kinds, among them, of course, the ungreased bullock carts; and members of three nations, English, Spanish and German, squeezed, crushed and cursed one another as they proceeded across. This procession had gone on since the morning, and yet the cavalry had to wait until evening before they could continue their advance.

Colonel George Napier, of the 52nd Light Infantry, recalled that:

> We had just time to pass the Tagus by the bridge of Arzobispo before Soult made his appearance, and the Light Brigade under General Craufurd was ordered to gain the bridge of Almaraz by a forced march, in order to prevent the French from crossing there and seizing the Pass of Mirrabet. This was done exactly as ordered, and the whole of Marshal Soult's plan of operation being frustrated ...

Mortier's cavalry patrols appeared only two hours after the last Riflemen of the rearguard had crossed the bridge at Arzobispo just after midday on 4 August. Lieutenant FitzClarence wrote: 'So nearly had the enemy intercepted our retreat that at dusk his cavalry interchanged some shots with our advanced posts close to Arisbispo and carried off one of our videttes.' It had been a very narrow escape.

The Puente del Arzobispo and the Rio Tagus.

Such was the breakdown in the supply of food that Brigadier Craufurd exceptionally gave orders that the men could kill any animals they found grazing in the woods and: 'By rare good fortune our men encountered a herd of swine which were set upon and many of the luckless pigs were killed, cut up, cooked and eaten in an incredibly short time.'

As a result of the death of Major General Mackenzie at Talavera, Wellesley elevated Robert Craufurd to the command of 3rd Division, with the Light Brigade taking the place of Mackenzie's depleted brigade alongside Donkin's, which was, of course, referred to by one and all in the Light Brigade as 'the Heavy Brigade'. Together the two brigades marched under Craufurd to the bridge at Almaraz on 5 August. They were to secure the crossing of the Tagus there, including a bridge of boats, and the Pass of Mirrabet, which if in the hands of Marshal Ney's VI Corps would threaten Wellesley's right flank. Meanwhile, the rest of the army headed south-east along the great road in the direction of Truxillo. Defence of the bridge at Arzobispo had been taken over by the Spanish.

Without Wellesley's support and with the French closing on his army from both directions, General Cuesta had also been forced to head for Arzobispo and its access to the safety of the south bank of the Tagus. In doing so, however, he abandoned the 1,500 British wounded left at Talavera. Cuesta was roundly condemned for this action by Wellesley and his army at the time and in most accounts written since. The fact is, however, that if Wellesley had to 'fly' for the safety of the Tagus in order to avoid being caught between two enemy forces, then for exactly the same reason Cuesta had to march for Arzobispo and safety as well. The remaining accusation is that the Spanish could have evacuated more of those that were capable of being moved, having provided only 'ten or a dozen carts'.[4] It would seem that in the scramble to get the Army of Extremadura on its belated march to Arzobispo, some Spanish wagons marched west empty.

When the French returned to Talavera, however, they treated the British casualties in Salamanca as best they could, given the limited medical resources of a Napoleonic army. Wellesley had written to the French and received from Marshal Mortier in return an assurance that the British wounded would be properly looked after and:

> we shortly afterwards learned from Mr Dillon, an assistant commissary who had been taken at Talavera, but being a civilian, had been set at liberty, that the marshal had fulfilled his promise, and that the officers and men were doing well.

Still unwilling to concede that he would have to give up the fight and retreat, Cuesta stood at Arzobispo throughout 5 August. This was in a thoroughly dangerous position with the Tagus and its single, narrow bridge behind him,

Marshal Ney, commander of VI Corps.

but Mortier, with his force still arriving, did not attack and the Army of Extremadura was able to cross to the southern bank. During 6 August the Spanish rearguard, still north of the river, skirmished with the French V Corps and it too eventually withdrew across the river covered by batteries of guns sited in redoubts.

The Loyal Lusitania Legion

The only element of Wellesley's force left north of the Tagus was Sir Robert Wilson's Legion. Since the British army marched into Spain it had been operating very effectively in the hills and mountains to Wellesley's left, with the French believing that they were at least twice as strong as they actually were. The Legion, numbering just over 3,000 men, consisted of its own two

Sir Robert Wilson wearing a staff officer's coat and his Peninsular honours and awards.

battalions and cavalry, with the addition of the Portuguese 5th Caçadores[5] and the Spanish regiments of Seville and Mérida. They had occupied Madrid for a short while and presented a threat in the aftermath of the battle on the 28th that contributed to the French withdrawal. News of Soult's move south and the redeployment of the allied armies west to escape Soult's trap created a dangerous situation for the Legion, which had been advancing towards Escalona, as explained by Scott Lillie and Mayne:

> Sir Robert found that General Cuesta had unexpectedly retired from Talavera the day after Lord Wellington, and that the enemy had advanced again to it.
>
> In consequence of these unexpected circumstances the Loyal Lusitanian Legion endeavoured, by long marches through the mountains, to

return to the British Army at Oropesa, from which we were sixty miles the day that General Cuesta evacuated Talavera, but we found that the road to Oropesa was in the enemy's possession, and that it was then too late to retire by Arzobispo. We were consequently in an alarming situation, having no retreat left unoccupied by the enemy; however, *nil desperandum*, we determined on forcing our way across the [Rio] Tietar towards the mountains which separate Estremadura from Castile.

With the Legion having headed north and clashed with a French detachment at Aldea Nueva, the French realised that they now had the opportunity to destroy Wilson's force that had tied down 10,000 French troops at critical stages of the campaign. Consequently, the Legion was soon fighting its way through a scattered enemy corps and they:

> were reduced to the necessity of making forced marches to the mountains, but we found that the town of Viranda, through which we were to pass, and at which we arrived at night, was occupied by the enemy in force, and we were under circumstances, induced to attempt carrying it by storm. We moved on quickly towards the gates, the 5th Caçadores forming the advance, but we were soon perceived by the sentries placed at the gates, and fired upon, which immediately alarmed the garrison: however we forced our way forward to the town, and found the garrison collected in the streets, who poured in a heavy volley amongst us, which was returned in an irregular manner by the 5th Caçadores, who were in front, and who had halted, and appeared unwilling to proceed in consequence of the hot fire kept up by the enemy, the darkness of the night, and narrowness of the streets.
>
> Sir Robert Wilson therefore ordered forward one of the battalions of the Loyal Lusitanian Legion from the rear, who eagerly advanced, proud of the circumstance, and of their selection on the occasion, and gallantly moved forward until they were brought in front, when they immediately poured in a well-directed volley, and coming down instantly to the charge, advanced with cheers upon the enemy, whom they threw into greatest confusion, and drove before them at the point of the bayonet.
>
> Having thus fortunately succeeded in affecting this important passage, we marched on without delay or interruption, the enemy having dispersed in all directions, and our loss on this occasion being inconsiderable.

Having forced their way through Viranda and eluded the French pursuit on several occasions in the mountains, Sir Robert Wilson saw Ney's corps marching north to the Puerto de Baños, where the Legion offered battle in a favourable position. In the ensuing action the French suffered heavy

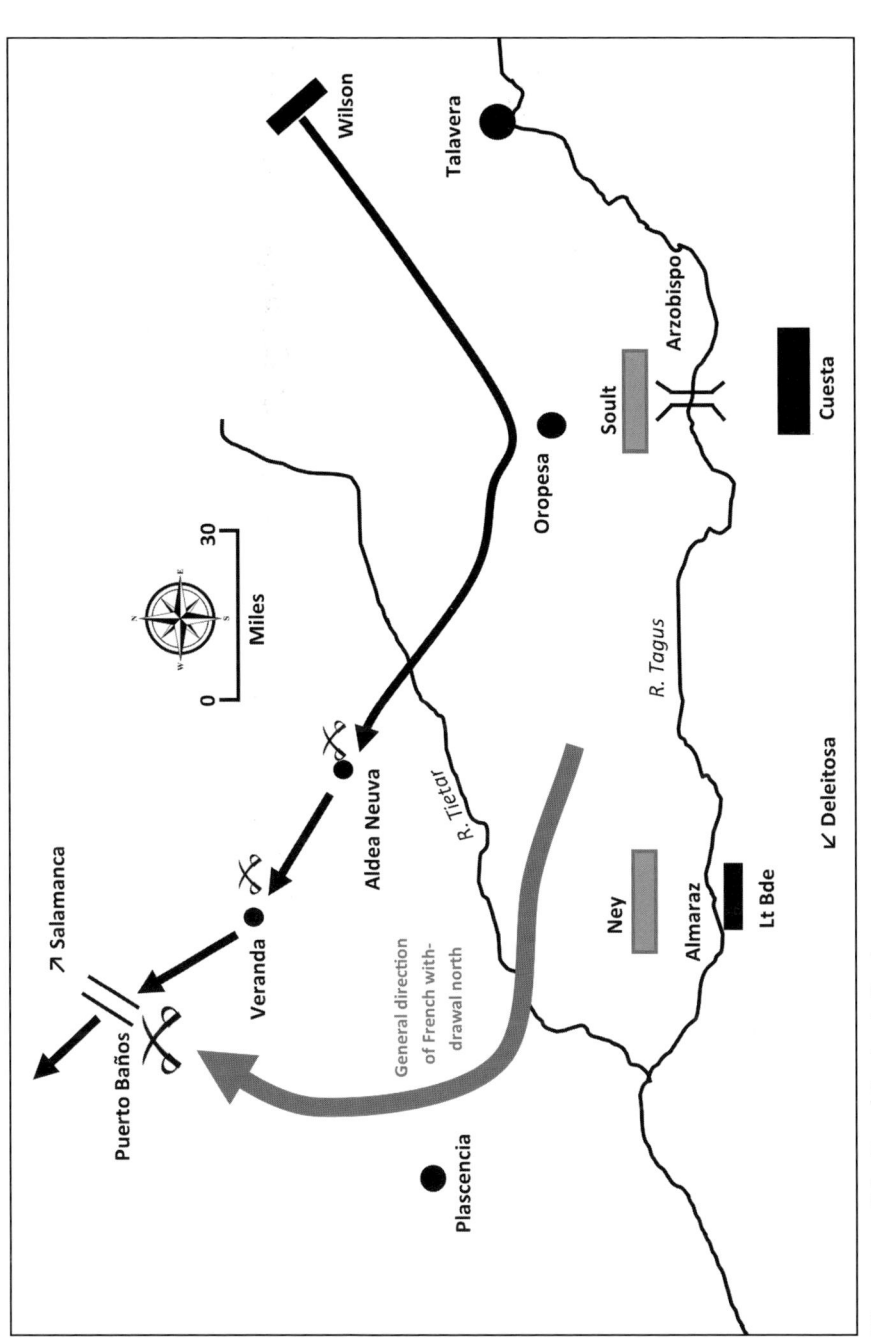

The escape of the Loyal Lusitania Legion.

A French column attacks preceded by its drummers beating the *Pas de Charge*.

casualties before, with their superior numbers, they were able to outflank Wilson's position, but the Legion was able to withdraw and continue its march to safety, having drawn away a substantial French force.

The March to Almaraz

After only a few hours' rest at Arzobispo, Craufurd's 3rd Division, minus artillery, began another forced march at midnight on the 4th/5th. This time it would be of two days to Almaraz and its ford via what were little more than mountain tracks. Lieutenant Leach wrote:

> After a thirteen hours' march through a mountainous, barren, unproductive country, affording no provisions of any sort except now and then a large, coarse description of pea, parched to a cinder by the sun, and an occasional God-send of wheat, found in the ungleaned fields near the line of march, we took up our ground for the night in a wild, uncultivated ravine, from which, I am inclined to think, the most enthusiastic admirer of romantic scenery would have made his escape without delay, from the fear of starvation.
>
> 6th. Daybreak found us again in the act of scrambling over the mountains, and with pretty nearly the same sort of diet as on the preceding day – boiled wheat and dried peas, without salt, bread, or meat. Spring water tolerably abundant, as rivulets were found in the numerous ravines. I cannot call to my recollection having ever witnessed a day's march where so many men left the ranks from fatigue. Many hundreds of the

The Withdrawal to Portugal 219

Brigadier General Robert Craufurd was in temporary command of the 3rd Division but was supplanted by General Hill. Craufurd became a divisional commander again when the Light Brigade was increased in size the following spring.

division were left in the mountains to find their way to Almaraz at their leisure, or, rather, as soon as exhausted nature had rallied. The unavoidable scarcity of food will account for all this, in addition to the length and severity of the marches in the hottest part of Europe, and over the most execrable roads.

Leach goes on to state that initially only fifty riflemen reached the remnants of the bridge and, more importantly, the ford at Almaraz, to join the handful of Spanish militia holding the vital Tagus crossing. In burning heat and famished, the remainder of the 95th and other battalions straggled in over the next twenty-four hours. A combination of excessive labour and marching over a protracted period, with inadequate food, produced this inevitable straggling. In these circumstances the normally strictly applied instructions detailed in Craufurd's standing orders of giving men tickets authorising them

Lieutenant Jonathan Leach of the 1st 95th Rifles. He later commanded a company in that battalion. He is pictured here waring the Tarleton helmet, a part of an officer's home service uniform during the early days of the regiment.

to fall out and handing musket or rifle along with knapsack to another soldier until the man returned, broke down.

The Rifle Brigade's historian recorded details of the march on 6 August:

> At 3.30 a.m. on the 6th the march was resumed and at 6 p.m. the Light Brigade reached Romangordo and bivouacked near it, Donkin's Brigade bivouacking at Las Casas del Puerto. The 95th [Rifles] pushed forward to the broken bridge of Almaraz and took up the outpost line, Soult's outposts being visible along the northern bank of the river [from 12 August]. This day's march was a tiring one and numbers of men of the different regiments in both brigades dropped on the road from excessive fatigue and the intense heat of the sun.[6]

Again, having beaten Ney's advance guard to another key point, Almaraz, by a matter of hours, the first priority was to take up the bridge of boats, which was a precious commodity for crossing the river by artillery, supplies and the army's baggage. Craufurd was instructed not only to dismantle the bridge but to move the components to a point on shore where the pontoons could not be damaged by French artillery fire.

Leach described the Light Brigade's routine for the next two weeks:

> The main body of the division encamped near the village of Las Casas del Puerto, in the formidable pass through which runs the road from Badajoz to Madrid, by the bridge of Almaraz. A more extensive and

An engraving taken from St Clair's picture of the Rio Tagus at Almaraz.

A rifleman stands sentry on a piece of high ground.

The bridge at Almaraz today.

magnificent prospect than that which one looks down on from this pass it is difficult to imagine. Our battalion was kept in advance during our stay in this position and was encamped in an olive-wood near the village of Ramon Gordo, in readiness to support the two companies which were always on picket near the ford. Every evening at sunset we left the olive-grove and lay down by our arms on the bank of the river near the pickets, returning to our campground at sunrise.

Action at Arzobispo

With Oropesa in French hands and the British having crossed the Tagus, the Army of Extremadura had also marched for Arzobispo on 4 August, where having been joined by Bassecourt's division, they clashed with Marshal Mortier's advanced guard. Cuesta stood in an exposed position on the northern bank of the river throughout the 5th, while the French marched hard to concentrate. By the following day, however, Cuesta's desire for battle had evaporated and he finally crossed the Tagus and occupied far less dangerous defences covering both the bridge and river. By the time the French arrived in force, the Spanish were across the river leaving only rearguards.

Cuesta had strengthened his position with several dominating redoubts mounting his heavy guns. These defences forced Soult to stay his hand but the troops the marshal could see deployed were in fact only a strong rearguard of Bassecourt's infantry and Alburquerque's cavalry. The rest of the Army of Extremadura was on the march into the mountains to Mesa de Ibor. Soult was, however, not inactive and dispatched patrols to find a ford, which was located to the east, when French patrols spotted Spanish cavalrymen watering their horses in mid-stream. Intelligence officers were dispatched to check the viability of the Azutan Ford that night, enabling Soult to make a plan for a *coup de main* attack the following day.

On 8 August, Soult ordered Ney's VI Corps to counter-march to the west with the aim of seizing the crossing at Almaraz, while his II Corps would advance on the relatively lightly held river line, which was covered by a regiment of Spanish cavalry and three battalions of infantry, with the remainder of the enemy cavalry and infantry further back in several farms and hamlets.

Soult had maintained an appearance of inactivity during the morning while forming his columns in cover ready to attack between 1300 and 1400 hours. This was a time when he was sure the habitual Spanish siesta would further reduce the alertness of Bassecourt's infantrymen and Alburquerque's cavalrymen. The plan was for the advance on the ford by twelve regiments of cavalry led by La Houssaye's dragoons, followed by the light cavalry brigades of Lorge and of II and V corps. Girard's infantry division was to provide a brigade to support the cavalry and another to attack the bridge itself. The attack was to be covered by a rapid deployment of all available artillery in order to bombard the Spanish artillery redoubts, thus covering the approach of the rest of the force.

The French forcing of the Tagus at Arzobispo.

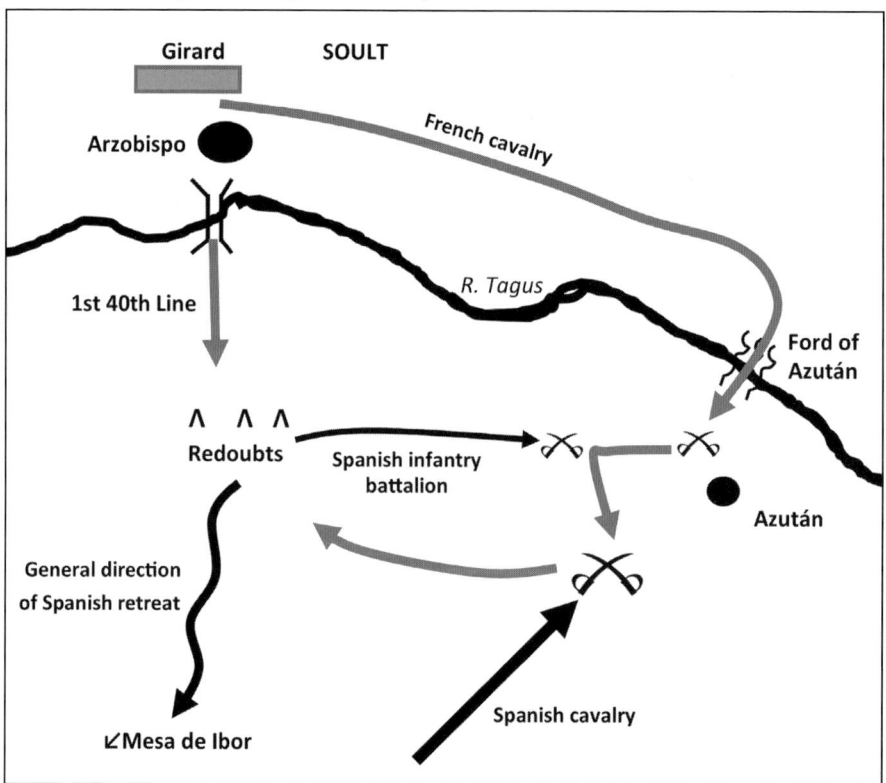

At 1330 hours the leading brigade of dragoons broke cover from behind the village of Arzobispo and headed straight for the ford. They were crossing before the Spanish could react and belatedly deploy. With the leading brigade of dragoons across the river in the ensuing melee, outnumbered Spanish hussars were routed, and the dragoons fell on an enemy infantry battalion as it was forming square, and this too was cut up. Meanwhile, the rest of the 4,000 French cavalry were crossing the Tagus and a battalion of French infantry attacked the narrow bridge covered by several companies of voltigeurs

The uniform of a mounted trooper of the French 4th Dragoons.

and a pair of horse artillery batteries. With the French infantry rushing across the bridge and the mass of enemy cavalry in danger of enveloping them, the other two Spanish battalions, having fired a volley, fled, abandoning the artillery. Consequently, Girard's infantry division was also across the river without significant loss but with the Spanish troops covering the river defeated, the remainder of the rearguard – roused from their siesta – were rapidly forming.

The infantry was quickly accoutred and deployed in line while the cavalry bridled, saddled and mounted their horses, with Alburquerque demanding that they advance forthwith. The result was that, with the exception of the Extremaduran Hussars, who had recovered from their earlier reverse, the Spanish cavalry bore down on La Houssaye's dragoons in a disorderly mass, which broke against the formed ranks of the French dragoons. The defeat of Alburquerque's cavalry, despite the hussars' best efforts, was sealed by the arrival on the flank of one of the French light cavalry brigades. The remaining four infantry battalions promptly withdrew to the rocky high ground, where they were largely immune from pursuit by the French cavalry.

Soult's *coup de main* had been a complete success with minimal loss and now he ordered the cavalry to pursue the Spanish rearguard, which in a series of running fights lost heavily. The Spanish losses amounted to 800 killed and wounded, with 600 men and 400 horses captured. The pursuit continued to the foot of the mountains, where the infantry of Cuesta's main body held the passes. Among the slow-moving baggage were most of the guns that IV Corps had lost in the battle on the afternoon of the 28th. Thanks to a lack of draft

A Spanish militia infantry column led by grenadiers wearing bearskins.

animals and a shortage of gunners, these artillery pieces were crawling along at the rear of the army's column and once back in his possession, Sébastiani disingenuously claimed not to have lost any guns at Talavera!

On arriving at Mesa de Ibor, Cuesta deployed his army into another very strong position in the mountains, where his army would in nearly all circumstances be safe from the overextended French corps. Marshal Soult immediately saw the natural strength of the position and again forbore from attacking and, thwarted, sought to recast his plans.

The March to Truxillo

Meanwhile, the progress of the main body of the British army to the southwest via Deleitosa, some 9 miles south of Almaraz, was scarcely less testing than that of the 3rd Division to Almaraz. Crossing the grain of the country, the army laboured uphill before descending sharply into valleys on terrible roads. Captain Ross, of the Royal Horse Artillery, detached from the Light Brigade, described the route as being across 'mountains which it is hardly possible to suppose artillery could have been got over'. Indeed, the problems were severe and it took the army's main body two days to march just 17 miles. Sergeant Stevenson recalled that:

> One day we crossed a small rivulet and mounted a hill, that took up nearly the whole day to climb; we were forced to put a double number of horses, and a great many men besides, to convey our artillery: and a six pounder, never in ordinary circumstances requiring more than four horses, now during the ascent proved quite as much as eight horses and a hundred men could move, often bringing them to a standing pull.

Riding with the headquarters staff, Lieutenant FitzClarence had the ability denied to those foot slogging to take in the scene:

> As we moved over the high ridges, we had a most extensive view across the place we had traversed a fortnight before from Placentia, and saw the glittering of arms. And the rising dust of the French columns advancing on Oropesa.
>
> Colonel Waters and Captain Mellish crossed the river [Tagus], and reconnoitred the last of these columns, and learned from the peasants that it was the third of the same size that had passed within the preceding three days; thus fully confirming the information of three corps having been directed on our rear.

Schumann shared a little food with a friend during the March on 6 August:

> In order to eat in secret he went behind a bush, for if the famished men had seen him with it he would have run the risk of being half killed for a

piece of bread. At two o'clock we again went forward over frighteningly steep hills. The dust raised by the cavalry was suffocating. It was dark when we reached a small town on the banks of the River Ibor, and we found shelter in an uninhabited farm house, where we slept on a bare floor. Fatigue parties were busy until late in the night dragging the guns one after the other over the steep heights.

The army was bitter at the way it had been let down by Cuesta and the Spanish establishment, and the soldiers roundly ignored edicts on treatment of the allied population's property and 'looting on pain of death'. Discipline in the British army in the face of terrible hunger was evaporating rapidly and Wellesley noted that: 'They plunder in the very presence of their officers.' One soldier wrote in his memoirs that:

Most of the villages of our Spanish Allies were deserted. By way of thanks we plundered them, and carried away window frames, doors and furniture to the bivouacs as fuel, for Spain is very poor in wood. In this way whole villages were deprived of their roofs.

General Wellesley arrived at Truxillo ahead of his army on the 7th, from where he wrote to General O'Donoju at Cuestas headquarters, reporting that: 'The whole army has passed over the worst part of the road. One division is still at Mesa de Ibor [25 miles distant as the crow flies] but the artillery is by this time at Campillo [20 miles] ...' Wellesley was now safe, as the French were now in no state to pursue the allies south of the Tagus or force the issue at Almaraz. Soult's infantry was exhausted, his cavalry horses were in an increasingly poor condition and French supplies were also running short. Consequently, an advance into an area known to have been already stripped of food by Victor during the spring was not a practical course of action in any case.

Captain the Honourable Alexander Gordon, one of Wellesley's junior ADCs,[7] described in a letter to his sister from Deleitosa the uncertainty in the headquarters at this time:

Here we shall remain some days to see what the Enemy will attempt. The Spanish Army remain at the Bridge of Arazbispo to defend it, all the bridges lower down at Alcantra are broke and they say there is no ford. We watch the River closely. Under such circumstances it is hard to say what the enemy will do; they are collecting their whole force from every part of Spain against us ... I rather think we will retire upon Portugal.[8]

Of the 2,500 sick and wounded evacuated with the army on its withdrawal from Talavera, 2,000 eventually reached Deleitosa, with an estimated 500 men dying en route or being captured by the French north of the Tagus.

Gordon noted: 'Sick and wounded poured in daily, looking famished and cadaverous. Many of them had had nothing but water for three days. The whole army was suffering from fever and dysentery.'

On 13 August at Jaraicejo on the road from Deleitosa to Truxillo, Gordon wrote again, this time to Lord Aberdeen:

> Here [Deleitosa] we remained for some days and should have remained longer but moved here to give way to the Spaniards. Their Army in the first instance was to defend the Bridge of Arazobispo and to have destroyed [it] … Soult having followed the Spanish as far as the pass from Arazobispo [Mesa de Ibor] found it too strong, recrossed the river and are now on their way to the frontiers of Portugal.

This latter point is indicative of the continuing uncertainty in Wellesley's headquarters; would Soult follow the emperor's intent and invade Portugal, or would the state of his army mentioned above preclude invasion? It only later became known that the other marshals had refused to co-operate with Soult's plans, preferring to return to their own fiefdoms. In other words, there no longer being a threat to Madrid, the crisis had passed and co-operation between the marshals ebbed away. Ney, for instance, was keen to escape from Soult's command and get back to the Asturias. King Joseph's papers also reveal that he and Marshal Jourdan would not have authorised an invasion of

(Left) An officer's cross belt plate of the 3rd Foot Guards. (Right) The plate worn on the 1906 pattern regimental cap by grenadier and centre companies.

Portugal, which would have stripped away troops needed to hold down the parts of Spain they occupied and to counter the Spanish armies that still held out in the corners of the country.

Almaraz

While the rest of the army rested for a few days at Deleitosa and Truxillo, Brigadier General Craufurd and the 3rd Division were joined at Almaraz after several days by not only their own stragglers but artillery and the 1st Hussars KGL. The latter were to provide patrols out to the Tagus fords on either flank in order to prevent a surprise attack, as a survey of the Tagus by Royal Engineer officers concluded that in the summer, the river could easily be crossed by small bodies of light troops at any number of places east towards Arzobispo. Craufurd's infantry and guns were concentrated nearer the main crossing point, as described by Ensign Brumwell, of the 43rd Light Infantry, in a letter home:

> In the daytime we were under the trees upon the top of a large mountain, and in the dark of the evening we were marched down, with two pieces of artillery, near to the river and remained there all night. On the opposite side the French had an army. It was supposed that they would come across the river, it being fordable at almost every place.

Marshal Ney, however, despite having a sketch map of the major fords' location, reported to Soult that his patrols had been unable or perhaps unwilling to find a ford. Consequently, the most memorable event for the Light Brigade during their time at Almaraz was hunger! Rifleman Costello said that '… living here became truly savage'. The fact that the French were suffering as badly was of little consolation. Sergeant Thomas Garrity recalled that:

> One of these spots we called Mount Misery. Many a time we have breakfasted upon acorns or oak-nuts beaten down by the Spanish swineherds for the use of the hogs. A goat's offal sold at this time for four dollars, or about double the usual price for the whole animal; and men and officers strove to outbid each other in the purchase of this wretched pittance.

The 1st 95th Rifles named their bivouac 'Dough Boy Hill' after the barely palatable dumplings made with scavenged peas ground into flour, chopped straw and water. Much of the blame for cramps and the 'flux' the riflemen suffered from was attributed to these cakes, which were either boiled or cooked on camp kettle lids. The brigade's nightly deployment area down by the river was known as 'Starvation Valley' by the perpetually hungry soldiers. During this period an officer of the 1st KGL Hussars wrote indicating that it wasn't just the rations that caused sickness; 'Our water was furnished by

Rifleman Costello in later life.

A section of Light Infantry march through a Spanish town.

stagnant ditches full of leeches, &c. into the throats of the men, occasioning perpetual bleeding'.

This was the first occasion in which the Light Brigade's piquets were, for an extended period of time, as described by Brumwell 'but a small distance from the enemy's' and a mutual understanding developed with the enemy piquets to their mutual convenience. It subsequently became a feature of the Peninsular War that went beyond simple 'live and let live', to include warning each other of a serious intent to attack, through to, on occasions, sharing campfires or shelter from the elements and the exchange of food, tobacco and drink.

The bugle horn badge worn by light infantry and rifles, plus light companies of other infantry battalions.

Chapter Eleven

The End of the 1809 Campaign

At a point that Wellesley clearly regarded the campaign as being all but over, he summed up the situation in a dispatch to London:

> To: Viscount Castlereagh.   Deleytosa, 8th Aug. 1809.
> I have but little to add to my public dispatch of this date, which I hope will justify me from all blame in the eyes of His Majesty's Ministers, excepting that of having trusted the Spanish General in anything. We should have been safe, if I could have prevailed upon him to occupy Baños, as it ought to have been; and we should have avoided the disgrace of the loss of the hospital, if he had sent away General Bassecourt on the night of the 30th or on the morning of the 31st, or if he had maintained his post at Talavera.

Ensign Aitcheson, of the 3rd Guards, voiced the concerns of much of the army in a letter home in response to overblown tributes in the press and family letters. Of the campaign as a whole, despite his junior rank Aitcheson was not sparing in his analysis or criticism!

> The truth must at last appear. I expected it would and I was prepared for all the clamour at present at home. How I pity fallen greatness – for rapidity of movement and able dispositions in a battle my Lord Wellington certainly merits much applause, but the late campaign in Spain has diminished in a considerable degree the credit for Generalship which he acquired by the brilliant success that attended his former operations.
>
> There is now but one opinion of the late campaign ... In arranging and directing his operations with the Spaniards my Lord Wellington appears entirely to have forgot the indolent habit and inactive disposition of the people with whom he had to co-operate, nor does he appear to have bestowed much consideration on the nature of the country through which he had to march, and the small supply, nay, *extreme deficiency* of medical stores showed he entertained no apprehension of a reverse – in short, ere he had quitted Abrantes with his army, he had already in imagination triumphed in Madrid.
>
> This hazardous boldness and apparent confidence of the chief had the effect to produce a corresponding feeling in the troops yet flushed with recollection of their former success – attack and victory became

synonymous in idea, and although the letters of Sir John Moore proclaimed the reception we were likely to experience from the Spaniards ... [we were] impatient only for the day we should measure our strength with that of the enemy.

The grand error of our Commander-in-Chief seems to me to have been too much reliance on the professions of ability and execution in Spain and the Spaniards – from this has resulted the discomfiture of the combined army. But I am also of an opinion the great miseries which our troops have suffered are in no small degree to be attributed to a presumption of infallibility, which Lord Wellington appears to have entertained for his own plans.

Such criticism, or as Wellesley referred to it, 'croaking', was common in letters of the time but was far less in evidence in memoirs written after the war, when it was greatly muted.

The March Back to the Borders

On 11 August Wellesley wrote to Cuesta from Truxillo, stating that the army was 'perishing for the want of food' and that 'for me to remain any longer in a country in which no arrangement has been made for the supply of provisions to the troops' was impossible and that he would have to withdraw to Badajoz.

The white undress uniform and cap worn over the regimental coat for fatigues and duties.

Captain Gordon, not constrained by diplomatic language and sounding dangerously like a 'croaker', wrote home:[1]

> We received not the least assistance from the Country and have actually been near starved; [the] Government will soon be obliged to believe what the whole Army said last year of the Spanish cause and what is the opinion of the Commander and everyone in this.

While the British negotiated with the Army of Extremadura for another week, the suffering of the army was far from over. Schaumann is again our commentator:

> The heat increased every day, and there was not a drop of rain to refresh us. If a storm rose in the west the distant mountains held it off, and while it increased the heaviness of the air, not a spot of rain came our way. The drought was so intense that our eyelids smarted; the ink thickened on our pens as fast as we wrote, and our skins, burnt by the sun, peeled off our noses and upper lips. Shaving and washing, and particularly drying ourselves with a coarse towel, became extremely painful. Every soldier stuck an olive leaf or a piece of paper on his under lip to prevent it from bursting.

Another officer added that: 'Grass and scrub fires along with vermin of every stinging, biting and sucking variety abounded in the bivouacs.'

Lieutenant FitzClarence noted that such was the state of the army's supply that: 'Sir Arthur ordered with justice, that the stoppage for the troops usually of sixpence a day for their provisions, should only be threepence from 27 July till further orders.'

On 19 August Wellesley terminated the fruitless discussions with General Cuesta, and his letter to London makes the army's situation clear:

> Starvation has produced such dire effects upon the army, we have suffered so much, and have received so little assistance from the Spaniards, that I am at last compelled to move back into Portugal to look for subsistence. There is no enemy in our front of any consequence: Ney is gone back into Castille; Soult is at Plasencia; Mortier at Oropesa, Arzobispo, and Navalmoral; Victor's corps is divided, being half of it at Talavera, and half in La Mancha with Sébastiani. They cannot say we were compelled to go therefore by the enemy, but by a necessity created by the neglect of the Spaniards of our wants.

Having concentrated his army around Truxillo, Wellesley had no choice but to order a resumption of the army's march back to the borders and the fortress of Badajoz, where a supply line via Elvas to Lisbon was established on 2 September. Such was the state of the army the march could only be

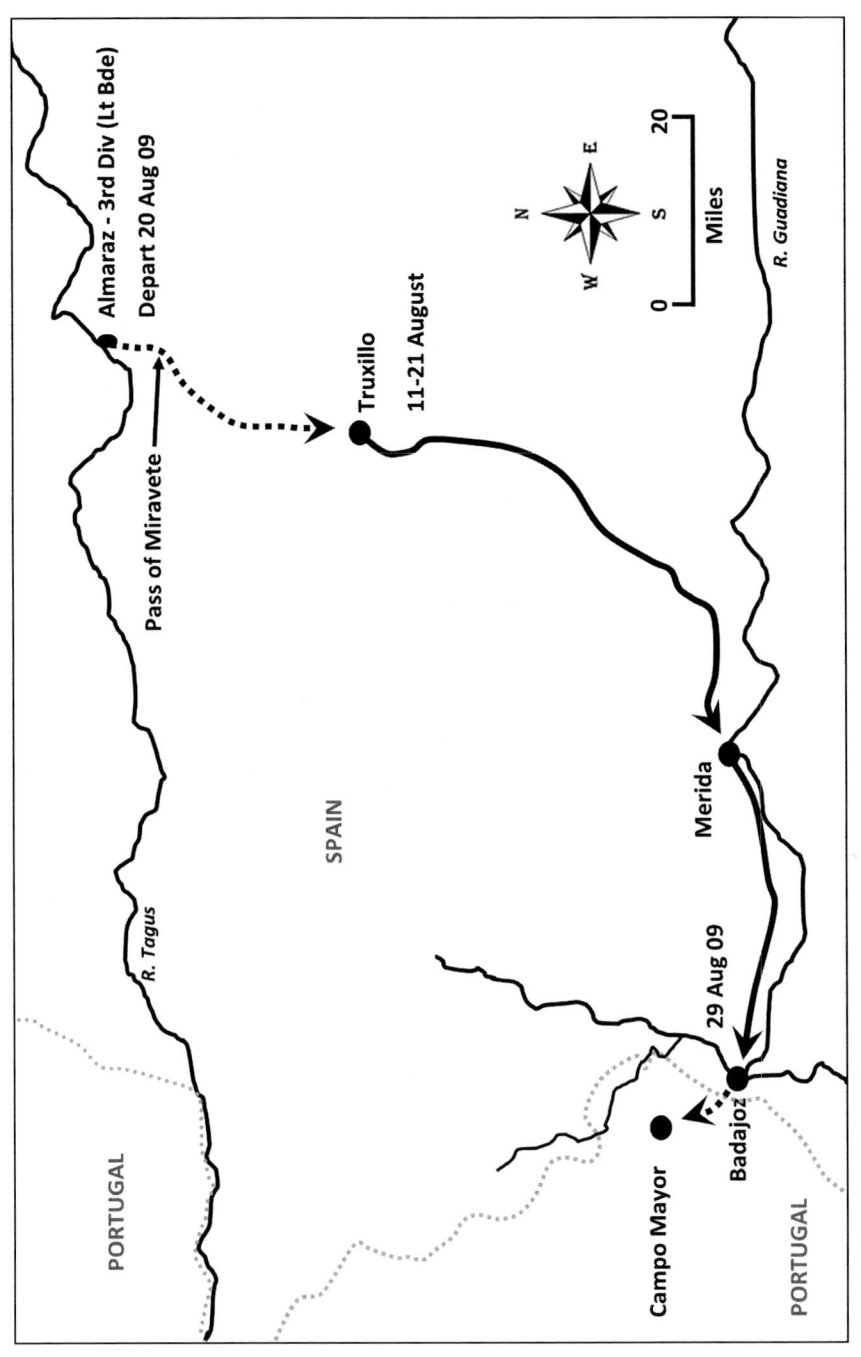

The withdrawal to Portugal.

conducted in short stages and consequently, though less than 90 miles, most brigades took over ten days to reach Badajoz.

Sergeant Garrity, of the 43rd Light Infantry, recalled the march of the Light Brigade from Almaraz:

> On the 20th of August the main body of the British army quitted Jaraicejo and marched by Truxillo upon Merida. Our brigade, under General Crauford [sic], being relieved at Almaraz by the Spaniards, took the road of Caceres to Valencia de Alcántara; but at the pass of Mirrabet we discovered how much we had suffered. Our brigade, which only a few weeks before, had traversed sixty miles in a single march, were now with difficulty, and after many halts, only able to reach the summit of the Mirrabet, although only four miles from the camp; and the side of that mountain was covered with baggage, and the carcases of many hundred animals that died in the ascent.

Militarily, Wellesley would probably have preferred to withdraw into Portugal to rest and refit his army, but politically he had to remain in Spain to preserve the alliance with the Central Junta. From positions around Badajoz, he could threaten the Tagus Valley and ultimately Madrid, which had the effect of forcing King Joseph to maintain two corps in the Tagus valley to watch the British and garrison the crossing point of Almaraz. This, of course, aided the Central Junta by reducing the number of French troops available to bring other parts of Spain under Joseph's control.

While at Badajoz, word reached Lieutenant General Sir Arthur Wellesley that he had been elevated to the peerage. News of the victory at Talavera had been received in London quickly and prompted the British Government to confer on him the title Viscount Wellington. Having few connections with England, Wellington, a small town in Somerset, had been chosen as his seat. In addition, the Central Junta of Spain gave the new peer the title of captain general. While the newly ennobled peer was receiving plaudits, General Cuesta had a stroke at Mesa de Ibor, which further immobilised him and as excoriating criticism within both Spanish and British circles of his conduct of the campaign grew, he resigned his command. He was given the governorship of Spain's Mediterranean Balearic Islands but having had another stroke in 1810, Cuesta died the following year.

Soult's force had withdrawn north to Salamanca, and he returned to France on leave, handing over command of II Corps to General Marchand. The French were not planning any offensive moves until the promised reinforcements from Germany had arrived, but the Central Junta had other ideas. Even though Wellington, as he was now styled, had via the Portuguese Regency, refused to take part in Spanish schemes, the Junta persisted with its plans. Consequently, the French were surprised when General Del Parque advanced

King Joseph's position was consistently undermined by his brother's intervention in affairs in Spain and the persistent state of competition between his marshals and general.

on Salamanca from the Spanish fortress of Ciudad Rodrigo with 21,500 men. Marchand marched his 13,200-strong division south to Tamames, where he was defeated by Del Parque and the French divisions dispersed to hold down the country were unable to prevent the Spanish recapturing Salamanca.[2] Del Parque's liberation of the city was, however, only temporary as the French concentrated to drive the Spanish back, but inevitably this was at the cost of abandoning large swathes of territory further north to the guerrilla bands. The maxim that the French only held the ground within a musket shot of their positions was already becoming clear. In this case Don Julian Sanchez, a former Spanish sergeant, nicknamed *El Charro* (the Cowboy) took the opportunity to raise a significant guerrilla force that was to aid Wellington on northern borders for the next few years.

Guadiana Fever

Meanwhile, the British army remained in Spain around the border fortification of Badajoz, where far from recovering its health after the privations of the campaign, the army, on the unhealthy banks of the Rio Guadiana, suffered from 'Guadiana Fever'; a combination of dysentery and a kind of malarial dysentery. Wellington, despite his renowned cast iron constitution, was among those who became 'very ill with ague' in late September.

The sickness carried many men to hospital and their graves. In the case of Rifleman Costello, for example, the fever lasted for six weeks, with recurring episodes for a year afterwards. Colonel George Napier wrote:

> The hospital was established at Elvas, and there five or six thousand gallant British soldiers breathed their last. It was dreadful to see the dead cart go round the town three times a day, loaded with dead bodies all naked, and tumbled into a hole outside town, from whence the smell was horrid, notwithstanding all means were tried to prevent it.

Second Captain George Jenkinson, of Ross's troop, Royal Horse Artillery, wrote home in mid-October describing the impact of the fever on his troop:

> Our situation is lamentable, we have lost 12 of our best men, and have at present 30 sick, the majority of which I fear will never recover, and that diminution of men, with the loss of 40 of our very finest horses, will give you an idea of the condition we are in.

The 43rd Light Infantry alone lost four sergeants and 106 rank and file during their stay at Campo Mayor. The fever persisted until the cooler weather of late autumn reduced its incidence.

From Badajoz Captain Gordon wrote to Lord Aberdeen that: 'In the present state of things we certainly could not undertake the offensive again in Spain. I imagine the plan of our government is to defend Portugal as long as we can, and then retire.' This is exactly what was intended by Wellington, insisting as he always had that Portugal was defensible.

1810 in the Peninsular

In the aftermath of his victories over the Austrians and Wagram, the prompt return of the British to the Peninsular and the insult to his imperial dignity of the battles of Oporto and Talavera, Napoleon was stung into action. Preparations for a new campaign in the Peninsular during 1810 with Napoleon at the head of his army were soon under way. Wellington also fully expected

240 *The Talavera Campaign, 1809*

Napoleon to turn his attention to personally 'throwing the leopard into the sea'. However, the requirements of state and a new wife, the Austrian princess Marie-Louise, saw the emperor handing over command to an aging and reluctant Marshal Masséna.

During the autumn of 1809, the question was which of the three practical invasion routes west from Spain into Portugal would the French use? The two southerly routes via Badajoz and further north the Tagus valley had both been stripped of food necessary for an army that lived off the land, which left

Napoleon and Marie-Louise of Austria in the gardens of the Tuileries.

The Spanish General Staff

A Spanish general staff had been formed under the venal and corrupt Godoy, Prince of Peace, as early as 1801 but under his control nepotism and fraud remained rife across the Spanish army. The poor performance of General Cuesta and the manner in which Venegas disobeyed orders and failed to co-operate for his own ends during the Talavera Campaign, plus the lack of a Central Junta with any authority, prompted the introduction of a new General Staff in 1810.

A Spanish general (right) and an officer of the General Staff. His coat has the light blue facings of a staff officer and he wears a light blue sash.

> Selected officers of ability rather than social background and wealth, were gathered from all arms into the General Staff from across the Spanish armies. However, so deeply rooted were many of the problems, this did not prove to be an instant panacea but was in reality the beginning of a slow process of transformation and improvement in command and organisation.
>
> As the war came to an end, Fernando VII returned to Spain and set about reversing the liberal reforms of the previous five years and abolishing constitutional government in favour of the absolute monarchy he had left in 1808. Among the institutions he supressed in 1814 was the Spanish General Staff.

the most northerly route via the respective border fortresses of Ciudad Rodrigo and Almeida and the Douro Valley. When clear indications were reported that the French were mounting invasion preparation around Salamanca, in December 1809 Wellington marched his army north away from the unhealthy Guadiana valley to winter quarters in the Beira region of northern Portugal. During the spring of 1810, Craufurd, now commanding a Light Division, provided the army's outposts on the Agueda–Azab line, observing Masséna's lacklustre siege of Ciudad Rodrigo before in July 1810 the French finally again advanced into Portugal. Despite defeat at Buçaco, French confidence that they would soon be in Lisbon was dashed when they encountered the fully manned Lines of Torres Vedras barring their way.

Elsewhere during 1810, while Marshal Masséna invaded via northern Portugal, marshals Soult, Victor and Sébastiani moved south to confront Generals Alburquerque and Aréizaga in Andalucía. This rich part of Spain fell into their hands, but they failed to capture Cadiz. In the north-east of the Peninsular marshals Suchet and Augereau attempted to subdue Catalonia and Aragon and then turned their attention south to Valencia.

Appendix I

An Example of Wellesley's General Orders

This, one of many issues between the two 1809 campaigns, demonstrates both the commissaries' lack of knowledge of their duties in the field and how specific procedures were in the process of being developed by General Wellesley at an early stage of campaigning in the peninsular.

G. 0.   Abrantes, 8th June, 1809.

1. The regiments will make a requisition upon the Commissary at Abrantes for a sufficient number of pairs of shoes to complete them to two good pairs each man; the period of the delivery of those shoes will be notified in General Orders; they will be paid for at the rate of 6s. 6d. per pair. The regiments not already completed with bill-hooks, canteens, haversacks, and camp kettles, according to the General Orders of the 31st ult., will make a requisition upon the Quartermaster-General at Abrantes for the same: the period of the delivery of those articles will likewise be notified in General Orders.

2. Various complaints having been made to the Commander of the Forces of the irregularity of the delivery of articles from the commissariat, the following rules are to be observed upon that subject in future:-

3. When articles are delivered to troops from a general store, the Commissary-General must, if possible, have two or more stores for the delivery of each article, viz., forage, corn, wood, meat, bread, and wine.

4. He must signify to the Assistant-Commissaries of brigades and regiments at which store, and where situated, troops in the brigade or regiment will receive their supplies, and in what order by brigades, and at what hour, the supplies will be delivered to the troops of each brigade or regiment at each store.

5. In general, however, it is better the troops of each brigade or regiment should receive their supplies at the brigade or regimental store.

6. When the army will halt, a commencement must be made to make the deliveries at the commissaries' stores at daylight, and the delivery must be continued without interruption, till the whole of the troops to receive their supplies at such store shall have received them. The soldiers of each

brigade or regiment will attend to receive the supplies at the hour appointed for them precisely, and not before.

7. The meat for the troops must invariably be delivered to them from a brigade or regimental store, and should be killed on the preceding night, or at daylight in the morning, when the army halts. When it marches, the order of the 5th of May comes in force and the meat should be delivered, killed and cooked as soon as possible after the orders for marching are given out.

8. When the army marches, the Commissary-General should notify as soon as possible to the Assistant-Commissaries of brigades and regiments of cavalry where the store of each article of supply for the troops will be made to each brigade or regiment. The deliveries on marching days must commence as soon as possible after the troops reach their ground.

9. It is obvious, however, that on marching days it is still more important than it is on halting days that the delivery should be made from a brigade or regimental, rather than a general store.

10. The Assistant-Commissaries with regiments of cavalry and brigades must not be changed, unless the change is notified in General Orders.

11. The Assistant-Commissaries with brigades and regiments of cavalry must take care to obtain copies of all General Orders from the Brigade-Majors or Adjutants respectively. The Commissary-General is responsible that all other officers of the department, not attached to brigades or regiments of cavalry, have copies of the General Orders.

ARTHUR WELLESLEY.

Appendix II

Orders of Battle – Talavera

British Army
(Lieutenant General Sir Arthur Wellesley[1])

Cavalry Division (Lieutenant General Payne) (Total: 2,969)

Fane's Brigade
3rd Dragoon Guards (525)
4th Dragoons (545)

Anson's Brigade
23rd Light Dragoons (459)
1st Light Dragoons KGL (451)

Cotton's Brigade
14th Light Dragoons (464)
16th Light Dragoons (525)

1st Infantry Division (Lieutenant General Sherbrooke) (Total 5,964)

H. Campbell's Brigade
1/Coldstream Guards (970)
1/3rd Guards (1,019)
5/60th (1 company 56)

Langwerth's Brigade
1st KGL Line (604)
2nd KGL Line (678)
KGL Light (1 company 51)

Cameron's Brigade
1/61st Foot (778)
2/83rd Foot (535)
5/60th (1 company 51)

Löw's Brigade
5th KGL Line Bn (610)
7th KGL Line Bn (557)

2nd Infantry Division (Major General Hill) (Total 3,905)

Tilson's Brigade
1/3rd Foot (746)
2/48th Foot (567)
2/66th Foot (526)
5/60th (1 company 52)

R. Stewart's Brigade
1/29th Foot (598)
1/48th Foot (807)
1st Bn of Detachments (609)

3rd Infantry Division (Major General Mackenzie) (Total: 347)

Mackenzie's Brigade
2/24th Foot (787)
2/31st Foot (733)
1/45th Foot (756)

Donkin's Brigade
2/87th Foot (599)
1/88th Foot (599)
5/60th (5 companies 273)

4th Infantry Division (Brigadier A. Campbell) (Total: 2,960)

A Campbell's Brigade
2/7th R Fusiliers (431)
2/53rd Foot (537)
5/60th (1 company 64)

Kemmis's Brigade
1/40th Foot (745)
97th Foot (502)
2nd Bn Detachments (625)
5/60th (1 company 56)

Artillery:

British batteries (681)
Lawson's (6 × 3-pounders)
Sillery's (5 × light 6-pounders, 1 × howitzer)
Eliott's (5 × light 6-pounders, 1 × howitzer)

KGL Batteries (330)
Rettberg's (5 × heavy 6-pounders, 1 × howitzer)
Heyse's (5 × heavy 6-pounders, 1 × howitzer)
Engineers (22)

Army total: 20,578

* * *

Spanish Army of Extremadura
(General Cuesta y Fernández de Celis)

Vanguard (Brigadier General Zayas) (41 Infantry Battalions 26,000)
2nd Volunteers of Catalonia
2nd Bn Cazadores de Barbastro
Cazadores de Campo-Mayor (1 bn)
Cazadores de Valencia y Alburquerque (1 bn)
2nd Bn Voluntarios de Valencia

1st Division (Major General Marques de Zayas)
Cantabria Infantry Regiment (3 bns)
Granaderos Provinciales (1 bn)
Canarias Infantry Regiment (1 bn)
Tiradores de Mérida (1 bn)
Provincial de Truxillo (1 bn)

2nd Division (Major General Iglesias)
2nd Majorca Infantry Regiment (1 bn)
Velez-Malaga Infantry Regiment (3 bns)
Osuna Infantry Regiment (2 bns)
Voluntarios Estrangeros (1 bn)
Provincial de Burgos (1 bn)

3rd Division (Major General de Portago)
Badajoz Infantry Regiment (2 bns)
2nd Antequera Infantry Regiment (1 bn)
Imperial de Toledo (1 bn)
Provincial de Badajoz (1 bn)
Provincial de Guadix (1 bn)

4th Division (Major General Manglano)
- Irlanda Infantry Regiment (2 bns)
- Jaen Infantry Regiment (2 bns)
- 3rd Seville Infantry Regiment (1 bn)
- 1st Bn Leales de Fernando VII (1 bn)
- 2nd Volunteers of Madrid (1 bn)
- Voluntarios de la Corona (1 bn)

5th Division (Major General Bassecourt)
- Real Marina, 1st Infantry Regiment (2 bns)
- Africa Infantry Regiment (1 bn)
- Murcia Infantry Regiment (2 bns)
- Reyna Infantry Regiment
- Provincial de Siguenza (1 bn)

1st Cavalry Division (Lieutenant General de Henestrosa)
(14 Cavalry regiments Tayal approx. 6,000)
- Rey Cavalry Regiment
- Calatrava Cavalry Regiment
- Voluntarios de España
- Imperial de Toledo
- Cazadores de Seville
- Reyna Cavalry Regiment
- Villaviciosa Cavalry Regiment
- Cazadores de Madrid

2nd Cavalry Division (Lieutenant General Duque de Alburquerque)
- Carabineros Reals (1 sqn)
- Infante Cavalry Regiment
- Alcántara Cavalry Regiment
- Pavia Cavalry Regiment
- 1st Hussars of Extremadura
- 2nd Hussars of Extremadura

* * *

The French Army
(King Joseph and Marshal Jourdan)

I Corps (Marshal Victor)

1st Division (General de Division Ruffin) (Total: 5,286)

General de Brigade
- 9th Légère (3 bns)
- 24th Line (3 bns)

General de Brigade Barrois
- 96th Line (3 bns)

2nd Division (General de Division Lapisse) (Total: 6,862)

General de Brigade Laplannes
- 16th Légère (3 bns)
- 45th Line (3 bns)

General de Brigade Solignac
- 94th Line (3 bns)
- 95th Line (3 bns)

3rd Division (General de Division Villatte) (Total: 6,135)

General de Brigade Cassagne
- 27th Légère (3 bns)
- 63th Line (3 bns)

General de Brigade Puthod
- 94th Line (3 bns)
- 95th Line (3 bns)

Corps Cavalry (General de Brigade Beaumont) (Total: 980)
  2nd Hussars
  5th Chasseurs à Cheval

IV Corps General de Division Sébastiani

1st Division General de Division Sébastiani (Total: 8,118)
  General de Brigade Rey
    28th Line (3 bns)
    32nd Line (3 bns)
  General de Brigade Liger-Belair
    58th Line (3 bns)
    75th Line (3 bns)

2nd Division General de Division Valance (Total: 1,600)
  4th Polish Regt (2 bns)

3rd Division General de Division Leval (Total: 4,537)
  Oberst von Porbeck
    2nd Nassau Regt (2 bns)
    4th Baden Regt (2 bns)
    Baden Foot Bty (8 × 6-pounders)
  General de Brigade Grandjean
    Hesse-Darmstadt Gross und Erbprinz Regt (2 bns)
    Frankfurt Bn
  General de Brigade Chassé
    2nd Dutch Regt (2 bns)
    3rd Dutch Horse Bty
      (6 × 6-pounders)

Corps Cavalry General de Brigade Merlin (Total: 1,188)
  General de Brigade Strolz
    10th Chasseurs à Cheval
    26th Chasseurs à Cheval
  General de brigade Ormancy
    Polish Chevaux-Léger-lancier Regt
    Westphalian Chevaux-Léger Regt

Cavalry:

1st Dragoon Division (General de Division La Tour-Maubourg) (Total: 3,279)
  1st Dragoon Regt
  2nd Dragoon Regt
  4th Dragoon Regt
  9th Dragoon Regt
  14th Dragoon Regt
  26th Dragoon Regt

2nd Dragoon Division (General de Division Milhaud) (Total: 2,356)
  5th Dragoon Regt
  12th Dragoon Regt
  16th Dragoon Regt
  20th Dragoon Regt
  21st Dragoon Regt
  3rd Dutch Hussar Regt

Notes

Chapter 1: The Peninsular, 1809

1. General Maximillian Foy, *Junot's Invasion of Portugal 1807–1808*. Published posthumously by Baudouin Frères, 1827.
2. Now known as Forte de Santa Catarina in Figueira da Foz. The fort had originally been captured and held by students from Coimbra University.
3. In 1802 King George III, largely at the instigation of Admiral John Jervis, Earl of St Vincent, granted the Marines the Royal prefix.
4. Leach, *Rough Sketches of the Life of an Old Soldier* (Longman, London, 1831).
5. Though outnumbered, only five battalions and the four companies of the 2nd 95th played an active part in the battle.
6. Castlereagh's dispatch of 25 September 1808.
7. A distance of 380 miles via Talavera rather than approximately 250 miles on the more direct routes via Ciudad Rodrigo. Splitting the army was a mistake based on poor information; the roads through northern Portugal were in fact perfectly practicable for artillery.

Chapter 2: The Douro Campaign

1. Wellesley on the Douro in 1809 is a campaign in its own right and is deserving of its own dedicated study. It is only covered alongside the Talavera Campaign for context.
2. Oman noted: of Wellesley's twenty-one British battalions, ten were 2nd battalions (of the 7th, 9th, 24th, 30th, 31st, 48th, 53rd, 66th, 83rd, 87th), two were single-battalion regiments (the 29th and 97th), three first battalions (of the 3rd, 45th and 88th), two Guards' battalions (1st Coldstreams and 1st Scots Fusiliers), two 'battalions of detachments,' one a 3rd battalion (27th), one a 5th battalion (60th).
3. Waters was a staff officer in the Adjutant General's Department in Wellesley's headquarters and ranked as a captain in the 1st of Foot and as a lieutenant colonel in Portuguese service. In addition to normal staff work as an Assistant Adjutant General, he became one of the renowned exploring officers.

Chapter 3: Campaign Planning and Preparation

1. General Mackenzie's headquarters was at Abrantes. His Lisbon covering force of some 8,000 British and Portuguese consisted of Fane's British heavy cavalry brigade, Mackenzie's own British infantry brigade, and Captain May's battery. The Portuguese troops under command were a cavalry brigade (five squadrons of dragoons), an infantry brigade, and two artillery batteries.
2. Napier WFP, *History of the War in the Peninsular and in the South of France*, Vol. II (Constable, London, 1992).
3. The monastery is now a Parador.
4. According to General Orders of 31 May, 6,000 pairs of shoes had been brought up to the army to address the immediate needs. That same day Wellesley wrote to Castlereagh requesting 30,000 pairs, along with 1,500,000lb of biscuit for the men and 6,000,000lb of forage for the army's horses and mules.

5. Gurwood John, *Dispatches of Field Marshal Duke of Wellington*, Vol. 3 (Parker Furnival & Parker, London, 1844).
6. Schaumann, August, *On the Road with Wellington, The diary of a war commissary* (Heineman Ltd, London, 1924).
7. Sherer, Joseph Moyle, *Recollections of the Peninsular* (Longman, London, 1824).
8. Cooper John, *Rough Notes of Seven Campaigns During the Years 1809–1815* (Spelmount, Staplehurst, 1996).
9. A corps of guides had been formed in September 1808, but this was an entirely new unit.
10. The Quarter Master General's role in the Peninsular Army is not analogous to that of the modern office of that name. Wellington only briefly flirted with the concept of a chief of staff, preferring to use the QMG as his senior staff officer. See SPG Ward, *Wellington's Headquarters* (Pen & Sword, 2017).
11. Urban points out that Scovell was a thoroughly competent Marlow officer but was without money or influence and that would have prevented his advancement. He was the natural choice.
12. Both Royal Horse Artillery batteries, Ross's A Troop, which would have a long association with the Light brigade/Division, and Bull's I Troop, both arrived with the army after Talavera.
13. The soldiers in the battalions of detachments mainly belonged to those battalions that had landed in Portugal during the summer of 1808, rather than those that arrived with General Baird via Corunna.
14. Wellington was still complaining about the performance of his divisional staffs in 1811. See Saunders, *Messana at Bay 1811* (Pen & Sword, Barnsley, 2021).

Chapter 4: The Campaign Opens

1. Aitchison, John, ed. Thompson, *An Ensign in the Peninsular War* (Michael Joseph, London, 1981).
2. Wellington Duke, *Supplementary Dispatches, Correspondence and Memoranda*, Vol. VI (John Murray, London).
3. Oman, Sir Charles, *A History of the Peninsular War*, Vol. II (Greenhill Books, London, 1995).
4. Leslie, Charles, *With the 29th Regiment in the Peninsula* (Leonaur, 2012).
5. *Dispatches*, Vol. II.
6. Wellesley, ed. Gurwood, *Wellington's Dispatches*, Vol. IV (John Murray, London, 1837).
7. Later Charles Vane, 3rd Marquis of Londonderry.
8. Londonderry, Lord, *Narrative of the Peninsular War, from 1808 to 1813*, Vol. 1 (Colburn, 1829).
9. This is the kind of operational detail that was often reprinted in newspapers. Much would be out of date by the time it reached Paris but nonetheless the arrival of reinforcements, etc, provided useful intelligence for the French.

Chapter 5: The Advance on Talavera

1. The English league is generally accepted as being 3 miles, while the Spanish legua was 2.6 miles.
2. Munster, Earl of (FitzClarence), *An Account of the Campaign in 1809* (Henry Colburn, London, 1831).
3. Despite the disadvantage of tall cavalry boots, French dragoons armed with a musket rather than the shorter carbine were expected to fight on foot as well as in the saddle.
4. Oman.
5. Ibid.

6. William Napier, having fought in nearly the whole campaign, was a confirmed Hispanophobe.
7. *Dispatches*.
8. The Legion was reinforced by the 5th Portuguese Caçadores and the Spanish regiments of Merida and Seville. The battalion of Caçadores were the only regular troops of the Portuguese Army to take part in the campaign.
9. Sidney, Rev. Edwin, *The Life of Lord Hill* (John Murray, London, 1843).
10. During the Napoleonic Wars grenadier companies formed on the right of battalions, while light companies did so on the left. When in mixed company, as in the Battalion of Detachments, they would deploy in numerical order from the right.
11. Companies made up of soldiers of the 79th Cameron Highlanders and the 92nd Gordon Highlanders. As many as 200 were taken prisoner – most escaped during the French withdrawal from the Medellín.
12. Quoted by Field, Andrew W, Girod, *Dix ans des mes Souvenirs militaires de 1805 à 1815* (Paris, 1873).
13. Cowdry, TE, *Incomparable, Napoleon's 9th Light Infantry Regiment* (Osprey, Oxford, 2012).
14. Saunders and Yuill, *The Light Division in the Peninsular 1808–1811* (Pen & Sword, Barnsley, 2020).
15. There was disagreement among those who took part in the march in their memoirs and letters over distance and hours marched. Furthermore, Napier's error in calculation has been built on and exaggerated to as much as 62 miles in twenty-six hours! Using contemporary and modern maps, the distance calculated to the battlefield is in line with Verner's 38–42 miles. For the full debate see Appendix III to Willoughby Verner, *History and Campaigns of the Rifle Brigade, Vol. 2, 1809–1813* (N&M Press reprint).

Chapter 7: The Day of Battle, 28 July 1809

1. Marshal Jourdan wrote in his memoirs, after the fact that he believed the Medellín to be far too strong to attack frontally, as attempted by Victor on the evening of 27 July and again on the morning of the 28th. He argued that: 'Hence the only prudent line was to take up position on the Alberche and await the effect of Soult's operation on the English rear.'
2. This in a nutshell is the issue that faced the French in Iberia throughout the war: Napoleon consistently exercised command and even in 1812 cast a shadow when he was in eastern Europe, marshals rarely co-operated, putting their own interests first and King Joseph, as a result, lacked any real authority to bring them to heel.
3. Beamish, Ludlow, based on the notes of Major von Holle, *History of the King's German Legion* (T. and W. Boon, London, 1832).
4. Letter from Hill to his sister 30 July 1809, quoted in *Short Memoirs of Eminent Men* (Society for Promoting Christian Knowledge, London, 1847).
5. Ellis, *letter* (Private collection, 30 July 1809).

Chapter 8: The Main Attack

1. Cooper, John, *Rough Notes on Seven Campaigns* (John Russel Smith, London, 1869).
2. 8-pounders as opposed to British 9-pounders. The guns were possibly disabled by spiking, i.e. driving a headless nail into the touch hole, more likely the infantry would have taken or broken the tools necessary for loading the gun, cut the teams' traces or burnt or otherwise spoiled the ammunition. It was also possible to destroy the barrel by loading multiple charges and firing the gun, but this needed specialist knowledge.
3. The normal establishment for a French foot artillery battery was eight guns. Cooper mentions twelve guns captured in his account, while others state six.

4. Chambray, General Marquis de Georges, *Quelques réflexions sur l'infanterie de nos jours, et en particulier sur l'infanterie Française et sur l'infanterie Anglais* (Paris, 1829).
5. Evidence is that Wellesley remained on the Medellín, from where he could observe the centre of the battlefield and the French approach. He almost certainly sent an ADC with word to General Sherbrooke.
6. Stevenson, John, Ed Glover, *The 3rd Guards in Time of War 1793–1814* (Ken Trotman Publishing, Huntingdon, 2019).
7. Napier, WFP, *History of the Peninsular War, Vol. II* (Constable, London, 1992).
8. Charles Oman places full credit for saving the day on Mackenzie's Brigade. 'for twenty minutes there was the most furious musketry battle in the British right centre. Mackenzie himself fell, and his three battalions lost 632 men out of about 2,000. ... on this point, the battle was saved: the main credit must go to Mackenzie's brigade, which has never received the praise that was its due, for its general was killed and thus no report from the 3rd division was sent into Wellesley, who omitted all mention of its doings in his Talavera dispatch. It is never too late to do homage to forgotten valour, and to call attention to a neglected feat of arms. The services of the 24th, 31st, and 45th saved the day for Britain.'
9. This is where the larger figure of twelve guns probably comes from. Joseph, Jourdan and senior artillery officers went to some pains to conceal the loss of the guns from Napoleon and recovered most of them later in the campaign. This enabled them to reduce the losses to two guns.
10. Rudnicki, Trans Lalowski, ed. North, *Memoirs of a Polish officer in Spain*, Napoleon Series – Research, accessed July 2022.

Chapter 9: The Final Phase and the Aftermath of Battle

1. There has been some confusion here with some historians interpreting the term 'regimental square' as being a single square. The term 'regimental square' in French drill books, however, means three separate squares so deployed to avoid shooting at each other should enemy cavalry ride between them.
2. Only the northerly extremity of the Taberna is still visible. The section where the Anson's cavalry action took place is now submerged under the Portina reservoir.
3. K Wojciechowski's and W Dobiecki's memoirs.
4. Merlin's brigade consisted of four small regiments totalling 1,188 (Oman) sabres and suffered just forty-eight casualties, one suspects mostly from artillery.
5. Quoted in Lipscombe, *Wellington's Guns* (Osprey, Oxford, 2013).
6. There were no eagles captured at Talavera. In popular culture the one captured by Bernard Cornwell's character Sharpe is fictitious.
7. *Mémoires de Joseph, Vol. 4.*

Chapter 10: The Withdrawal to Portugal

1. Page, Julia (ed.), *Intelligence officer in the Peninsular, Letters & Diaries of Major The Hon. Edward Charles Cocks 1786–1812* (Spellmount, Tunbridge Wells, 1986).
2. Sherer, Joseph Moyle, *Recollections of the Peninsular* (Longman, London, 1824).
3. Garrity, Sergeant, *Memoirs of a Sergeant, The 43rd Light Infantry During the Peninsular War* (Nonsuch Publishing, Stroud, 2005).
4. FitzClarence.
5. The 5th Caçadores, a light infantry battalion, was the only Portuguese battalion to take part in the Talavera Campaign. One force of Portuguese was under Marshal Beresford further north but the majority of the army was still training.

6. Verner, Willoughby, *History and Campaigns of the Rifle Brigade 1800–1813, Vol. 2* (N&M reprint).
7. Then a captain in the 3rd Foot Guards and a junior AC. He remained a part of Wellesley's military 'family' throughout the Peninsular War, rising to the rank of lieutenant colonel. He was mortally wounded at Waterloo.
8. Muir, Rory (ed.), *At Wellington's Right Hand, The Letters of Lieutenant Colonel Sir Alexander Gordon 1808–1815* (Army Record Society, 2003).

Chapter 11: The End of the 1809 Campaign

1. Wellesley, particularly in the early years of his command, was consistently plagued by letters home, some of them his senior officers, predicting defeat and in some cases optimistically hoping for an early return home. The authors of these letters, which often circulated in society drawing rooms or found their way into newspapers, were referred to as 'croakers' by Wellesley.
2. Captain Gordon ADC to Wellington somewhat ungenerously commented that: 'The Spaniards are quite up about this paltry victory the Duke del Paque has gained.'

Appendix II: Orders of Battle – Talavera

1. Oman. The British order of Battle is compiled from the returns of 25 July 1809.

An Officer of the 95th Rifles.

Index

I Corps 18, 27, 37, 38, 39, 43, 55, 62, 65, 84, 97, 135, 199, 247
II Corps 16, 18, 21, 26, 27, 203, 205, 206, 237
IV Corps 63, 71, 76, 92, 95, 97, 135, 137, 155, 176, 226, 248
V Corps 33, 203, 214, 224
VI Corps 30, 33, 231, 205, 213, 214, 224
9th Légère (The Incomparable) 119, 120, 123, 124, 126, 133, 139, 145, 146, 153, 179, 247
16th Légère 106, 109, 248
24th Line 120, 139, 140, 146, 147, 184, 247
96th Line 120, 139, 140, 143, 182, 247

Abrantes 27, 41, 43, 47, 48, 57, 67, 68, 192, 233, 243, 249
Aitcheson, Ensign 62, 75, 78, 160, 175, 250
Alacántra 33, 35, 26, 37, 39, 237
Alberche, Rio vii, 65, 70, 75, 79, 84, 86, 88, 91, 97, 98, 101, 105, 106, 109, 110, 112, 134, 150, 152, 154, 189, 192, 195, 198, 251, 252
Alburquerque, Duke of 83, 86, 97, 185, 223, 224, 226, 242, 246, 247
Almaraz, Bridge of 33, 39, 55, 63, 66, 68, 79, 212, 213, 218–23, 224, 227, 228, 230-2, 237
Anson, Brigadier 84, 86, 97, 106, 179, 181, 182, 185, 208, 245, 252
Arzobispo bridge & village 211, 212, 213, 216, 218, 223, 224, 225, 230, 235
Austerlitz 1

Bassecourt, Gen 153, 179, 205, 208, 209, 223, 224, 233, 247
Baylen 5, 7
Beaumont, Brig Gen 135, 248
Beresford, Marshal 18, 19, 26, 27, 63, 197, 205, 208, 252

Berlin Decrees 1
Bingham Col 156, 159, 190, 197, 210
Bivouacs 47
British Army:
  1st Division 11, 88, 98, 112, 160, 164, 165, 198
  2nd Division 53, 98, 112, 114, 127, 142, 246
  3rd Division 33, 46, 88, 97, 105, 106, 108, 112, 170, 213, 218, 219, 227, 230, 252
  4th Division 53, 109, 112, 155, 160, 176, 177, 247
  2nd Cavalry Brigade 59
  Guards Brigade 164–8
  Light Brigade 49, 51, 52, 55, 76, 111, 126–34, 192–6, 211, 212, 213, 219, 221, 227, 230, 231, 237
  14th Light Dragoons 21, 45, 245
  16th Light Dragoons 45, 168, 171, 188, 190, 245
  23rd Light Dragoons 50, 79, 83, 181–5, 245
  Corps of Mounted Guides 48–9
  2nd Coldstream Guards 165, 189, 246, 249
  3rd Guards 62, 75, 95, 136, 160, 162, 165, 174, 177, 233, 245, 252
  7th R. Fusiliers 47, 136, 155, 156, 159, 176, 197, 246, 249
  29th Foot 79, 89, 90, 112, 114, 122, 123, 125, 137, 139, 140, 141, 142, 164, 170, 179, 181, 188, 190, 197, 199, 205, 245, 249, 250
  24th Foot 106, 120, 160, 164, 173, 182, 245, 249, 252
  31st Foot 107, 173, 245, 249, 252
  43rd LI 31, 52, 53, 55, 126, 191, 192, 194, 196, 201, 211, 230, 237, 239, 252
  45th Foot 107, 109, 116, 173, 245, 249, 252

255

48th Foot   24, 50 114, 121, 125, 139, 142, 147, 164, 170, 171, 172, 173, 174, 245, 249
52nd LI   51, 52, 55, 126, 192, 194, 196, 212
53rd Foot   46, 156, 157, 159, 176, 190, 246, 249
60th Rifles   5, 107, 109, 117, 162, 164, 165, 245, 246, 249
61st Foot   50, 79, 169, 245
66th Foot   168
87th Foot   46, 109, 245, 249
88th Connaught Rangers   46, 107, 109, 245, 249
92nd Gordon Highlanders   53, 122, 126, 251
95th Rifles   5, 14, 51, 52, 54, 55, 122, 126, 127, 191, 193, 194, 195, 196, 219, 220, 221, 231, 247, 249, 254
Brown Bess musket   178

Campbell, Brig A.   112, 155, 156, 159, 162, 170, 176, 177
Campbell, Brig H.   145, 195
Casa de Salinas   105–9, 114, 117, 134, 135, 152, 175, 195
Cascajal, Cerro de   112, 116, 119, 120, 134, 135, 137, 140, 145, 146, 147, 150, 153, 155, 169, 179, 182, 189, 198
Castelo Branco   51, 192
Castlereagh, Lord   10, 15, 16, 41, 42, 43, 46, 153, 197, 206, 207, 233
Charleville musket   178
Ciudad Rodrigo   9, 65, 75, 205, 238, 242, 249
Cocks, Capt Somers   168, 188, 196, 203, 252
Coimbra   18, 19, 26, 41, 46, 249
Commissariat   viii, 9, 44, 47, 243
Continental System   1
Convention of Cintra   6, 16
Cooper, Sgt   47, 48, 59, 136, 155, 157, 164, 176, 197, 250, 251
Corunna   10, 11, 12, 14, 16, 18, 52, 53, 194, 250
Cotton, Gen   55, 59, 60, 79, 114, 164, 168, 170, 210, 245
Cradock, Gen   14, 18, 19, 53
Craufurd, Brig Gen   51, 52, 76, 110, 111, 126, 129, 192, 194, 195, 196, 212, 213, 218, 219, 221, 230, 242

Cuesta, Gen   18, 33, 37, 38, 39, 40, 41, 42, 43, 44, 55, 63, 65, 68, 70, 71, 75, 78, 79, 80, 81, 84, 86, 88, 89, 91, 93, 95, 96, 97, 98, 101, 105, 112, 116, 118, 152, 153, 187, 198, 201, 205, 298, 210, 211, 213, 215, 216, 223, 227, 228, 234, 235, 237, 241, 242

Donellan, Col   121, 125, 170, 171, 172, 173, 174
Donkin, Col   46, 106, 107, 112, 115, 117, 213, 221, 245
Dos de Mayo (Rebellion)   47
Douro Campaign   15–32, 33, 48, 50

Elley, Col Sir John   183, 184, 185

Ferdinand VII, King   2
Fifth Coalition   15, 33, 45
FitzClarence   21, 22, 24, 25, 80, 81, 82, 83, 84, 88, 107, 109, 133, 134, 135, 147, 150, 154, 169, 183, 186, 187, 209, 212, 227, 235, 250
Flogging   47
French Army:
   I Corps   18, 27, 37, 38, 39, 43, 55, 62, 65, 84, 97, 135, 199, 247
   II Corps   16, 18, 21, 26, 27, 203, 205, 206, 237
   IV Corps   63, 71, 76, 92, 95, 97, 135, 137, 155, 176, 226, 248
   V Corps   33, 203, 214, 224
   VI Corps   30, 33, 203, 205, 213, 214, 224
   9th Légère (The Incomparable)   119, 120, 123, 124, 126, 135, 139, 145, 146, 153, 179, 247
   16th Légère   106, 109, 248
   24th Line   120, 139, 140, 146, 147, 184, 247
   96th Line   120, 139, 140, 142, 182, 247
Frere, Mr (diplomat)   62, 65, 91, 93, 205

Galicia   11, 16, 20, 26, 27, 28, 30 33, 40, 62, 74, 203
Gamonal   81, 86
Girod, Lt   123, 125, 126, 133, 251
Grand Battery   135, 154, 179, 182
Grant, Lt Col   33, 37
Guadiana, Rio   43, 57, 63, 239, 242

Index 257

Hill, Gen 11, 18, 23, 24, 90, 112, 116, 120, 121, 122, 126, 127, 140, 142, 145, 146, 170, 214, 245, 251

Intelligence, British 21, 26, 62, 91, 114, 140, 203, 205, 352
Intelligence, French 28, 33, 62–3, 96, 224, 250

Joseph, King vii, 2, 18, 33, 38, 31, 49, 55, 57, 62, 63,71, 84, 96, 97, 119, 134, 135, 147, 150, 152, 173, 175, 179, 186, 187, 188, 197, 198, 205, 207, 229, 237, 238, 247, 250, 251, 252
Jourdan, Marshal 39, 62, 135, 147, 152, 153, 187, 188, 189, 201, 202, 205, 229, 247, 251, 252
Junot, Gen vii, 1, 2, 6, 249
Junta (various) 3, 5, 10, 11, 28, 39, 40, 41, 42, 43, 63, 65, 68, 70, 73, 74, 91, 205, 237, 241

Kemmis, Brig Gen 53, 112, 176, 246
King's German Legion 21, 45, 83, 93, 105, 109, 117, 120, 121, 126, 150, 168, 169, 170, 179, 181, 182, 185, 230, 245, 246
   1st Hussars KGL 45, 93, 105, 109, 181, 182, 185, 230
   1st Light Bn KGL 143, 245
   1st Lin Bn KGL 168
   5th Line Bn KGL 143, 144, 245

Lapisse, Gen 35, 36, 37, 39, 106, 135, 140, 143, 144, 155, 161, 162, 163, 168, 171, 173, 247
Leith Hay, Lt 86, 88, 89, 98, 105, 114, 115, 126, 137, 140, 141, 142, 145, 164, 170, 179, 182
Leslie, Lt 66, 79, 81, 89, 114, 115, 116, 120, 123, 139, 141, 144, 199, 250
Lisbon 1, 2, 3, 5, 6, 9, 14, 16, 18, 33, 37, 48, 50, 51, 52, 53, 59, 84, 126, 192, 236, 242, 249
Low, Brig Gen 120, 143, 168
Loyal Lusitania Legion 35, 57, 96, 186, 207, 214–18, 251

Mackenzie, Brig Gen 18, 33, 37, 41, 76, 86, 97, 105, 106, 107, 109 112, 152, 160, 170, 173, 174, 192, 213, 245, 249, 252

Madrid 3, 11, 33, 39, 52 57, 58, 62, 71, 76, 78, 81, 83, 84, 86, 91, 201, 207, 209, 215, 221, 225 233, 237, 247
Mayne, Col 35, 39, 41, 215
Medellín, Cerro de 55, 86, 112, 114 116–26, 127, 133, 134, 137–45 146, 147, 150, 153, 164, 169, 170, 171, 179, 183, 185, 185, 186, 189, 196, 198, 251, 252
Meyers, Col 156, 157
Milhaud, Gen 152, 187, 248
Mirrabet, Pass of 212, 213, 237
Moore, Gen Sir John 3, 6, 7, 8–14, 15, 16, 33, 41, 51, 53, 134, 194, 234
Mortier, Marshal 33, 203, 205, 206, 212, 213, 214, 223, 235
Mules 48, 65, 66, 75, 101, 208, 212, 249
Murray, Col 21, 25, 49, 72, 250, 251

Napoleon 1, 2, 3, 7, 10, 11, 15, 16, 18, 30 33, 38, 39, 40 47, 135, 136, 178, 198, 199, 201, 203, 239, 240, 251, 252
Ney, Marshal 27, 30, 33, 203, 205, 213, 214, 216, 221, 224, 229, 230, 235
Northern Plain 153, 179, 180, 184, 185, 198

O'Donoju, Gen 70, 75, 76, 86
Ompteda, Capt von 120
Oporto 5, 16, 18, 19, 20, 21, 22, 25, 26, 33
Oropesa 79, 80, 81, 129, 208, 209, 210, 211, 216, 223, 227, 235

Pajar de Vergara 112, 135, 153, 155, 159
Piquets & outposts vii, 5, 35, 47, 62, 106, 110–11, 120, 133, 150, 155, 198, 232
Plascencia 43, 55, 76, 79, 91, 189, 205, 206, 208, 211, 235
Plundering, British 46
Portina Brook vii, 109, 112, 114, 120, 126, 133, 134, 139, 140, 150, 154, 155, 162, 168, 169, 173, 186, 192, 198, 252
Puerto de Baños 205, 206, 208, 216

Quarter Master General 49, 59, 182, 210, 243, 250

Rations, Spanish supply of viii, 38, 41, 65, 66, 67, 68, 75, 76, 91, 101, 198, 208, 213, 234, 235
Regimental baggage 101–3
Reinforcements (1809) 4, 5, 49, 51, 250

Roliça 5, 6
Royal Navy 2, 5, 6, 11, 20
Ruffin, Gen 119, 212, 134, 135, 139, 140, 143, 144, 145, 146, 153, 179, 185, 247

Schaumann, Commissary 45, 59, 79, 93, 98, 101, 181, 203, 211, 235, 250
Scott Lillie, Major 96, 215
Scovell, Capt 49, 50
Sébastiani, Gen 33, 57, 63, 70, 72, 76, 78, 95, 97, 135, 152, 155, 161, 162, 175, 1746, 227, 235, 242, 248
Seville 43, 62, 65, 91, 215, 247, 251
Sierra de Segurilla 112, 153, 179, 184
Soult, Marshal 11, 16, 18, 19, 21, 22, 23, 25, 26, 27, 33, 39, 42, 48, 62, 135, 150, 153, 189, 203, 203, 206, 207, 208, 209, 210, 211, 212, 215, 221, 223, 224, 226, 227, 228, 229, 230, 235, 237, 242
Spanish Army 72–4
  Army of La Manche 33, 57, 63–5, 78, 95, 150
  Army of Extremadura 18, 33, 39–40, 41, 44, 55, 70, 76, 79, 84, 97, 105, 112, 198, 208, 213, 214, 223, 235, 246
Spencer, Gen 3, 5
Stewart, Brig C. 68, 69, 70, 71, 80, 84, 93, 134, 209
Stewart, Brig R. 53, 112, 114, 115, 117, 122, 125, 137, 141, 170, 179, 196, 245, 252

Tagus Valley 18, 27, 33, 34, 35, 37, 40, 43, 47, 55, 57, 63, 65, 78, 112, 192, 222, 205, 237, 240
Tagus, Rio 3, 27, 33, 35, 39, 41, 42, 43, 47, 55, 59, 63, 71, 75, 79, 84, 86, 93, 98, 187, 208, 211, 212, 213, 214, 219, 221, 223, 224, 225, 227, 228, 230
Thomar 45, 59
Tilson, Brig Gen 114, 122, 137, 140, 245
Toledo 30, 63, 78, 93, 96, 150, 247
Tour-Maubourg, Gen la 35, 83, 84, 85, 97, 135, 170, 248
Truxillo 213, 227, 230, 234, 235, 237, 246

Venegas, Gen 57, 63, 70 76, 78, 91, 95, 150, 153, 188, 201, 207, 241
Victor, Marshal 18, 27, 33, 35, 37, 38, 39, 41, 42, 44, 55, 62, 63, 64, 68, 74, 75, 79, 84, 86, 88, 89, 91, 95, 96, 97, 116, 117, 119, 125, 134, 135, 137, 139, 146, 147, 150, 152, 153, 173, 185, 188, 189, 188, 199, 228, 235, 242, 247, 251
Villatte, Gen 135, 153, 179, 24

Wellesley's Campaign Plan 41–3
Wilson, Sir Robert 57, 71, 96, 186, 207, 214, 215, 216, 218

Zayas, Gen 83, 97, 246